Getting to Know Allah

Legacy Edition

Bernard Payeur
& Lucette Carpentier

Front cover photo by A. S.

ISBN: 978-1-928023-09-8

Note for Librarians: A cataloguing record for this book is available from Library and Archives Canada at www.collectionscanada.gc.ca/amicus/index-e.html.

© Copyright 2015 Bernard Payeur

All rights reserved. No part of this publication may be reproduced, stored in a retrieval system, or transmitted, in any form or by any means, electronic, mechanical, photocopying, recording, or otherwise, without the written prior permission of the author.

Boreal Books
www.boreal.ca

Getting to Know Allah is an extract from the Legacy Edition of Pain, Pleasure and Prejudice, a comprehensive review of the Koran.

Other extracts from Pain, Pleasure and Prejudice

Shared Prophets

Women and the Koran

The Islamic Hereafter

Jihad in the Koran

From Merchant to Messenger

CONTENTS

A Belated Acknowledgement 11

Revelations and Generalizations 15
   Three Translations, One Interpretation 20

INSIGTHS INTO OMNIPOTENCE 23

Allah's Mercy 25
   A Conditional Type of Mercy 26
   Terrified Into Believing 29
   Allah's Way of Old 34
   Unbelievers Not by Choice 34

Salih and the Destruction of Thamud 37
   Al-Rass 43

Allah Days 45
   A Litany of Death and Destruction 46
   Allah's Covenant with His Prophets 53
   The World Before and After the Messengers 53
     Why No Roofs and Stairways of Silver 54
     Messengers to the Common People 55
   Allah Days or the Nearer Punishment 56

Allah and the Crime of No Longer Believing 57
   The Example of Pharaoh 57
   Repentance Denied 58
   "Kill them wherever you find them" 59
   Telling Apostates and Believers Apart On Judgement Day 61

Allah vs. Alleged Associates 62
   The Largest and Heaviest of Gods 62
   Phantasmagorical Creations of God and Man 64
   "Is there, then, another god with Allah?" 69
   Goddesses and the Fathers Who Worshipped Them 70
   Children! Do Not Obey Parents Who Worship Other Gods 72
   Gog and Magog 73
     Alexander and the Wall 73
     The True Promise 75

Allah's Parables 77
   Slaves in Parables 84
   Intriguing Comparisons and Mixed Metaphors 86
   Allah, Two Boys and a Dog 91

Allah's Do Not Do List 95
- Grave Sins - An Introduction 95
- The Greatest Sin of All 96
- The Top 40 97
- 10 Made Up Sins 98
- Tips for Avoiding the Grave Sins 99

Allah and the Ptolemaic Universe 102
- The Near-Earth Constellations 105

Allah and the Shape of the Earth 107
- Floating On A Sea of Mud 107
- Pointed Revelations About a Flat Earth 108
- Who Stops the Sky From Falling? 110
- Full Circle in Seven Verses 111

Allah's Calendar 112
- The Names of the Months 114
- Year Zero 115

Allah and the Beginnings of Life 116
- A Fluid Beginning 116
- Bones Then Flesh 119
- Beware of the Clot 119
- It's All About the Sperm 120
- Things Which Don't Come in Pairs 121
- Allah as Proof that Imperfection Is Pervasive 122

Allah and the Jinn 123
- The Myth and the Reality 123
- How the Jinn Heard About the Koran etc. 125
- Jinn and Men Together on Judgement Day 129
- Messengers to the Jinn 129
- The Jinn and the Prophet's Grandfather 130

Allah and She Who Blows in Reeds 132

Allah and the Unseen 134

Self-Sufficient Heart Reader 138

Allah's Bounties 141

The Rainmaker 146

Allah on the Present Life 152

Contents

Signs, Signs, Everywhere Signs 154
  Not Doing What is Being Asked as a Sign 158
  Why No Signs for the Messenger 159

Allah the Eternal Adolescent 161
  Doomed Children at Play 162
  The Responsible Adult vs. The Adolescent: 163
  More Destruction, Less Creation 165
  Playing With Toys 166
  Hooked On Praise 167

I AM THE GREATEST! WORSHIP ME! 169

Prayers 171
  One-on-One With Allah 171
  Negotiating the Prayers 172
  The Call to Prayer 179
  Prayers in War and Peace 181
  An Answer to a Prayer 184
  The Night too is for Praying 186
  The Prayer of the People of Paradise 186

Pilgrimages – The Hajj and the Umrah 187
  The Importance of Mecca 188
  Safa and Marwa 191
  Deaths, Molestations and Managing the Hajj 192
    Safely accommodating millions more pilgrims at the Hajj 194
  The Anthropological Impact of the Hajj 195
  Post Pilgrimage Rituals and Early Departures 197

Ramadan 199
  Ramadan in the Land of the Midnight Sun 201

IF TRUTH BE TOLD 203

Allah Does Not Care for Homosexuals 205
  Crime and Punishment 208
  Where Homosexuals Go When They Die 209

Allah Despises the Riba-Eaters 210
  The Prophet as Borrower 213

Allah Loves His Messenger Perhaps More Than He Loves Orphans 214

Allah Loves His Cattle; Dogs, Not So Much 216
  An Ode to Cattle 216
  Domesticated in Paradise 216
  Water, Men and Cattle 217
  Allah on the Versatility of His Cattle 219
  Slicing the Ears of Cattle 220
  Dogs in a Cattle World 221

Allah's Charity Is Not All It Seems 224

Oaths Can Be Broken 227

Immutable Truths About Slavery 231
  A God's Dilemma 231
  Why Slavery Cannot Be Simply Abolished 235
  Slavery and the Prophet 236

The Babylonian Exile and the Roman Diaspora 239

Trees to Impress a God 241

You Are What You Eat 244
  The Table Is Set 244
  Answering a Question with a Question and Pork is for Other Gods 248
  Vegetarians are not Muslims 249
  What Do the Jews Have To Do With It! 251
  Where You May Dine 253
  Why Some Gods Go Hungry 253

Two Once Extraordinary Verses About Tolerance 254
  Revelation 2:62 255
  Revelation 109:6 257

Tidbits Meccan Surahs 260

Tidbits Medinan Surahs 283

AFTERWORD 293

It Wasn't Always Like That 295
  Arabs, Before and After 295
  Competing World Views 299
  The Cartoon Protest 301

APPENDICES 303

Pillars 305

   Pillars of Faith 305
   Pillars of Islam 305

The First Koran 307

A Belated Acknowledgement

She is Lucette Carpentier. She kept her maiden name. I would not have had it any other way. Without Lucette's knowledge, intellectual honesty and the human warmth and understanding she brought to our relationship there would have been no *Getting to Know Allah* or any of our other books on Islam and the Prophet Muhammad.

In this cowering new age where drawing an innocent cartoon, or offering a contrary opinion on a blog about a man who would have us believe he was on speaking terms with God tasked with delivering His definitive instructions for mankind, is a death defying act, I thought it prudent not to acknowledge her contribution until now.

The buzz of the alarm clock was my signal to get up and go downstairs to make the coffee. Ten minutes later, a warm cup of coffee in each hand, I would make my way back up the stairs, leaving one cup on the desk in my home office, and the other on her bathroom vanity. Back in the bedroom I would open the curtains, then walk over to the bed to kiss her good morning.

She would shower and get dressed and I would drive her to her job on Parliament Hill, a ten minute drive. For 35 years, she was one of the fifty or so elite professionals who provide translation and simultaneous interpretation to the House of Commons, the Senate of Canada, Parliamentary and Cabinet Committees and Party Caucuses.

After a hurried goodbye and have a nice day – Wellington Street, in front of Parliament, is a busy street in the morning – I would make my way back home and begin my day's work, which, for ten years or more, was researching and writing *Pain, Pleasure and Prejudice*.

When she got home at the end of the day, depending on the season, and the weather, we would sit on the front porch with a glass of wine and some munchies and she would review and comment on my day's work. I always had a copy of Fakhry's interpretation of the Koran on my lap ready to answer her questions. This was when her Master's in Linguistics, specialty *Translation,* came in handy.

Sipping her wine she would patiently explained some of the nuances of Fakhry's translation that I had failed to grasp or that I might have misunderstood.

We agreed on most things when it came to Islam and the threat it posed to Western Civilization, except that it would all come to pass, that the moderates would win the day and the March of Civilization would continue and we would not see the *Enlightenment,* which ushered in the *Age of Reason,* undone.

If our discussion became too animated and we could not find common ground we changed the subject, if only temporarily. For example, she had never watched *Let The Quran Speak,* a half-hour program hosted by Shabir Ally, President of the Islamic Information and Dawah* Centre in Toronto, then broadcasted across Canada most Saturday nights on Vision TV. This Saturday's topic was the controversial verse 4:34 which condones the beating of a spouse who disobeys her husband, or whose husband fears she will disobey.

> 4:34 Men are in charge of women, because Allah has made some of them excel the others, and because they spend some of their wealth. Hence righteous women are obedient, guarding the unseen (their sex) which Allah has guarded. And those of them that you fear might rebel, admonish them and abandon them in their beds and beat them. Should they obey you, do not seek a way of harming them; for Allah is Sublime and Great!

When we came upon the program, Shabir Ally was being questioned by a young woman wearing the traditional headscarf (chador) on the meaning of what is often referred to as the "wife beating verse".

Ally was not put off by her questions and appeared comfortable with being interviewed by a female. He offered an explanation which I had never heard before, or come across in my research on the Koran. He said that verse 4:34 had to be looked at in a much wider context, and in that wider context Allah did not sanction the beating of one's wife, but instead, instructed the community to protect and look after wives.

Lucette was impressed by Ally's restrained and positive interpretation of a revelation which, when taken at face value, gives a husband, not only the right, but a God-given responsibility to physically discipline his wives for both real and imagined transgressions against him or against God.

The discussion of Shabir Ally's interpretation of verse 4:34 would lead us to the trial of Galileo charged with heresy for supporting Copernicus' theory that the earth revolved around the sun.

In the Bible, it is written that during the Israeli conquest of Palestine God ordered the sun to stand still in the sky for a day so the Israelites could complete the extermination of the Amorites.

A Belated Acknowledgement

> Then spoke Joshua to the Lord in the day when the Lord delivered up the Amorites before the children of Israel, and he said in the sight of Israel, Sun, stand thou still upon Gibeon; and thou Moon, in the valley of Ajalon.
>
> And the sun stood still, and the moon stayed, until the people had avenged themselves upon their enemies. Is not this written in the book of Jasher? So the sun stood still in the midst of heaven, and hasted not to go down about a whole day (Joshua 10: 12-13).

God had commanded the sun to stand still, not the earth. To accept Galileo's explanation would have meant, for Christians raised on the literal interpretation of the Bible, that the Bible was wrong. This was unacceptable to pope Urban VIII. It was not that Urban VIII did not believe in the Copernican system, he simply wanted Galileo to keep quiet while the Church guided the faithful to a new interpretation of the scriptures concerning the sun interrupting its race across the sky for twenty-four hours.

My wife thought that Shabir Ally was just doing what the informed leadership in Rome had done, gradually getting the believers to abandon a simplistic, literal interpretation of the Koran. Lucette was the optimist in our more than thirty year marriage.

I did not agree. When it comes to women's rights and religion, I argued that this was a doomed strategy, and in any event, women should not have to compromise on fundamental issues such as equality in the hope that one day, an enlightened male religious leadership will consider them equal in every way.

She said I was being obstinate and unrealistic. To avoid going to bed upset, we decided to watch the Australian Open where an obstinate and determined Greek Cypriot, Marcos Baghdatis, beat the overwhelming favourite, number two seed American Andy Roddick.

As *Pain, Pleasure and Prejudice* has grown from a few hundred pages to today's comprehensive guide, not only to the Koran, but the life and times of the Prophet Muhammad, that optimisms has waned, but she remains steadfast in her commitments and true to her beliefs.

If we can, believers and non-believers, have the type of discussions Lucette and I had about Islam – taking time-outs if the discussion gets too animated – then her optimism that a modern interpretation of the Koran and mutual respect and understanding will eventually overcome fanaticism and intolerance may be validated and nothing would make her and me happier in this world or the next.

Bernard Payeur
October 17, 2015

Revelations and Generalizations

Revelations and Generalizations is the opening explanatory chapter of *Pain, Pleasure and Prejudice*. What is written there about the why, the wherefore and the methodology used in that ground-breaking publication is applicable to *Getting to Know Allah*.

THE PEOPLE

114 An-Nâs

*In the Name of Allah,
the Compassionate, the Merciful*

114:1 Say: "I seek refuge with the Lord of the People,

114:2 "The King of the people,

114:3 "The God of the people,

114:5 "From the evil of the slinking whisperer [Satan],

114:6 "Who whispers in the breasts of people,

114:7 "Both jinn and men."

Both jinn and men! That is it, the last verse of the Koran. What a read! What a revelation! What is a jinn? Jinns are spirits that inhabit another dimension. There are good and evil jinns. The caricature of the genie is probably based on this creature of the Koran.

When I decided to read and study the Koran with the intention of writing about it, I was determined to get a Muslim's interpretation, an interpretation that could only be viewed as being favourable to Islam. I also wanted a translation that was easy to read and understand. The translation that seemed to satisfy these requirements was an interpretation by Majid Fakhry, Emeritus Professor of Philosophy at the American University of Beirut, which has the seal of approval of Al-Azhar University of Egypt, a world-renowned center for Islamic study for more than 900 years.

Messrs Garnet Publishing Limited, with reference to your

letter dated 5 July, 2000, in respect of your request that this department (Islamic Research) may review your book titled: An Interpretation of the Qur'an, English Translation of the Meanings. A Bilingual Edition translated by Majid Fakhry.

After having reviewed this book as requested we have the pleasure to declare that we have no objection to approve this book and put it in circulation or introduced for republication.

Islamic Research Academy, Al-Azhar University

In the translator's own words "we have tried to express ourselves in a simple, readable English idiom." Publishers Weekly wrote of Fakhry's notable accomplishment: "Succeeds in expressing the meanings of the original Arabic in simple readable English."

My goals in reading the Koran were diverse. At the top of my list was gaining an understanding of what makes this book so special; to understand what makes the religion based on its content so attractive to so many and yes, to satisfy my curiosity about what God sounds like, or more accurately, reads like. I also read the Koran in the hope of dispelling some prejudices and apprehensions that I had developed after reading about Islam from authors, devoted Muslims most of them, who had mostly nothing but praise for Allah and His "perfect religion".

Pain, Pleasure and Prejudice is the culmination of more than ten years of work and study. I believe it is the most honest, forthright, complete review ever attempted by a non-Muslim of Allah's and His anointed Messenger's legacy: the Koran. This appraisal takes Allah and the Prophet Muhammad at their word, as does most of the Muslim world, and so should you. Although I consider myself well versed (no pun intended) in the Koran and the life and times of the Prophet Muhammad, in *Pain, Pleasure and Prejudice* you will not be subjected to drawn-out discussions about Allah's Revelations. I prefer letting Allah and His Messenger speak for themselves, offering only a layman's opinion, or an expert's explanation, where I feel one is warranted.

When Fakhry's crisp translation is not sufficient, it is Moududi I most often turn to. Abul A'la Moududi's (also spelt Maududi) [1903-1979] credentials as a pre-eminent Islamic scholar are impeccable: journalist, theologian, Muslim revivalist, Islamist philosopher, first recipient of the *King Faisal International Award* for his services to Islam and Islamic studies. Of the more than 120 books he wrote, he is most famous for his magnum opus *The Meaning of the Qur'an*.

The Koran is the book upon which the Taliban, the Islamist fundamentalist movement which ruled most of Afghanistan from

1996 until 2001, based their concept of God's government on earth. The Taliban, like all believers, were, and are required to at least attempt to commit to memory the entire Koran. Believers are also expected to accept Allah's Revelations in their totality without question. This has not been my approach in presenting my impressions, the impressions of a former Catholic, now an agnostic, on first reading the Koran.

As an unbeliever, I hope I can safely express my opinions about the Koran and the Prophet Muhammad, although nothing is certain. It is an unfortunate fact of life that authors who choose to write about Islam, the Koran or the life of the Prophet Muhammad must tread carefully lest the believers perceive their writings as an insult to Islam. I hope that I have achieved that fine balance, if such an equilibrium is even possible.

Translations of the Koran are usually called interpretations because believers claim that only the Arabic version of the Koran can convey the true meaning of God's words. If you can't read the Koran in the original, they say, you are bound to misinterpret Allah's words. Do they have a point, or is it just a pre-emptive rationalisation? A pre-emptive excuse for some of the frightening revelations contained within the Muslim Holy Book. Revelations that may leave some unbelievers wondering if it is God's words they are reading or those of His nemesis?

The Koran is written in verses or ayats, therefore it is true that you will not be able to appreciate the rhythm and rhyme that only the original can convey, but any good translation will be able to communicate the meaning of the poet's words and the meaning of the words is what you should be concerned with.

An English translation of the Koran will run to about 77,700 words; the approximate size of a standard 300 page book. A book, Allah reveals, in which you can study "Whatever you choose."

> 68:35 Shall We consider those who submit like those who are criminals?
>
> 68:36 What is the matter with you; how do you judge?
>
> 68:37 Or do you have a Book in which you study?
>
> 68:38 Wherein there is whatever you choose.

It is a bold statement for a relatively small book where boundless repetitions use up print space that could, perhaps, be put to better use.

The Koran is made up of 114 chapters or surahs. When referring to chapters of the Koran, I use the Arabic transliteration (converting from one alphabet to another) of chapter, which is surah. Each surah is further divided into verses. I have chosen to remain with the English understanding of what is an ayat.

There are 6,346 verses in the Koran if you include the 112 unnumbered Basmalahs, the formula-invocation "in the name of Allah, the Compassionate, the Merciful" which appears at the beginning of every chapter of the Koran except the first and the ninth.

In *Pain, Pleasure and Prejudice* I refer to verses by the surah number and verse; for example, verse 2:282. Or by surah name and verse: *The Cow, verse* 282. A verse can be just a few words long or more than 200 words such as verse 2:282, the longest verse in the Koran which deals, in part, with the virtue of good bookkeeping practices and why, when it comes to transactions involving money or chattel, a woman on her own cannot be trusted to accurately remember things.

Towards the end of some chapters you will find supplementary material following a squiggly line (~~~). It is additional information which I consider important that could not be conveniently presented in footnotes.

Just a few editorial notes before we get down to business and let God speak for Himself. All quotes from the Koran are from Majid Fakhry's interpretation unless otherwise indicated. Text added by Fakhry within a quoted verse to improve understanding is enclosed within square "[ ]" brackets. Other clarifications by Fakhry, including footnotes, are enclosed in round "( )" brackets. On rare occasions, you will find italicised bracketed comments within a verse. These are the author's.

Any underlining of words in verses for emphasis is my doing not Fakhry's. I hope that Majid will forgive me if I have substituted the more familiar Koran for Qur'an when quoting verses and comments from his "English translation of the Meanings."

At the beginning of twenty surahs, following the invocation *In the Name of Allah the Compassionate, the Merciful*, are letters, or groups of letters of the alphabet e.g. Alif - Lam - Ra. According to some Islamic scholars, these letters are abbreviations or Muqatta'at, of Arabic words, in this instance, the English meaning can be interpreted as "I am Allah, the Most Seeing." Other Islamic scholars, according to Fakhry, believe they are "secret symbols with which the Angel Gabriel opened the revelation or surah in question." I have included these letters or groups of letters in quoted verses where they appear.

Where warranted, verses are accompanied by sayings or descriptions of actions of the Prophet called hadiths (Ahadith is often use to indicate the plural form, but not here). Hadiths, of which there are tens of thousands, are hearsay evidence collected approximately 200 years after the Prophet's passing of what God's Messenger said and did, including the silent approval of actions done in his presence. An authentic (sahih) or good (hasan) hadith i.e. one that can be traced to a witness of what the Prophet said or did, or did not do, via of chain of reliable transmitters, is usually considered a legal precedent if it does not contradict the Koran[1].

Much of what Allah reveals of his Koran is in the form of telling His Messenger what to say in what are responses or appear to be responses to questions or observations from believers and unbelievers listening to the Prophet deliver the latest batch of revelations delivered by Allah's intermediary Messenger, the angel Gabriel. When you encounter the word "say" followed by a colon in a revelation (with no other qualifier such as "they" e.g. "they say" or on a rare occasions "you said") unless otherwise indicated you may assume it to be Allah telling His Messenger what to say. Examples:

> 3:98 Say: "O People of the Book, why do you disbelieve in the Revelations of Allah, when Allah witnesses whatever you do?"

> 3:99 Say: "O People of the Book, why do you debar those who have believed from the Path (the religion) of Allah, seeking to make it crooked, while you are witnesses (while you know it is the right religion)? Allah is not unaware of what you do!"

Is it favored or favoured? Majid Fakhry rendered his excellent translation of the Koran into British English e.g. favoured as opposed to favored.

> 17:40 Has your Lord, then, favoured you with sons and taken to Himself females from among the angels? Surely, you are uttering a monstrous thing.

Not only have I not changed Fakhry's translation to conform to American English (that was unthinkable), but I have, in my accompanying narrative, chosen to remain with British English, with an occasional inadvertent foray into Canadian English (yes, there is such a thing). The same for hadiths. In quoting the sayings and recollections of the actions of the Prophet I have chosen to remain with the English of the translators and their often confusing punctuation and grammar.

---

[1] Sunni Islam considers the hadiths collected by six men ((al-Bukhari, Imam Muslim, At-Tirmidi, Ibn Majah, Abu Dawood and An-Nisa'i) with the al-Bukhari collection being the largest and considered the most authoritative as the "six canonical collections." Imam Bukhari (d. 870) is said to have gathered over 600,000 hadiths of which 7,275 are considered authentic. The Koran and these "hadith collections" inform every facet of a believer's existence.

One final editorial observation: all quoted verses have been carefully reviewed to ensure that Fakhry's interpretation has been faithfully rendered. Many verses such as 44:43-44 must be read together to form a complete sentence or thought; therefore, do not assume a typographical (typo) or grammatical error if a verse does not end with the expected punctuation.

> 44:43 The Tree of Zaqqum (the Tree of Bitterness) will certainly be
>
> 44:44 The food of the sinner.

Finally, some of the quoted verses from Fakhry's interpretation of the Koran have no closing quotes and it has to do with an often misunderstood rule of English grammar. If the material being quoted is more than one paragraph .i.e. verses, you can get away with only opening quotation marks (") at the beginning of each verse and only supply closing quote (") at the end of the complete multiple paragraph quotation.

Three Translations, One Interpretation

Is it a translation or an interpretation?

Fakhry:

> 14:33 And He has made subservient to you the sun and the moon pursuing their courses, and subjected also the night and the day.

Yusuf Ali's translation closely parallels Fakhry's; the main difference being "subjected to you" instead "subservient to you" and "also" is enclosed in quotes.

> 14:33 And He hath made subject to you the sun and the moon, both diligently pursuing their courses; and the night and the day hath he (also) made subject to you.

In his translation of revelation 14:33, Muhammad Assad uses square brackets to show what he believes Allah means by "subservient".

> 14:33 And has made the sun and the moon, both of them constant upon their courses, subservient [to His laws, so that they be of use] to you; and has made the night and the day subservient [to His laws, so that they be of use] to you.

All three rendering of revelation 14:33 could be considered translations, but perhaps not a fourth by M. M. Pickthall, a Christian convert to Islam who modelled his translation on the old English of the King James Bible.

14:33 And maketh (sic) the sun and the moon, constant in their courses, to be of service unto you, and hath made of service unto you the night and the day.

All translations consulted in the extensive research for *Pain, Pleasure and Prejudice* are from pre-eminent Islamic scholars of the Koran.

INSIGTHS INTO OMNIPOTENCE

13:13 And the thunder sounds His praise and the angels, too, in awe of Him. And He sends forth the thunderbolts smiting with them whomever he pleases. Nevertheless, they dispute with Allah, but he is Mighty in prowess.

Allah's Mercy

20:5 The Compassionate has sat upon the Throne.

20:6 To Him belongs what is in the heavens, and what is in the earth, and what is in between them, as well as what is beneath the ground.

20:7 If you speak aloud, He surely knows the secret and what is even more hidden.

20:8 Allah, there no god but He. His are the Most Beautiful Names.

The *Compassionate* and the *Merciful* are two of the "Most Beautiful Names" of the official ninety-nine names of God. *Compassionate* and *Merciful* are the ostensibly laudable attributes of Allah most often mentioned in the Koran, and by a wide margin. The flattering invocation "In the Name of Allah, the Compassionate, the Merciful" begins every chapter of the Koran except chapter 1, *The Opening* and chapter 9, *Repentance*. Nonetheless, the reader is reminded at least twice in the first chapter (only seven verses) of Allah's merciful and compassionate nature.

THE OPENING[2]

1 Al-Fâtihah

1:1 In the Name of Allah, <u>the Compassionate, the Merciful</u>,

1:2 Praise be to Allah, the Lord of the Worlds,

1:3 <u>The Compassionate, the Merciful</u>,

1:4 Master of the Day of Judgement,

1:5 Only You do we worship, and only You do we implore for help.

1:6. Lead us to the right path,

---

[2] Also referred to as the *Chapter of Prayer* because it is repeated in every one of the five daily prayers.

> 1:7 The path of those You have favoured Not those who have incurred Your wrath or have gone astray.

The ubiquitous phrase begins every surah of the Koran except chapter 1 and chapter 9, Repentance. The reason put forward by some Islamic scholars why the phrase, *In the Name of Allah, the Compassionate, the Merciful* does not appear at all in chapter 9, *Repentance,* is because *Repentance* is mainly about making war. In war, Allah expects no mercy and compassion to be shown to those who will not submit to His Will.

In any event, a compassionate and merciful god is not the impression that a first time reader of the Koran is left with. Quite the opposite! This is not to say that Allah is not a compassionate and merciful god, He is; but it is a conditional type of mercy and compassion.

A Conditional Type of Mercy

> 17:80 Say: "My Lord, make my entry a truthful one and my going out a truthful one, and grant me from you a supporting power."
>
> 17:81 And say: "The truth has come and falsehood has perished. Falsehood is ever perishing."
>
> 17:82 And We reveal of the Qur'an that which is healing and merciful to the believers, and it yields nothing but perdition for the wrongdoers.

In the Name of Allah, the Compassionate, the Merciful is also the phrase that you hear Muslims repeating over and over during their daily prayers, and almost every time the name Allah is mentioned in print or during a conversation. This phrase in particular leaves a lay reader of the Koran somewhat perplexed for these are not qualities we associate with Allah as our reading takes us further into the Koran and the mindset of its Author[3]. Only thirteen verses into the Koran (6,333 revelations to go) and it starts, verse 2:7.

> 2:6 Those who have disbelieved, whether you warn them or not, they will not believe.
>
> 2:7 Allah has sealed their hearts and their hearing; their sight is dimmed and a terrible punishment awaits them.

---

[3] Scholars, including the pre-imminent medieval erudite Abul Hasan al-Ash'ari (b. 873 - d. 941) have argued that the Koran has no author, that, like Allah, it is eternal; always was, always will be.

2:8 There are some who say: "We believe in Allah and the Last Day;" but they are not real believers.

2:9 They seek to deceive Allah and the believers, but they deceive none other than themselves, though they are not aware of that.

2:10 In their hearts is a sickness; so Allah has increased their sickness. A painful punishment awaits them because of their lying.

More than six thousand verses later and Allah is still at it, talking about punishment and pain and burning people – men, women and children – in a raging fire. If *compassionate* is defined as being aware of the suffering of an other and wishing to relieve it and *merciful* as being unconditionally kind and forgiving then these are not the virtues we would associate with the author of the following verses about roasting a man over an open fire, with his wife, tethered like an animal, supplying the firewood that fuels the flame that is burning her husband.

THE FIBRE

111 Al-Masad

In the Name of Allah,
the Compassionate, the Merciful

111:1 Perish the hands of Abu Lahab, and may he perish too;

111:2 Neither his wealth nor what he has earned will avail him anything.

111:3 He will roast in a flaming fire,

111:4. And his wife will be a carrier of fire-wood,

111:5. She shall have a rope of fibre around her neck.

Does it matter that Abu Lahab and his wife were inveterate enemies of Islam in the early days? If the treatment reserved for Abu Lahab, an uncle of the Prophet, and his wife was an exception to the definition of mercy and compassion, then perhaps the phrase most associated with Allah would not, for the non-believer, have such a hollow ring. Roasting in Hell for an eternity is the fate Allah reserves for all who refuse to believe in Him and His Messenger; a fiery fate for all unbelievers which Allah never tires of reminding the readers of the Koran. Often when you come across the many verses where Allah brags about His mercy and compassion He has just committed a merciless, pitiless act of grandiose proportions, or is about to.

Islamic tradition informs us that Allah showed what non-Muslims would consider compassion and mercy for an unbeliever only once. He spared His Prophet's parents the torment of Hell after His Messenger was seen weeping over the tomb of his mother at Medina. When asked by people who were near him at the time why he was crying, he replied, it was because he had just seen his parents burning in hell. Allah would bring both parents, Abdullah and Amina, back to life temporarily so that they could become Muslim and enter Paradise.

Allah is adamant! His Messenger's parents notwithstanding, all unbelievers – whether they are your children, your mother or your father – are to be shown no compassion or mercy.

Another Islamic tradition maintains that when Allah saw His Messenger praying for a beloved, recently deceased uncle who had sheltered him, protected him from his enemies, been a father to the young Muhammad, whose own father died before he was born, he was scolded by the angel Gabriel. The angel, in no uncertain terms, informed the Prophet that Allah did not want to see His Messenger praying for an unbeliever ever again (his uncle Abu Talib died an unbeliever). He reminded the Prophet that it was all pointless anyway, since unbelievers automatically go to Hell.

The further you get into the Koran the more you have difficulty accepting the contradiction of a god who claims to be compassionate and merciful while revelling in the pain He will cause you if you die an unbeliever. Then you remember; <u>Islam is all about loyalty</u> and the whole thing starts making sense ... *again*. Those who intone *In the Name of Allah, the Compassionate, the Merciful* during prayer and at other occasions are reminding Allah that the price of their loyalty is the compassion and mercy He has promised to those who remain loyal and die believing in Him and Him only.

Allah will handsomely reward and forgive the sins of those who believe in Him and His Messenger and are ruthless with those who don't.

> 48:29 Muhammad is the Messenger of Allah and those who are with him are hard on the unbelievers, merciful towards each other. You will see them kneeling and prostrating themselves, seeking bounty and good pleasure from Allah; their mark is upon their faces, as a trace of their prostration. That is their likeness in the Torah and their likeness in the Gospels; just as a seed which puts forth its shoot, strengthens it and grows stout, then rises straight upon its stalks, delighting the sower, to vex thereby unbelievers. Allah has promised those who believe and do the righteous deeds forgiveness and a great wage.

Terrified Into Believing

You don't necessarily remain loyal to Allah because you love Him and He loves you[4]. You fear and respect Him for what He will do to you if you don't. The punishment reserved for Abu Lahab and his wife is just one of many graphic and cruel reminders scattered throughout the Koran of the price you will pay if you break your oath of loyalty to Allah. These pitiless Koranic images forever etched in the mind of the believer, never letting him or her forget that this god does not fool around when it comes to those who would dare not to submit to His Will.

When reading the Koran you have to get used to the violent imagery, just like more than a billion Muslims around the world who must recite verses just as horrifying as the one about the fate of the Prophet's uncle as part of their daily prayers to Allah. Writer and Islamic scholar Yahiya Emerick estimates that twenty-five percent of the Koran is concerned with visions of heaven and hell, mostly hell. And in these visions of hell, Allah is almost always torturing some unfortunate unbeliever with His favourite instrument of torture: *Fire*.

Fire seems to hold a mesmerizing fascination for Allah, an almost Zoroastrian-like fascination. In Fakhry's translation of the Koran, whenever Hell's fire is mentioned, it is written with a capital "F". This may just be his way of showing respect for Allah's beloved "Fire". When talking about sending unbelievers into the Fire, Allah's rationalisation is nearly always the same; unbelievers have it coming, they deserve to spend an eternity roasting in Hell for not believing in Me and my Messenger.

The opening surah of the Koran is repeated in every one of the five daily prayers. It is also recited on occasions of any significance, and at the commencement of a Muslim's daily activities. While two of the first three verses, verses 1:1 and 1:3 mention Allah's compassionate and merciful nature, every time a Muslim recites the seven verses that make up the first surah, *The Opening*, he is also

---

[4] A rare expression of affection for other than His Messenger, the Prophet Muhammad, followed by the ubiquitous boast from the All-Compassionate about generations He annihilated as a warning for generations to come.

> 19:96 Those who believe and do what is right, the Compassionate will favour them with love (His Love and that of their fellow creatures).
>
> 19:97 For We made it easy (the Qur'an) [to understand] in your own tongue, so as to announce the good news to the God-Fearing and warn trough it (the Meccan unbelievers).
>
> 19:98 And how many generations before them We have destroyed! Do you perceive any one of them or hear any sound of theirs?

reminded by the seventh verse that unbelievers are not deserving of Allah's compassion or mercy.

> 1:6 Lead us to the right path,
>
> 1:7 The path of those You have favoured Not those who have incurred Your wrath or have gone astray.

Allah promises a "terrible punishment" for those with whom He is displeased. The description of the pain He will inflict as revealed in the Koran more than lives up to that promise. Robert Redeker, a philosophy teacher, writing in *Le Figaro* described the Koran "as a book of incredible violence." And it is. And the violence, more often than not, when it is Allah talking about what He will do to those who will not submit to His will, as mentioned earlier, usually involves fire. Allah first mentions fire as His favourite instrument for torturing unbelievers early on in chapter 2, *The Cow*, after daring anyone to produce better verses than Him.

> 2:23 If you are in doubt as to what We have revealed to Our Servant (the Prophet Muhammad), then produce a surah similar to it and call upon your witnesses other than Allah (that is, the gods you associate with Allah), if you are truthful.
>
> 2:24 If you do not do that, and surely you will not, then guard yourself against the Fire whose fuel is men and stones, prepared for the unbelievers.

And how much time will you spend being consumed by a fire that is fuelled by "men and stones"?

> 2:39 And [as to] those who have disbelieved and denied Our Revelations, they are the people of Hell, wherein they will dwell forever.

Even if the topic is not unbelievers, as in the following verse where Allah warns the faithful not to use an expression His Messenger dislikes because the Jews frequently used it as a term of reproach, He can't resist mentioning what a painful punishment awaits the unbelievers. He does this all the time.

> 2:104 O believers, do not say (to our Messenger): "Ra'ina [listen to us] but Unzurna [look at us] and listen." And for the unbelievers a painful punishment is destined.

Allah, like the cat that teases the mouse it will eventually have for lunch, sometimes likes to have fun with the unbelievers, giving them a false sense of security, before tossing them into Hell where they will burn for an eternity. A revelation that gives us a glimpse into Allah's duplicitous, some would say, playful nature.

> 17:18 He who desires the transitory life, We hasten to him and to whomsoever We desire whatever We please. Later We consign him to Hell in which he will burn despised and rejected.

But it is mostly a lack of patience with unbelievers that we associate with Allah. The punishment can't be too soon for these wretched souls.

> 2:161 Upon those who disbelieve and die as unbelievers is the Curse of Allah, the angels, and the whole of mankind.
>
> 2:162 They abide forever in it (Hell); their punishment will not be reduced, nor will they be given any respite.

This punishment is a courtesy from a god who never tires of reminding the reader of His *compassionate and merciful* side just after he has condemned an unbeliever to an eternity of agony.

> 2:163 Your God is one God. There is no God but He, <u>The Compassionate, the Merciful.</u>

The creator and controller of the universe no less.

> 2:164 In the creation of the heavens and the earth; in the alternation of night and day; in the ships which sail in the sea with what profits mankind; in the water which Allah sends down from the sky in order to bring the earth back to life after its death and disperses over it every type of beast; in the continuous changing of winds; and in clouds which are driven between heaven and earth[5] – surely in these are signs for people who understand.

Having believed in other gods won't cut you any slack with Allah (revelation 2:167) after all He has done for you. It's into the Fire with you, and saying you are sorry for backing the wrong god will only make Him angrier.

> 2:165 Yet, there are people who set up equals to Allah (*false gods*), whom they love as they love Allah. Those who believe, however, have greater love for Allah. If only the evil-doers could understand, upon seeing the punishment, that all power is Allah's and that Allah is Stern in punishment.

---

[5] In the Koran, Paradise is just above the clouds.

> 2:166 Those who were followed will disowned those who followed them when they will see the punishment and their relations with each other will be severed.
>
> 2:167 Those who followed will say: "If only we could go back (to life on earth) we would disown them as they disowned us." Thus Allah will show them their works as sources of deep regret. And they will never come out of the Fire[6].

Another verse confirming that you will be joined in the Fire by the false gods you once worshipped.

> 21:98 "You and what you worship, besides Allah, are the fuel of Hell, and into it you shall all descend."

Sometimes you get the impression that Allah is looking for any excuse to mix people and Fire. In the next verse, He puts Fire into people.

> 2:174 Those who conceal anything from the Book which Allah has revealed and sell it for a small price will swallow nothing but fire in their bellies. Allah will not speak to them on the Day of Resurrection, nor will He purify them (from their sins), and their punishment is very painful.

Some will burn for an eternity because they differed about what is in *the Book*.

> 2:175 It is those who prefer to commit error rather than seek guidance, and incur punishment in place of forgiveness. How bold they are in the face of the Fire!
>
> 2:176 That is because Allah has revealed the Book with the truth; and those who disagree about the Book are in great dissent.

And so it goes ... We are just a few verses into the second chapter of the Koran and already the *Compassionate* is talking incessantly about roasting people. He will finally give it a rest more than one-hundred chapters later, more than six thousand verses later with the story of the hapless Abu Lahab roasting over an open fire with wood that his wife is forced to provide.

Wood!!! Didn't Allah say in verse 2:24 that men and stones were his favourite combustibles: "... guard yourself against the Fire whose fuel is men and stones"? Yes, and in a subsequent verse he reiterates

---

[6] Both the false gods and those who worshipped them will have Hell for a permanent home.

his preference for people as the ideal combustible to burn other people.

> 3:10 As to the unbelievers, neither their riches nor their children will avail them anything against Allah; in fact, they shall be the fuel of the Fire.

Maybe it was an act of kindness to Abu Lahab's wife who may not have been up to the task of stoking the fire that was barbecuing her husband with unbelievers, or her children depending on your interpretation of "their children will avail them anything against Allah; in fact, they shall be the fuel of the Fire." Or maybe, for Allah, wood and unbelievers are one and the same. Consider verse 8:37 where Allah talks about piling those who disbelieve like a cord of wood before casting them into the Fire.

> 8:36 Indeed, the unbelievers spend their wealth to bar [people] from Allah's Path. They will continue to spend it, but it will become a source of anguish for them; then they will be vanquished. And those who disbelieve shall be gathered in Hell.

> 8:37 So that Allah might separate the foul from the fair and place the foul, one upon the other, piling them up all together and casting them into Hell. Those are truly the losers.

I think it is safe to assume that due to the frequency of calling unbelievers fuel for His Hell that it is people who are Allah's favourite combustible. Refuse to believe in Allah or His Messenger and you become a burnable piece of trash, a piece of wood, a log just waiting to be cast, without ceremony or remorse, into Hell's Fire. A terrible dreadful place, Allah will remind us, where Satan himself would not want to spend any time.

You have to admire the genius of Allah in creating a Hell that is self-sustaining. People on fire burning other people and being burnt in return by other people being consumed by flames; only a god could have thought of that. I must admit that the more I advanced into the Koran, the more I came to appreciate the Gospels with their quiet, subdued message about loving your neighbour and turning the other cheek, with only scattered references to punishment for sinners, as opposed to Allah's constant, relentless, unremitting, cruel condemnation of anyone who won't accept Islam, His "perfect religion", as his or her religion.

In case you should forget about Allah's favourite fuel you will be reminded again and again … and again.

Allah's Way of Old

> 40:81 And He shows you His Signs. Which Signs of Allah will you then deny?
>
> 40:82 Have they not travelled in the land, then, to see what was the fate of those who preceded them? They were more numerous than they and had greater power and influence in the land. Yet what they used to earn availed them nothing.
>
> 40:83 Then, when their Messengers came to them with the clear proofs, they rejoiced in the knowledge they had and were afflicted with that which they used to mock at.
>
> 40:84 But when they saw Our Might, they said: "We believe in Allah alone and disbelieve in that we used to associate with Him."
>
> 40:85 Yet, their belief, upon seeing Our Might, did not profit them. It is Allah's Way of old regarding His servants; and the unbelievers shall be lost there and then.

Moududi on "Allah's Way of old":

> "The standing Law of Allah": the Law that repentance and faith are beneficial only till the time man is not seized by the torment of Allah or death. Believing or repenting after the torment has arrived or the signs of death have appeared, is not acceptable to Allah.

Unbelievers Not by Choice

The difficulty in getting more people to accept his claim that he is God's Messenger, and that the Message he is delivering is from the Almighty himself, via the angel Gabriel, caused the budding Prophet, on more than one occasion, to doubt his ability to fulfil his mission.

Numerous times, Allah, to shore up His favourite servant's morale, will explain to him that, if some people refuse to believe and obey him, it has nothing to do with the superbly drafted message and the excellent delivery. It is because He wants it that way; that it is all part of the Plan as He explains in the surah Yâ Sîn, which the Prophet called the Heart of the Koran.

> **It was narrated that Anas said:**
>
> "The Prophet (peace and blessings of Allaah (sic) be upon him) said: 'Everything has a heart and the heart of the Qur'an (sic) is Ya-Seen. Whoever recites Ya-Seen (sic),

Allaah will record for him the reward of reading the Qur'aan ten times.'"

al-Tirmidhi

In Yâ Sîn, Allah will again remind His Messenger that those whom He does not want as believers, such as the arrogant, He causes to remain unbelievers. In "the Heart of the Koran" Allah reveals, He has restrained the arrogant from becoming believers by placing "invisible shackles upon their necks down to their chins; and so their heads are held high". And to be absolutely sure the arrogant never believe, He has "placed in front of them a barrier and behind them a barrier" and "covered their eyes so they do not see" and are, therefore, oblivious to His Signs.

36 YÂ SÎN

*In the Name of Allah,
the Compassionate, the Merciful*

36:1 Yâ - Sîn (came to be one of the Prophet's names)

36:2 By the wise Qur'an.

36:3 You are truly one of the Messengers.

36:4 Upon a straight path.

36:5 It is the Revelation of the All-Mighty, the Merciful.

36:6 To warn a people, whose fathers were not warned and so they are heedless.

36:7 The sentence has been passed against most of them, for what they do not believe.

36:8 We have placed shackles upon their necks down to their chins; and so their heads are held high.

36:9 And We placed in front of them a barrier and behind them a barrier and We have covered their eyes so they do not see.

36:10 It is the same whether you warn them or do not warn them, they will not believe.

36:11 You only warn him who follows the Reminder and fears the All Compassionate though unseen. Announce to him, then, the good news of forgiveness and a generous wage.

In surah 10, *The Cave*, the "barrier" becomes "coverings upon their hearts", revelation 18:57.

18:56 We do not send Messengers except as bearer of good news and warners; yet the unbelievers dispute with falsehood, to refute the truth thereby; and they take My Revelations and what they were warned about as an object of mockery.

18:57 And who is more unjust than one who, upon being reminded of his Lord's Revelations, turns away from them, and forgets what his hands have done? We have placed coverings upon their hearts lest they understand it (the Qur'an), and put a deafness in their ears. If you call them to the guidance they will never be guided.

18:58 And your Lord is All-Forgiving and Merciful. Were He to call them to account for what they have earned, He would have hastened their punishment. However, they have an appointment from which they will find no escape.

18:59 And those towns, We have destroyed them when they did wrong, and We set for their destruction an appointed time.

If only those Allah wishes to lead will be led, it only makes sense for Allah to tell His Messenger to preach, so to speak, to the choir in revelation 36:11 as He does in revelation 18:28.

18:27 Recite what was revealed to you from your Lord's Book; no one can alter His Words, and from Him, you will find no refuge.

18:28 And confine yourself to those who call upon their Lord, morning and evening, desiring His Face. And let not your eyes wander away from them, desiring the finery of the present life. And do not obey him whose heart We have made heedless of Our Remembrance, he has followed his own desires, and his case has become hopeless.

Salih and the Destruction of Thamud

26:208 We have never destroyed a city, but it had prior warners,

26:209 As a reminder; and We have never been unjust.

"The Thamud were a people of ancient Arabia who were known from the 1st millennium BC to near the time of Muhammad. Although they are thought to have originated in southern Arabia, Arabic tradition has them moving north near Mada'in Saleh a pre-Islamic archaeological site."Wiki The Thamud were wiped out by Allah for not heading the warning of a prophet not found in the Bible, the Arab prophet Salih.

The Destruction of Thamud is also an exception to Allah's predilection for committing genocide because people called one or more of His messengers liars. Nonetheless, the destruction is just as ghastly and the reason for the destruction of the people of Thamud is about as petty as petty gets where gods are concerned.

"Away with…" is how Allah ends many of His stories about the civilizations He destroyed thereby demonstrating a somewhat uncaring, not to say callous, attitude towards the thousands of men, women and children He slaughters at a moment's notice and on the flimsiest of pretences; in the case of the people of Thamud, for an injury done to His camel, a white she-camel just like His Messenger's favourite camel.

Thamud, it would appear, had an army, just like Pharaoh's, which, like Pharaoh's was to no avail when confronted with Allah's Wrath.

85:17 Have you heard the story of the hosts (*armies*)?

85:18 Of Pharaoh and Thamud.

85:19 Yet, the unbeliever continue to denounce.

85:20 While Allah, from behind them, is All-Embracing.

Allah revels in the destruction of Thamud in at least nine surahs.

Surah 7, The Ramparts

In *The Ramparts* Thamud is destroyed by an earthquake.

> 7:73 And to Thamud [We sent] their brother Salih. He said: "O my people, worship Allah; you have no other god but He. A clear proof from your Lord has now come to you. This is Allah's she-camel, to be a sign onto you; so let it graze in Allah's Land and do not cause her any harm; for you will be then be seized by a very painful punishment.
>
> 7:74 "And remember how He made you as successors after 'Ad, and established you in the land, wherein you built yourselves castles on its plains and hewed the mountains into houses. Remember then Allah's Bounties and do not corrupt the earth with mischief."
>
> 7:75 The arrogant dignitaries among his people said to some of those who had believed and were deemed to be weak: "Do you know that Salih is sent forth from his Lord?" They said: "Indeed, we believe in what he has been sent with."
>
> 7:76 The arrogant dignitaries said: "In that which you have believed, we definitely disbelieve."
>
> 7:77 So they hamstrung the she-camel and defied their Lord's Command and said: "O Salih, bring upon us what you are promising us, if you are one of the Messengers."
>
> 7:78 Whereupon the earthquake overtook them, and so they lay prostrate in their own homes.
>
> 7:79 Then he turned his back on them and said: "O my people, I have delivered to you my Lord's Message and given you advice, but you do not like the givers of advice."

Surah 11, Hud

In *Hud,* it's "the [thundering] cry"!

> 11:61 And to Thamud [We sent] their brother Salih. He said: "O my people, worship Allah; you have no other god but Him. He brought you out from the earth and made you inhabit it; so ask His forgiveness and repent onto Him. My Lord is indeed close at hand and answers [the prayer]."
>
> 11:62 They said: "O Salih, we set our hopes on you before this. Do you forbid us to worship what our fathers worshipped? We are indeed in grave doubt regarding what you are calling us to."

> 11:63 He said: "O my people, what if I am in possession of a clear proof from my Lord, and He has accorded me a mercy of His Own? Who then will protect me from Allah if I disobey Him? Surely, you will only compound my perdition.
>
> 11:64 "O my people, here is the she-camel of Allah, a sign onto you. Let her graze in Allah's land and do not do her any harm, lest a swift punishment should overtake you."

After someone cuts the camel's hamstring, Salih tells the people of Thamud that they only have three days to live.

> 11:65 However, they hamstrung her, and so he said: "[You can] stay in your houses [only] for three days. This is a promise which will not be belied."
>
> 11:66 Then, when our Command came, We saved Salih and those who believed with him, by a mercy of Our Own, from the disgrace of that day. Your Lord is truly the Strong, and Mighty.
>
> 11:67 And the evildoers were overtaken by the [thundering] cry and they lay prostrate in their own homes,
>
> 11:68 As if they never dwelt therein. Truly, Thamud disbelieved their Lord. Away with Thamud!

Surah 17, The Night Journey

The night journey is a reference to the night the Prophet flew to heaven on a horse name Al Burak to meet with God. In this two revelation account of the destruction of Thamud, Allah alludes to this short time get-together when He gave His Messenger a glimpse of Hell and the tree at the bottom of Hell – the Tree of Zaqqum, "the tree cursed in the Qur'an" in revelation 17:60 – which will provide the food for the sinners e.g. the people of Thamud.

> 17:59 Nothing prevents Us from sending the signs except that the ancients denied them. We gave to Thamud the she-camel as a manifest sign, but they maltreated her. We do not sent the signs except to warn.
>
> 17:60 [Remember] when We said to you; "Your Lord encompasses mankind. We did not make the vision We showed you except as a trial to mankind, and likewise the tree cursed in the Qur'an. We warn them, but that only increased their tyranny."

The resistance to the Message of Salih by the "tyrants" of Thamud was exceptional considering Allah's appalling description of His pitiless out-of-proportion punishment that the men, women and children of Thamud would experience for an eternity because of a regrettable prank.

Surah 26, The Poets

In *The Poets*, the people regret what they did to Allah's camel; but being sorry did not deter the wrath of the Compassionate.

26:141 Thamud denounced the Messengers as liars.

26:142 When their brother Salih said to them: "Do you not fear God?

26:143 "I am a faithful Messenger to you.

26:144 "So fear Allah and obey me.

26:145 "I do not ask you any wages for this; my wage is with the Lord of the Worlds.

26:146 "Will you be left herebelow in peace?

26:147 "In gardens and springs;

26:148 "And plantations and palm trees, whose shoots are tender?

26:149 "And will you hew skilfully houses in the mountains?

26:150 "So fear Allah and obey me.

26:151 "And do not obey the orders of the extravagant;

26:152 "Who work corruption in the land and do not make amends."

26:153 They said: "You are certainly a man bewitched.

26:154 "You are only a mortal like us. Produce, then, a sign, if you are truthful."

26:155 He said: "This is a she-camel; this has a drinking day, and you have a fixed drinking day.

26:156 "Do not cause her any harm, or else the punishment of a Great Day will smite you."

26:157 However, they hamstrung her, and became full of remorse.

26:158 Then, punishment smote them. There is surely in that a sign; and most of them were not believers.

26:159 Your Lord is truly the All-Mighty, the Merciful.

Surah 27, The Ants

The destruction of Thamud in *The Ants* is the only recollection where the she-camel is not mentioned. In *The Ants* Allah reveals that it was nine wrongdoers who were responsible for His genocidal wrath and that He did it, in part, to prove that He was a better schemer.

27:45 And We have sent to Thamud their brother Salih, saying: "Worship Allah"; and lo and behold, they split into two groups fighting each other.

27:46 He said: "O my people, why do you hasten the evil course before the fair? If only you would seek Allah's Forgiveness, that perchance you may receive mercy!"

27:47 They said: "We augured ill of you and your companions." He said: 'Your bird of omen is with Allah, but you are a people who are being tested."

27:48 And they were in the city nine individuals, who worked corruption in the land and did not set things right.

27:49 They said: "Swear one to the other by Allah: We will attack him and his family at night; then we will tell his guardian: 'We did not witness the slaying of his family, and we are indeed truthful.'"

27:50 They schemed a scheme and We schemed a scheme, while they were unaware.

27:51 See, then, what was the outcome of their scheming; We destroyed them together will all their people.

27:52 Their houses are in ruin, on account of their wrongdoing. There is in that a sign for a people who know.

27:53 And we delivered those who believed and were God-fearing.

Surah 41, The Well-Expounded

The shortest account of the obliteration of Thamud:

41:17 But as for Thamud, We extended guidance to them; yet they preferred blindness to guidance, and so the thunderbolt of humiliating punishment seized them on account of what they used to earn.

41:18 And We delivered those who believed and were God-Fearing.

Surah 51, The Scattering Wind

The Thamud disappeared from history shortly before the Prophet Muhammad arrived on the scene; it was not the next genocide after that of Noah's people as might be assumed from, revealed truth 51:46. It may simply be the Almighty reminding the believers of His favourite act of wanton destruction of a sinful people.

51:43 And in Thamud, when it was said to them: "Enjoy yourselves for a while."

51:44 Then, they disdained arrogantly the command of their Lord, and so the thunderbolt struck them, while they looked on.

51:45 They were unable to stand upright, and they were not victorious.

51:46 And We destroyed the people of Noah before that. They were indeed a sinful people.

Surah 54, The Moon

In *The Moon*, Allah recalls the many people He has destroyed, including the people of Thamud, for not believing in Him.

54:23 Thamud denounced the warnings as lies.

54:24 So they said: "Shall we follow a lone mortal from among us? We are indeed in error and folly.

54:25 "Has the Reminder been sent down upon him alone among us? No, he is an arrogant liar."

54:26 They will surely know tomorrow who is the arrogant liar.

54:27 We shall send the she-camel as a test for them; so watch them and be patient.

54:28 And tell them that the water is to be divided between them, each drinking in turn.

54:29 They called their companion, and so he took charge and hamstrung [her].

54:30 How then were My Punishment and My Warnings?

54:31 We released upon them a single cry and they became like the stubble of a corral-builder.

Surah 91, The Sun

In the *Sun*, Allah's camel's drinking time is part of the test.

> 91:11 Thamud have denounced, due to their arrogance.
>
> 91:12 When their most vicious citizen emerged.
>
> 91:13 Then Allah's Messenger said to them: "Beware of Allah's she-camel and her drinking time."
>
> 91:14 They called him a liar and hamstrung her; whereupon their Lord destroyed them for their sins and settled the matter;
>
> 91:15 And He does not fear its sequel.

Al-Rass

Allah, in bragging of his destructions of the people of Thamud and 'Ad and the genocide of countless "generations in between", in two revelations (25:38, 50:12) in Fakhry's translation mentions "the companions of al-Rass" as being another people and/or city He has annihilated. In three other translations (Pickthall, Shakir and Khan) it is "the dwellers in ar-Rass" or "dwellers of the Rass", therefore it is safe to assume that Rass is a reference to another unfortunate rational people who did not buy into Allah's Messenger's Message that they would be raised from the dead; so He killed every last one of them, including children who would not have had a clue as to what was being revealed.

> 25:38 And 'Ad, Thamud, the companions of al-Rass and many generations in between;
>
> 25:39 To each, We proposed similes and each We ruined utterly.
>
> 25:40 And they came upon the city (of Lot) which was drench by an evil rain. Did they not see it? No, they did not hope to be raised from the dead.

In Khan's translation "them" in revelation 50:12 are "the pagans of Makkah who denied you, O Muhammad SAW".

> 50:12 Prior to them, the people of Noah, the companions of al-Rass and Thamud denounced [the Prophets].
>
> 50:13 'Ad, Pharaoh and the brethren of Lot, too;

Some of the generations in between must have included "the Companions of the Thicket" and "the people of Tubba'".

50:14 And the Companions of the Thicket and the people of Tubba', they all denounced the Messengers and so My Warning was fulfilled.

Allah Days

30:42 Say: "Travel in the land and behold what was the fate of those who came before; most of them were idolaters."

30:43 So, set your face towards the true religion, before a Day from Allah comes, which cannot be turned back. On that Day they will be rent asunder.

There is Judgement Day, the aforementioned day yet to come "when they will be rent asunder"; then there are Allah Days, agonising days of death and destruction in the here-and-now, until the ultimate manifestation of the irrepressible omnipotent sociopath's wrath[7] is visited on an unsuspecting world signaling the end of times.

30:44 Whoever disbelieves, upon him shall recoil his unbelief and whoever does a righteous deed, it is for themselves that they will be preparing a comfortable abode.

30:45 That He may reward those who have believed and done the righteous deeds out of His Bounty. Indeed, He does not love the unbelievers.

30:47 We have, indeed, sent Messengers to their own people before you (*Muhammad*), and they brought them clear

---

[7] A psychiatrist was allegedly asked: "what is the difference between a psychopath and a sociopath?" His response: "A psychopath, if he wishes to kill you, will show up at your door and kill you and anyone with you; a sociopath will not bother showing up, he will simply destroy the neighborhood in which you live." From that perhaps insubstantial definition, Allah does fit the description of a sociopath as does His Messenger whose army did the killing.

Narrated Anas bin Malik:

Allah's Apostle reached Khaibar in the early morning and the people of Khaibar came out with their spades, and when they saw the Prophet they said, "Muhammad and his army!" and returned hurriedly to take refuge in the fort.

The Prophet raised his hands and said, "Allah is Greater! Khaibar is ruined! If we approach a nation, then miserable is the morning of those who are warned."

Bukhari 56.840

proofs. Then We revenged upon those who sinned, and it was incumbent on Us to give the believers support.

A Litany of Death and Destruction

> 14:5 We have, indeed, sent Moses with our Signs (sayings): "Bring your people out of the darkness and into the light and remind them of Allah Days (major events or calamities)." Surely in those are signs for every steadfast and thankful person.

As you may have begun to appreciate from reading about prophets from the Bible who, in the Koran, are responsible for the cruel death of countless men, women and children, you don't mess with Allah's Messengers. More revelations about a quick to anger deity and, in this instance, mostly anonymous Messengers who are the justification for His devastating Wraths.

> 40:21 Have they not journeyed in the land and seen what was the ultimate fate of those who came before them? Then Allah seized them because of their sins, and against Allah they had no protectors.

> 40:22 That is because their Messengers used to come to them with the clear proofs, but they disbelieved. So Allah seized them; He is indeed Strong, Terrible in retribution.

> 23:31 Then, We brought out after them another generation.

> 23:32 So, We sent them a Messenger of their own, saying: "Worship Allah, you have no other god than Him. Do you not fear [Allah]?"

> 23:33 Then the dignitaries of his people, who had disbelieved and denied the meeting of the Hereafter and whom We accorded ease in the present life, said: "This is, indeed, merely a mortal like you; he eats from what you eat and drinks from what you drink.

> 23:34 "If you obey a mortal like yourselves, you are surely the losers.

> 23:35 "Does he promise you that once you die and turn into dust and bones, you will be brought back?

> 23:36 "Far, far away is what you are promised!

> 23:37 "There is only this our earthly life; we die and we live, but we shall not be raised from the dead.

> 23:38 "He is only a man who fabricates lies about Allah and we will not believe in him."

The familiar unspoken demand from the Messenger that Allah murder every man, woman and child for the "dignitaries" calling him a liar.

> 23:39 He said: "Lord, support me against their calling me a liar."
>
> 23:40 He (Allah) said: "In a little while they will regret."
>
> 23:41 Then the Cry seized them justly, and so We turned them into scum. Away then with the wrongdoing people!
>
> 23:42 Then We raised up after them other generations.
>
> 23:43 No nation hastens its term; nor will they put it back.
>
> 23:44 Then We sent Our Messengers one after the other. Every time a Messenger came to his nation, they denied him. So We made them succeed one another and reduced them to mere tales. Away with the people who do not believe.

And you know what happened next. For Allah to destroy an entire generation, or a city it does not matter that within that generation or city, are good, if poor people; if the wealthy people don't do what they are told, it is death to everyone.

> 17:16 And when We want to destroy a city, We command those of its people who are given to luxury; but as they transgress therein Our sentence against it is pronounced and We utterly destroy it.
>
> 17:17 How many generations We have destroyed since Noah! It suffices that your Lord knows and sees the sins of His Servants.

Yet, Allah claims that He only destroys the wrongdoing people.

> 6:47 Say: "Tell me! If Allah's Punishment should seize you suddenly or openly, will any be destroyed other than the wrongdoing people?"
>
> 6:48 And We only send forth the Messengers as bearers of good tidings and warners. Those who believe and mend their ways have nothing to fear and have no cause to grieve.
>
> 6:49 But those who deny Our Revelations will be punished for having been sinful.

It's all about being humble.

> 6:42 We have indeed sent forth [Messengers] to other nations before you (*Muhammad*) and We afflicted them with misery and hardship that perchance they might humble themselves.
>
> 6:43 If only they humbled themselves when Our Punishment overtook them; but their hearts were hardened and the Devil made what they were doing seem fair to them.

Happy Days as a harbinger of Allah Days.

> 6:44 Then, when they forgot what they were reminded of, We opened wide for them the gates of everything [good]; so that as soon as they rejoiced at what they were given, We struck them down suddenly, and they were driven to despair.
>
> 6:45 Thus the remnant of the wrongdoing people were rooted out, Praise be to Allah, the Lord of the Worlds!

He destroys one generation, only to raise another which, in all likelihood, will suffer a similar fate at the hands of a petty, vengeful genocidal deity.

THE CATTLE

6 Al-An'âm

*In the Name of Allah,
the Compassionate, the Merciful*

> 6:1 Praise be to Allah, Who created the heavens and the earth and made the darkness and the light; yet the unbelievers set up equals to their Lord.
>
> 6:2 It is He Who created you from clay, then decreed a term [for you] and another set term with Him, but still you doubt.
>
> 6:3 He is Allah in the heavens and on earth. He knows your secrets and public utterances, and He knows what you earn (the good and evil you do).
>
> 6:4 And there comes not to them a revelation from Allah, but they turn away from it.
>
> 6:5 So, they denied the truth when it came to them; but surely the news of what they were mocking will come to them.

6:6 Do they not see how many generations before them We destroyed, after We had established them in the earth more firmly than We had established you, and how We let loose the sky upon them in torrents, and We made the rivers flow beneath them? Thus we destroyed them because of their sins. And after them We raised another generation.

THE RAMPARTS
7 Al-A'râf

*In the Name of Allah,
the Compassionate, the Merciful*

7:1 Alif - Lam - Mim - Sad.

7:2 [This is] a Book revealed to you (Muhammad); let there be no gall in your heart because of it. [It is revealed] so that you may warn with it, and as a reminder to the believers.

7:3 Follow what has been revealed to you from your Lord and do not follow other patrons besides Him. How little you heed the warning.

7:4 How many a town We have destroyed; Our might struck them at night or while they were napping.

5. Their only assertion when Our Might struck them was to say: "We have indeed been wrongdoers."

...

7:94 We did not send forth a Prophet to any city but afflicted its people with distress and suffering, that perchance they might humble themselves.

7:95 Then We changed their adversity into well-being, till they multiplied. They said: "Hardship and prosperity did visit our fathers." Then, We seized them suddenly, while they were unaware.

7:96 Yet had the people of the cities believed and feared Allah, We would have opened upon them blessings from the sky and the earth (rain from the sky, plants from the earth); but they denied [the Prophets], and so We destroyed them on account of their misdeeds.

The saddest thing about Allah Days is that they are pre-ordained, and there is nothing anyone can do to deter them. A town, a city, a civilization could not escape the cruel fate Allah had in store for it, as He explained to His Messenger, who may have wondered why, in his lifetime, God did not obliterate forthwith cities where people enjoyed life instead of humbling themselves before Him, as He had done before.

THE ROCK (THAMUD)
15 Al-Hijr

*In the Name of Allah,
the Compassionate, the Merciful*

15:1 Alif – Lam Ra.
These are the Verses of the Book and a manifest Qur'an.

15:2 Perhaps those who disbelieve wish they were Muslims.

15:3 Leave them to eat, enjoy themselves and let [false] hopes beguile them; for they will soon know.

15:4 We have never destroyed a town but it had a fixed decree.

15.5 No nation can hasten its term, nor defer it.

Death will not bring any relief for those who had the impudence to deny Allah's Messengers.

35:23 You are only a warner.

35:24 We have sent you forth in truth as a bearer of good news and a warner. There is not a nation to whom a warner has not come and gone.

35:25 If they denounce you as a liar; those before them have also denounced; their Messengers came to them with clear proofs, with scriptures and the illuminating Book.

35:26 Then I seized the unbelievers; how then was My wrath!

65:8 How many a city transgressed arrogantly the Command of its Lord and His Messengers; and so We brought it to account severely and punished it with an abominable punishment.

65:9 And so it tasted the bane of its deed and the outcome of its deed was perdition.

65:10 Allah has prepared for them a terrible punishment. So fear Allah, O people of understanding who have believed. Allah has sent down to you a reminder,

65:11 A Messenger, reciting to you the Signs of Allah fully

clarified; so as to bring those who have believed and done the righteous deeds from the shadows of darkness to light. He who believes in Allah and does the righteous deed, Allah will admit him into Gardens, beneath which rivers flow, dwelling therein forever. Allah has assigned to him a fair provision.

65:12 It is Allah Who created seven heavens and of the earth like thereof. The Decree descends among them all, that you might know that Allah has power over everything and that Allah has encompassed everything in knowledge.

In His would-be uplifting messages for His Messenger, who was being accused of spreading lies, parts of which was that he is in good company, Allah again demonstrates His trademark casual whimsical attitude to the taking of human lives.

22:42 If they denounce you as a liar, then the people of Noah, 'Ad and Thamud have denounced before them;

22:43 And the people of Abraham and the people of Lot, too;

22:44 And the people of Midian. And Moses was denounced. Then I reprieved the unbelievers; then I struck them down. How, then, was my punishment?

22:45 How many a city We destroyed when it was doing wrong; and now it has fallen down upon its turrets; and how many a deserted well, and lofty palace?

22:46 Have they not travelled in the land, so as to acquire hearts to reason with[8]; or ears to hear by? For it is not the eyes which are blind, but the hearts within the breasts.

22:47 They ask you to hasten the punishment. Allah will never break His Promise; but a day for your Lord is like a thousand years of what you reckon.

22:48 And how many a city have I reprieved, although it was unjust? Then I struck it down, and unto Me is the ultimate return.

The audacity of a god who dares to lay claim to being the embodiment of opposites, revelation 16:47.

16:45 Do those who devise evil feel assured that Allah will not cause the earth to swallow them up, or that punishment

---

[8] Like many classical philosophers, including Aristotle, Allah considered the heart the seat of reason, not the head and the brain contained within.

will not overtake them from whence they do not expect?

16:46 Or that He will not seize them in the course of their journeys, when they will not be able to escape?

16:47 Or that He will not seize then while in dread? Surely your Lord is Clement, Merciful.

It is a testament to the human race's resilience that even after reports of massive pitiless annihilations throughout the Koran of men, women and children in their homes, courtesy of a god who claims to be the epitome of Compassion and Mercy, the earth's population now surpasses six billion souls with unbelievers outnumbering believers by approximately four to one. This is not to say that Allah, whose patience and scheming is legendary, will not be in a position to redress this imbalance in a generation or two, or perhaps earlier, and do "Away with the people who do not believe", once and for all, for "they are, indeed, the companions of the Fire."

THE FORGIVER

40 Ghâfir

In the Name of Allah,
The Compassionate, the Merciful

40:1 Ha – Mim.

40:2 The sending down of the Book is from Allah, the All-Mighty, the All-Knowing.

40:3 The Forgiver of sins, Receiver of repentance, Terrible in retribution, the Bountiful. There is no god but He. Unto Him is the ultimate return.

40:4 No one disputes concerning the Signs of Allah, except the unbelievers; so do not be deceived by their wandering in the lands.

40:5 Before them, the people of Noah and the Confederates after them have denounced, and each nation sallied forth against their Messenger to seize him, and they disputed falsely to repudiate therewith the truth. Then I seized them. How, then, was my retribution?

40:6 And thus your Lord's Word against the unbelievers was fulfilled, that they are, indeed, the companions of the Fire.

Allah's Covenant with His Prophets

> 3:81 And when Allah made His Covenant with the Prophets, [He said]: "I gave you the Book and the Wisdom. Then a Messenger came to you confirming what you already possessed; so you must believe in him and give him support." He said: "Do you affirm this and accept my covenant on this matter?" They said: "We do affirm it." He said: "Bear witness and I will be with you one of the witnesses."
>
> 3:82 "Whoever turns his back thereafter; such, are the true sinners."

Allah's Covenant with His Prophets included His last and greatest Messenger, the one-and-only Prophet Muhammad.

> 33:7 And [remember] when We took from the Prophets their covenant and from you and from Noah, Abraham and Jesus, son of Mary, too; and We took from them a solemn covenant;
>
> 33:8 So as to question the truthful about their truthfulness, and He has prepared for the unbelievers a very painful punishment.

The World Before and After the Messengers

> 2:213 Mankind was one nation. Then Allah sent forth the Prophets as bearers of good news and warners. He sent with them the Book (the Scriptures) in truth, to judge between people regarding what they differed on. And none differed on it (religion) except those to whom it (the Book) was given after clear proofs had reached them, out of envy for one another. Allah, by His Will, guided those who believe to the truth on which they had differed. Allah guides whom He wills to the Right path.
>
> 2:214 Or do you suppose that you will enter Paradise before the example of those who came before you had reached you? They were stricken by privation and affliction and were so shaken that the Messenger and those who believe along with him said: "When is Allah's support coming?" Surely Allah's Support is close at hand.

If only ...

11:116 If only there had been among generations who preceded you (*Muhammad*) men possessing understanding and forbidding corruption in the earth, except for a few of them whom We saved! The wrongdoers continued to indulge in what they used to enjoy and, in fact, were wicked sinners.

11:117 And your Lord would not have destroyed the cities unjustly, had their inhabitants been righteous.

11:118 And had your Lord willed, He would have made mankind a single nation[9]; but they will continue to differ among themselves,

11:119 Except for those on whom your Lord has mercy. To that end He created them, and the Word of your Lord has been accomplished: "I will surely fill up Hell with jinn and humans all together."

11:120 And all We relate to you (*Muhammad*) of the tidings of the Messengers is to strengthen your heart; and you have received in these the truth, admonition and a reminder for the believers.

11:121 And say to the unbelievers: "Continue with what you are doing, and We shall continue with ours.

11:122 "And wait; we too are waiting."

11:123 To Allah belongs the Unseen in the heavens and on the earth, and to Him the whole affairs shall be referred. So worship Him and put your trust in Him; your Lord is not unaware of the things you do.

Why No Roofs and Stairways of Silver

Another way that Allah split up the one nation, apart from sending Messengers who sowed discord, was to deny people some of His Bounty such as "roofs of silver" and "adornment of gold" so that people would not be deluded into thinking that the here-and-now

---

[9] 10:19 Mankind were a single nation; then they differed. Had it not been for a prior order of your Lord, the matter over which they had differed would have been settled.

42:8 Had Allah wished, He would have made them a single nation, but He admits whom He wishes into His Mercy. Yet, the wrongdoers have no protector or supporter.

42:9 Or have they taken, apart from Him, other protectors? Surely Allah is the Protector and He revives the dead and has power over everything.

was a better place than the Hereafter. In modern vernacular, He was afraid of a single nation of materialists who sought only to live the good life in the here-and-now instead of seeking the good life in the Hereafter. This interpretation is similar to Moududi's.

> 43:32 Do they apportion the Mercy of your Lord? It is We Who have apportioned their livelihood among them in the present life and raised some of them in rank above others; so that some would be subservient to the others. Your Lord's Mercy is better than what they amass.

> 43:33 And were it not for fear that mankind would be a single nation, We would have assigned to those who disbelieve in the All-Compassionate, roof of silver for their houses and stairways upon which they ascend;

> 43:34 And portal for their houses and couches upon which they recline;

> 43:35 And adornment of gold; but all that is nothing but worldly enjoyment. Yet the Hereafter with your Lord is reserved for the God-fearing.

Messengers to the Common People

A little known fact, is that Allah also sent Messengers to the common people, the "common nations" in revelation 62:2. Common nation, al-Ummiyyun in Arabic, Fakhry notes "could also mean the illiterates, or the people of no revealed scripture, as against People of the Book, or Jews and Christians."

FRIDAY, OR THE CONGREGATION

60 Al-Jumu'ah

*In the Name of Allah,
The Compassionate, the Merciful*

> 62:1 Everything in the heavens and on the earth glorifies Allah, the King, the Holy One, the All-Mighty, the All-Wise.

> 62:2 It is He Who raised up from the common nations a Messenger of their own, reciting to them His Signs, purifying them and teaching them the Book and the wisdom, although they had been in manifest error before that;

> 62:3 And others from them, who had not joined them yet. He is the All-Mighty, the Wise.

62:4 That is Allah's Bounty which He imparts to whomever He pleases; and to Allah belongs the Great Bounty.

Allah Days or the Nearer Punishment

32:18 Is he who believes, then, like he who is a sinner? No, they are not equal.

32:19 As for those who believe and do the righteous deeds , they will have gardens of refuge to receive them, for what they used to do.

32:20 But, as for the sinners, their refuge is the Fire. Every time they want to get out of it, they are brought back and it will be said to them: "Taste the punishment of the Fire which you used to deny."

32:21 We shall surely let them taste the nearer punishment ("those calamities which afflict man in this world" *Moududi*), prior to the greater punishment, that perchance they might repent.

32:22 Who is more unjust than he who is reminded of Our Signs, then he turns away from them? We will certainly wreck vengeance upon the criminals.

Allah and the Crime of No Longer Believing

2:257 Allah is the Supporter of the believers. He brings them out of darkness into light. As for those who disbelieve, their supporters are the devils who bring them out of light into darkness. Those are the people of the Fire in which they shall abide forever.

5:54 O believers, whoever of you renounces his religion, Allah will certainly bring forth (replace them) a people whom He loves and they love him, humble towards the faithful, but mighty towards the unbelievers. They fight in the Way of Allah and do not fear anybody's reproach. That is a favour from Allah which He confers on whomever He pleases. Allah is Munificent, All-Knowing.

The Example of Pharaoh

If you are in a position do so, you do not wait on Allah's promise to replace those who renounce His religion, you must take matters into your own hands and expedite their becoming "people of the Fire". Apostasy i.e. abandoning your faith is a crime punishable by death; a gruesome death, based in part on what Allah said He would do to disbelievers in the Hereafter (revelation 88:24), and Pharaoh said He would do to his apostate magicians in the here-and-now when they professed their devotion to Allah after witnessing Moses' superior magic.

> 20:70 Then the magicians fell down prostrate. They said: "We believe [now] in the Lord of Aaron and Moses." .
>
> 20:71 He (Pharaoh) said: "Do you believe in him before I give you leave? It must be your chief who has taught you magic. I shall then cut your hands and feet on alternate sides, and I will crucify you upon the trunks of palm trees, and you will certainly know whose punishment is sterner and more lasting."

Religious leaders in Afghanistan did not demand that Abdul Rahman – an Afghan man sentenced to death for converting to Catholicism – be crucified and dismembered, but still insisted that he be tortured before the death sentence was carried out as called for by their interpretation of Islamic law. In the face of public outcry, and pressure from the Vatican, Rahman was allowed to emigrate to Italy to escape his death sentence.

A Canadian imam said that apostates deserved to die because of the embarrassment they cause Allah by leaving his perfect religion.

Can you return to the faith to save your life? The Salmon Rushdie experience would indicate that this is not always possible. Rushdie, after being declared an apostate for writing The Satanic Verses, offered a public apology and re-affirmed his commitment to Islam, to no avail. Khomeini's death sentence still stands.

Repentance Denied

In an extraordinary series of revelations, Allah seeks to explain his views on apostates, first promising to forgive those who "disbelieved after they had believed" and "repent afterwards", revealed truth 3:89; then, revealing the almost exact opposite, adding the qualifier about growing in disbelief, revealed truth 3:90.

> 3:86 How will Allah guide a people who disbelieved after they had believed and bore witness that the Messenger is true, and after the clear proofs had come to them? Allah will not guide the unjust people.

> 3:87 The reward of those people shall be that the curse of Allah, the angels and mankind as a whole shall be upon them.

> 3:88 They will abide therein forever; their punishment shall not be lightened and they shall have no respite.

He then softens his stance:

> 3:89 Except for those who repent afterwards and mend their ways; for Allah is Forgiving and Merciful.

Then the hard line again:

> 3:90 Surely those who disbelieve after believing, and then grow in disbelief, their repentance shall not be accepted. Those are the ones who have gone astray!

> 3:91 As for those who disbelieve and die as unbelievers, the earth's fill of gold will not be accepted from any of them,

"Kill them wherever you find them"

Some modern Islamic scholars, according to Ibn Warraq author of *Why I am not a Muslim* and *Leaving Islam: Apostates Speak Out*, argue that "in the Koran the apostate is threatened with punishment only in the next world"[10]. Such an argument could be made based on revelation 88:24 if you assume that in the preceding verses where Allah instructs His Messenger to "dominate ... him who turns away and disbelieves" is not an order to kill them if they don't desist in their disbelief.

> 88:17 Will they, then, not consider the camels, how they were created?
>
> 88:18 And heaven, how it was raised up?
>
> 88:19 And the mountains, how they were hoisted?
>
> 88:20 And the earth, how it was levelled.
>
> 88:21 So, exhort, you are a mere exhorter;
>
> 88:22 You are not supposed to dominate (compel, *Moududi*) them;
>
> 88:23 Except for him who turns away and disbelieves;
>
> 88:24 Then Allah will punish him in the most terrible way.
>
> 88:25 Indeed, unto Us is their return;
>
> 88:26 Then, upon Us rests their reckoning.

Mr. Warraq disagrees with this interpretation, as do most traditional Islamic scholars. Two compelling reasons being verse 4:89 and a hadith from the Prophet Muhammad that demonstrates that when it comes to apostates both Allah and His Messenger are of the same mind and unequivocally so.

Allah said:

> 4:89 They wish that you disbelieve, as they have disbelieved, so that you will all be alike. Do not, then, take any companions from them, until they emigrate in the Way of Allah. Then should they turn back, seize them and <u>kill</u>

---

[10] From a paper presented by Ibn Warraq at a panel discussion on "Apostasy, Human Rights, Religion and Belief" held at the 60th Session of the UN Commission on Human Rights in Geneva on April 7, 2004

> them wherever you find them; and do not take from them any companion or supporter;

The Prophet said:

> If a Muslim discards his religion, kill him. (*Bukhari:* 4.52.260).

In war, deserters are usually executed to deter others from abandoning the fight. Islam, since the Prophet's flight to Medina, year one in the Islamic calendar, has considered itself at war with the unbelievers until such a time as they have all submitted to the Will of Allah or have been killed or enslaved. Allah and His Messenger's demand that those who abandon the Faith, with the outcome of the war still undecided, may have to do with not weakening the war effort as desertions tend to do.

~~~~~~~~~~~~

Allah did make at least two exceptions to His general rule of killing apostates "wherever you find them."

> 4:90 Except for those who seek refuge with a people with whom you are bound by a compact, or come to you because their hearts forbid them to fight you or fight their own people. Had Allah wished, He would have made them dominate you; and then they would have certainly fought you. If, however, they leave you alone and do not fight you and offer you peace, then Allah allows you no way against them.

> 4:91 You shall find others who wish to be secure from you and secure from their own people; yet, whenever they are called back to sedition they plunge into it. If these do not keep away from you, nor offer you peace, nor hold their hands back, then seize them and kill them wherever you find them. Those, we have given you clear authority over them.

> 16:106 He who disbelieves in Allah after He has believed, except him who is compelled, but his heart remains firm in belief (will be forgiven); but those whose hearts rejoice in disbelief shall incur Allah's Wrath and a grievous punishment awaits them.

Apostates may not believe in the Hereafter, but the Hereafter will be waiting, but not in a good way.

16:109 There is no doubt that in the Hereafter they shall be the losers.

Telling Apostates and Believers Apart On Judgement Day

On Judgement Day those who believed then disbelieved will be easily identifiable for their face will turn black.

> 3:106 On the Day when some faces will turn white and others will turn black. As to those whose faces turn black [it will be said]: "Did you disbelieve after you had believed? Then taste the punishment because you have disbelieved."

As for those whose faces turn white, the next verse, a totally different outcome, which raises an interesting question: "Will the skin of the inhabitants of Paradise all be the same colour?"

> 3:107 But as for those whose faces turned white, they will dwell in Allah's Mercy (Paradise) forever.

> 3:108 These are the Revelations of Allah. We recite them to you in truth, and Allah does not desire any injustice for mankind.

> 3:109 And to Allah belongs what is in the heavens and on earth, and unto Him all matters shall be referred.

Abraham's father was not an apostate, but an unbeliever, and he too, the Prophet informs us, will have his face blackened on Judgement Day, confirming, perhaps, that only white and dark-skinned people sporting white faces will be allowed into Paradise.

> **Narrated Abu Huraira:**
>
> The Prophet said, "On the Day of Resurrection Abraham will meet his father Azar whose face will be dark and covered with dust ..."
>
> *Bukhari 55.569*

Whatever you do, don't die as an unbeliever if you were previously a believer. Allah and His Messenger despise apostates more than they despise people who never believed in the first place, and that is one scary thought indeed.

> 3:102 O believers, fear Allah as He should be feared, and do not die except as Muslims.

Allah vs. Alleged Associates

The Largest and Heaviest of Gods

In His hundreds of revelations about other gods, which often take the form of rants, Allah recurrently reveals the most about Himself, as is He does here about his size. If size does matter, Allah is one huge god indeed, revelation 39:67.

> 39:62 Allah is the Creator of everything and He is the Guardian of everything.
>
> 39:63 His are the keys of the heavens and the earth; and those who have disbelieved in Allah's Signs are the losers.
>
> 39:64 Say: "Do you, then, command me to worship anyone other than Allah, O ignorant ones?"
>
> 39:65 He has in fact revealed to you (Muhammad) and those who preceded you: "If you associate any others with Allah, He will frustrate your work and you will certainly be one of the losers."
>
> 39:66 Instead, worship Allah and be one of the thankful.
>
> 39:67 They have not recognized Allah's true measure. The whole earth shall be in His grasp and the heavens shall be rolled up in His Right Hand on the Day of Resurrection. Glory be to Him, and may He be exalted above what they associate with Him. [11]

Narrated Abdullah:

A (Jewish) Rabbi came to Allah's Apostle and he said, "O Muhammad! We learn that Allah will put all the heavens on one finger, and the earths on one finger, and the trees on one finger, and the water and the dust on one finger, and all

---

[11] From the size of Allah we can extrapolate the size of His throne, and from its size, the size of angels, as eight only will be required to carry it on Judgment Day.

> 69:17 And the angels shall be ranged around its borders, eight of whom will be carrying above them, on that Day, the Throne of your Lord.

the other created beings on one finger. Then He will say, 'I am the King.'"

Thereupon the Prophet smiled so that his pre-molar teeth became visible, and that was the confirmation of the Rabbi.

Then Allah's Apostle recited: "No just estimate have they made of Allah such as due to Him." (39.67)

Bukhari 60.335

Allah is also the weightiest of gods.

> 34:22 Say: "Call upon those you allege, apart from Allah. They do not possess the weight of a speck of dust in the heavens or on earth, and they have no partnership in either of them; nor is any of them a helper to him."

And Allah knows this for a fact, as those other gods have never asked for an audience with Him to offer their services.

> 17:42 Say: "If there were other gods with Him, as they say, then surely they would have sought access to the Lord of the Throne."

Except for being much bigger, Allah may not be that much different from you and me, revelation 7:195.

> 7:191 Do they associate with Allah those who can create nothing, while they, themselves, are created?
>
> 7:192 And they can neither help them nor help themselves.
>
> 7:193 And if you call them to guidance, they do not follow you. It is the same, for you, whether you call them or you remain silent.
>
> 7:194 Indeed those you call, apart from Allah, are servants like you; so call them and let them answer you, if you are truthful.
>
> 7:195 Do they have feet to walk with; do they have hands to smite with; do they have eyes to see with; or do they have ears to hear with? Say (O Muhammad): "Call your associate-gods, then plot against me and give me no respite."
>
> 7:196 My protector is Allah who sent down the Book and He protects the righteous.

Allah is a big and powerful god who could have stopped these other gods from causing their worshippers to murder their children but didn't:

> 6:137 And likewise, their associate-gods have insinuated to them the killing of their children, so as to destroy them and confound them in their religion. Had Allah pleased they would not have done it. So leave them (*Muhammad*) to their fabrications.

Phantasmagorical Creations of God and Man

> 17:22 Do not set up another god with Allah, lest you be despised and forsaken.

> 23:116 Glory be to Allah, the True King; there is no God but He. He is indeed the Lord of the Noble Throne.

> 23:117 He who calls, along with Allah, upon another god of whom he has no proof, his reckoning is with His Lord. Surely, the unbelievers will never prosper.

> 23:118 Say: "Lord Forgive and have mercy; for You are the Best of the Merciful."

Those other gods are not able to help themselves, let alone you!

> 7:197 And those you call, apart from Him, are not able to help you or even to help themselves.

> 7:198 If you call them to the guidance they do not hear; and you see them look at you, but they do not see.

What you must do, and why, and hope your brethren don't interfere.

> 7:199 Hold to forgiveness, enjoin the good and turn away from the ignorant.

> 7:200 And if a temptation from the Devil troubles you, seek refuge in Allah; He is truly All Hearing, All-Knowing.

> 7:201 Indeed, those who fear God, when a visitation from the Devil afflicts them, will remember [Allah's Commands], and behold they will see clearly.

> 7:202 But their brethren will plunge them further into error, and [then] they will not desist.

What you worship, apart from Allah, are misleading fantasies.

> 6:56 Say: "I have been forbidden to worship those you call upon apart from Allah." Say: "I do not follow your fancies, or else I would have gone astray and would not be one of the well-guided."

Those other gods may be a figment of someone's imagination; but you can't be too careful, Muhammad!

> 6:108 Do not curse those [deities] whom they call upon besides Allah, lest they wrongfully curse Allah without knowledge. Thus We have made the deeds of every nation seem fair to them; then unto their Lord is their return, and He will tell them what they were doing.

In another surprising revelation, Allah admits to creating the ostensibly non-existent competing and associated deities that He excoriates and demeans at every opportunity.

Before getting to this revelation, Allah will again remind His Messenger about some of the stuff He has created from nothing and the good He has done for mankind from the goodness of His Heart, and that this should cause people to reflect on how all this did not just happened, and it was not the work of other gods. This is the typical setup: self-aggrandisement followed by an attack on the gods people worship apart from Him.

The setup:

> 16:9 It belongs to Allah to show the Straight Path; some, however, deviate from it. Had Allah pleased He would have guided you all.

> 16:10 It is He who sends down water from the sky; from it you drink, and through it grow the plants on which you feed your cattle.

> 16:11 From it He brings forth for you vegetation, olives, palms, vines and all kinds of fruit. In that, surely, there is a sign for a people who reflect.

> 16:12 And He has subjected to you the night and the day, the sun and the moon; and the stars are subjected by His Command. In that there are signs for a people who understand.

> 16:13 And what He created for you in the earth is of multifarious colours; in that there is, surely, a sign for people who are mindful.

> 16:14 And it is He Who subjected the sea, so that you may eat from it tender meat and bring out from it jewelry for you to wear; and you see the ships cruising therein. [He subjected it for you] so that you may also seek His Bounty and give thanks.
>
> 16:15 And He laid up in the earth firm mountains, lest it shake under you; as well as rivers and pathways that, perchance, you may be guided.
>
> 16:16 And He [laid] landmarks; and by the stars they are guided.

The big question:

> 16:17 Now, is He Who creates like him who does not create? Do you not take heed?
>
> 16:18 Were you to count Allah's Blessings, you will not exhaust them. Allah is truly All-Forgiving, Merciful.
>
> 16:19 And Allah knows what you conceal and what you reveal.

The Admission:

> 16:20 Those they call upon, apart from Allah, do not create anything, but are themselves created.
>
> 16:21 [They are] dead, not alive, and they do not know when they will be raised from the dead[12].

Not only will they not be raised from the dead, they cannot, what should be obvious, raise you from the dead; Allah is the only god that can do that!

> 30:40 It is Allah who created you, then provided for you and Who will cause you to die, then bring you back to life. Is there among your associates any one (sic) who does any of this? Glory be to Him and may He be exalted above what they associate with Him.

Allah's favourite ending to any topic; it's all about the Hereafter, and often the arrogant who would deny His Revelations:

> 16:22 Your God is One God; those, then, who do not believe in the Hereafter, their hearts deny and they are arrogant.

---

[12] To be dead they must have once been alive, therefore, isn't Allah admitting to their existence and, whom will He raise from dead if this is not the case? Not to belabor the point, does not this also mean that the forefathers of the Arab pagans were not worshipping figments of their imagination?

16:23 Undoubtedly, Allah knows what they conceal and what they reveal. Indeed, He does not like the arrogant.

Many worshipped these lesser or associate gods for the reason some people worship saints, that they might intercede on their behalf with the top god, Allah. Their intent might have been well-meaning, but to Allah they were thankless liars, revelation 39:3.

THE TRONGS

39 Az-Zumar

*In the Name of Allah,
the Compassionate, the Merciful*

39:1 The sending down of the Book is from Allah, the All-Mighty, the Wise.

39:2 We have, indeed, sent down the Book to you in truth; so worship Allah professing the religion sincerely to Him.

39:3 Sincere religion truly belongs to Allah. Those who took other protectors, apart from Him, say: "We only worship them so as to bring us closer to Allah in rank." Allah surely judges between them with respect to what they differ upon. Allah surely does not guide him who is a thankless liar.

Allah makes it clear in the following revelations that the would-be intercessors are clueless and have no power to intercede; and that, if necessary it is assumed, He will intercede with Himself on your behalf, revelation 39:44:

39:43 Or have they taken intercessors, apart from Allah? Say: "Even if they have no power whatever and no understanding."

39:44 Say: "To Allah belongs all intercession. His is the dominion of the heavens and the earth. Then unto Him you will be returned."

And they are judges of nothing!

40:20 Allah judges rightly, but those upon whom they call, apart from Him, judge of naught. Allah is the All-hearing, the All-Seeing.

And they are creators of nothing; and unlike Allah, they are not "in possession" of a book containing the proof of what they advance, as revealed in another ubiquitous self-serving disclosure where He instructs His Messenger as to what to say.

35:40 Say: "Have you seen your associates upon whom you

call, apart from Allah? Show me what they have created on earth? Do they have any share in the heavens, or have We given them a Book, so that they are in possession of a clear proof therein? In fact, the wrongdoers only promise each other vanity."

Jesus among revelations about "gods who do not create anything":

THE CRITERION

25 Al-Furqân

*In the Name of Allah,
the Compassionate, the Merciful*

25:1 Blessed is He Who sent down the Criterion (a way to distinguish right from wrong *i.e. the Koran*) upon His servant (Muhammad), so as to be a warner for all mankind.

25:2 To whom belongs the dominion of the heavens and the earth and He has not taken to Himself a child, and has no associate in this dominion, and He created everything, preordaining it fully.

25:3 Yet they have taken, apart from Him, other gods who do not create anything, but are themselves created. They do not have the power to harm or profit themselves, nor the power over death, life or resurrection.

These imaginary other gods also know nothing of the Unseen, including "when they shall be resuscitated". Allah is initially unsure as to what they know about what only He knows, revelation 27:66.

27:65 Say: "No one in the heavens or on earth knows the Unseen, except Allah; and they will have no inkling when they shall be resuscitated.

27:66 Has their knowledge of the Hereafter continued? Nay, they are in doubt regarding it, or rather, they are blind to it.

Allah is a god who gives you all you ask for; and when you do get His blessings, including His lifting of adversity, don't make an offering to another god, they had nothing to do with it. If you do, your good fortune will be short-lived, and "soon you shall know" the punishment i.e. the *Fire*.

16:53 Whatever blessings you have is from Allah. Then, if adversity touches you, unto Him you turn for help.

16:54 Then, once He lifts the adversity from you, behold, some of you associate [other gods] with their Lord;

16:55 So as to deny what We gave them. Enjoy yourselves then, for soon you shall know.

16:56 And they set apart, for what they know not (their idols), a portion of what We have provided for them. By Allah, you will be questioned about what you fabricated.

39:8 If some adversity touches man, he will call upon his Lord, repenting unto Him; then, if He confers on him grace of His, he forget what he was calling for before that and assigns equals to Allah, so as to lead others astray from His Path. Say: "Enjoy your disbelief a little; for you are truly one of the companions of the Fire."

"Is there, then, another god with Allah?"

27:59 Say: "Praise be to Allah and peace upon those of His servants whom He has chosen. Is Allah better or those they associate with Him?"

27:60 Is He not the One Who created the heavens and the earth and sent down upon you water from the sky; and so We caused to grow thereby delightful gardens. It was not in your power to cause their trees to grow. Is there, then, another god with Allah? Yet, they are a people who assign to Him an equal.

27:61 Is He not the One Who made the earth a stable abode and created rivers flowing through it, created immovable mountains therein and created a barrier between the two seas[13]. Is there, then, another god with Allah? Yet, most of them do not know.

27:62 It is He who answers the one in trouble when he calls upon Him and lifts the adversity and appoints you as successors on earth. Is there then, another god with Allah? Little do you recollect.

27:63 He who guides you through the dark shadows of land and sea, and sends forth the wind as good news ahead of

---

[13] This is a reference to salt and fresh water. Allah is probably referring to the Black Sea which is a fresh water sea whose waters flow into the salty Marmara sea, then the Aegean and the Mediterranean. There is of course nothing to stop fresh water and salt water from mixing as it does in the Sea of Marmara leading to the sea being one third less salty than the oceans.

His Mercy. <u>Is there, then, another god with Allah?</u> No, He is exalted above what they associate!

27:64 He Who originates the creation, then brings it back, and Who provides for you from the heavens and the earth. <u>Is there, then, another god with Allah?</u> Say: "Produce your proof, if you are truthful."

Goddesses and the Fathers Who Worshipped Them

43:15 They have attributed to Him part of His servants. Man is indeed manifestly thankless.

43:16 Or has He taken for Himself daughters from what He creates, and favoured you with sons?

43:17 And when one of them is given the news of what he attributes the likes thereof (that is, daughters), to the All-Compassionate, his face becomes darkened and he is filled with gloom.

Moududi:

> Here, the folly of the polytheists of Arabia has been fully exposed. They said that the angels were the daughters of Allah. They had carved out their images as females, and these were their goddesses whom they worshipped.

43:18 What, one who is brought up in luxury but in the art of disputation is not well-versed?

Moududi:

> You have assigned to Allah the offspring that is by nature delicate, weak and frail, and adopted for yourselves the offspring that is bold, courageous and fearless.

43:19 And they have made the angels, who are servants of the All-Compassionate, females. What, have they witnessed their creation? Surely, their testimony will be written down and they will be questioned.

43:20 They say: "If the All-Compassionate had willed it, we would not have worshipped them." They have no knowledge of that at all; they are only lying.

43:21 Or have We given them a Book prior to this one (the Qur'an), so that they are clinging to it?

The Arab pagans worshipped what their fathers worshipped, and their fathers displayed none of Allah's biases against worshipping females.

> 43:22 No, they say: "We found our fathers upon this course, and we are actually following in their footsteps."
>
> 43:23 Likewise, We never sent forth a warner to any city before you (*Muhammad*), but its affluent chiefs have said: "We have found our fathers upon a certain course, and we actually following in their footsteps."
>
> 43:24 He said: "What if I were to bring you a more certain guidance than what you found your fathers upon?" They said: "We are definitely disbelievers in what you were sent forth with."

The leaders of these cities apparently preferred the gentle tutelage of female deities, even after Allah sent them Messengers with His Demand that He alone be worshipped and obeyed. Not to be denied, Allah reduced their cities to rubble, and, except for the Messengers and a few who accepted their ultimatum, killed every man, women and child.

> 43:25 So, We wrecked vengeance upon them. Behold, then, what was the fate then of those who deny.

A few more revelations about the fathers who dared to worship females, the father of Abraham being the most noteworthy.

> 43:26 When Abraham said to his father and his people: "I am certainly quit of what you worship;
>
> 43:27 "Except for Him Who created me. He will certainly guide me well."
>
> 43:28 And he made it an enduring word in his progeny, that perchance they might repent.

Allah made an exception for the fathers of the Arabs of Muhammad's time in the hope that they might repent

> 43:29 Yet, I gave these (*Meccans*) and their fathers some enjoyment, till the Truth and manifest a Messenger came to them.
>
> 43:30 But when the Truth came to them, they said: "That is sorcery, and we are definitely disbelieving therein."

> 43:31 They also said: "If only this Qur'an had been sent down upon some outstanding man from the two cities (Mecca and Ta'if)."

~~~~~~~~~~~~~~

It does not matter what a revelation or groups of revelations are ostensibly about, Allah will repeatedly find a way to make His deceptive alleged rivals the center of attention and those who worship them the object of His Wrath.

> 42:20 He who wishes the tillage of the Hereafter, We will increase his tillage, and he who wishes the tillage of the present life, We will give him thereof; but in the Hereafter, he will have no share.

> 42:21 Or do they have associates who enacted for them as a religion that for which Allah did not give leave? But for the Word of Decision (the final judgement), judgement would have been pronounced upon them. Surely, the wrongdoers will suffer a painful punishment.

Children! Do Not Obey Parents Who Worship Other Gods

Luqmân is a legendary figure in Islamic lore. He is regarded as a paragon of wisdom. Luqmân had some advice, familiar advice, for his son about "a mighty evil".

> 31:12 We have, indeed, imparted wisdom to Luqmân: "Give thanks to Allah." Whoever gives thanks, gives thanks only for his own good and whoever disbelieves will find Allah All-Sufficient, Praiseworthy."

> 31:13 And when Luqmân said to his son exhorting him: "My son, do not associate others with Allah; associating others [with Allah] is a mighty evil."

Allah will interrupt Luqmân with some advice of his own.

> 31:14 We have admonished man regarding his parents; as his mother bore him in weakness upon weakness, weaning him in two years: "Give thanks to Me and to your parents. Unto Me is the ultimate return.

> 31:15 "If they strive with you so as to associate with Me that of which you have no knowledge, do not obey them; but keep them company in the present world honourably. Follow the path of those who turn to Me. Then unto Me is your return, whereupon I will tell you what you used to do.

Luqmân again:

> 31:16 "O my son, if there be the weight of a mustard seed, whether in a rock, in the heavens or in the earth, Allah will bring it forth. Surely, Allah is Subtle, Well-Informed.
>
> 31:17 "Oh my son, perform the prayer, command the honourable and forbid the dishonourable and bear patiently what has befallen you. That is an instance of constancy in one's affairs.
>
> 31:18 "Do not turn your face away from people and do not walk in the land haughtily. Allah does not love any arrogant or boastful person.
>
> 31:19 "Be modest in your stride and lower your voice; for the most hideous voices is that of asses."

Gog and Magog

The story of Gog and Magog in the Koran bears a striking similarity to the tale told in the Alexander Romance, a collection of legends about the life of Alexander the Great. The chief source of Alexander Romance, according to the Encyclopedia Britannica is "a folk epic written by a Hellenized Egyptian in Alexandria during the 2nd century A.D."

Alexander and the Wall

According to Wiki, Alexander, in the Romance "came to a northern land devastated by incursions from barbarian peoples, including Gog and Magog. Alexander defends the land by constructing the Gates of Alexander, an immense wall between two mountains that will stop the invaders until the end times. In the Romance, these gates are built between two mountains in the Caucasus called the 'Breasts of the World'. This has been taken as a reference to the historical "Caspian Gates" in Derbent, Russia. Another suggested candidate is the wall at the Darial Gorge in Georgia, also in the Caucasus." Alexander built the wall between Gog and Magog and the rest of the world out of iron and brass.

> 18:94 They said: "O Dhul-Qarnayn (Alexander the Great), surely Gog and Magog are making mischief in the land. Shall we pay you a tribute so that you may build a barrier between us and them?"
>
> 18:95 He said: "What my Lord has empowered me to do is better. So help me forcefully and I will build a barrier between you and them.

> 18:96 "Bring me large pieces of iron." So that when he had levelled up [the gap] between the two sides, he said: "Blow." And having turned it (the iron) into fire, he said: "Bring me molten brass to poor on it."
>
> 18:97 Then, they (Gog and Magog) could neither scale it or make a hole through it.

As in the Alexander Romance, Allah expects His wall to last until the end-of-times when He will destroy it thereby allowing the warring factions to fight one another until the trumpet is blown signalling the coming of Judgement Day.

> 18:98 He said: "This is a mercy from my Lord; but when my Lord's Promise comes to pass, He will turn it into rubble, and the Promise of my Lord is ever true."
>
> 18:99 And on that day we shall make them surge upon one another, and the trumpet shall be blown, and we shall gather them together.
>
> 18:100 On that Day We shall boldly set Hell before the unbelievers.
>
> 18:101 Those whose eyes were closed to My Reminder (the Qur'an) and they could not hear [it].

Alexander's gates, for God's Messenger, were real, and visions of a breach in the barrier freaked him out, for it was a sign that Judgement Day was imminent!

> **Narrated Zainab bint Jahsh:**
>
> That the Prophet once came to her in a state of fear and said, "None has the right to be worshipped but Allah. Woe unto the Arabs from a danger that has come near. An opening has been made in the wall of Gog and Magog like this," making a circle with his thumb and index finger.
>
> Zainab bint Jahsh said, "O Allah's Apostle! Shall we be destroyed even though there are pious persons among us?"
>
> He said, "Yes, when the evil person will increase."
>
> Bukhari 54.565

Could Alexander be the servant who the unbelievers thought they could take as protector in the following revelation?

> 18:102 Have the unbelievers, then, supposed that they can take My servants besides Me, as protectors? We have

indeed prepared Hell for the unbelievers as an abode.

The True Promise

Allah's Gog and Magog are not a people, as in the Alexander Romance, but false gods who will join their followers in Hell if the phrase "Had those been real gods" in verse 21:99 is a reference to the infamous twosome as deities not tribes.

> 21:95 And it is forbidden that any city We have destroyed should come back.
>
> 21:96 Until Gog and Magog are let loose, and they slink away from every quarter.
>
> 21:97 Then the true promise will draw near; and, behold, the eyes of the unbelievers are staring [and they will say]: "Woe to us! We were heedless of this; no, we were wrongdoers."
>
> 21:98 You and what you worship, besides Allah, are the fuel of Hell, and into it you shall all descend.
>
> 21:99 Had those been real gods, they would not have gone down into it; yet they will all dwell in it forever.

The true promise is, of course, Judgement Day when imaginary gods and goddesses, and real gods like Gog and Magog will be mustered by the Compassionate, and one and all will deny they were ever worshipped by those they now consider their enemies.

THE SAND-DUNES

46 Al-Ahqâf

*In the Name of Allah,
the Compassionate, the Merciful*

> 46:1 Ha – Mim.
>
> 46:2 This is the revelation of the Book from Allah, the All-Mighty, the All-Wise.
>
> 46:3 We have not created the heavens and the earth and what is in between them except in truth and for an appointed term. Yet the unbelievers do not heed what they were warned against.
>
> 46:4 Say: "Have you considered what you call upon, apart from Allah? Show me what they have created of the earth, or whether they have a share of the heavens? Bring me a

Book before this one or some vestige of knowledge, if you are truthful?"

46:5 Who is farther astray than he who calls, apart from Allah, upon him who does not answer his call till the Day of Resurrection? They are even heedless of their calling.

46:6 And when people are mustered, they will be their enemies, and even their worship they will disclaim.

Judgement Day is when Allah's anger and pathological obsession with these other gods find it's fullest expression. For more about their fate and that of the people who worshiped them, read *The Islamic Hereafter*, Boreal Books, 2012.

Allah's Parables

47:1 Those who have disbelieved and barred others from the Path of Allah, He will render their works perverse;

47:2 But those who have believed and done the righteous deeds and believed in what was sent down upon Muhammad, which is the Truth from their Lord, He will remit their sins and set their minds aright.

47:3 That is because those who have disbelieved have followed falsehood, but those who have believed have followed the truth from their Lord. Thus does Allah frame the parables for mankind.

18:54 We have set out in this Qur'an, for the people, every manner of example; but man is the most contentious being.

18:55 Nothing prevents men from believing when the guidance comes to them, or from seeking forgiveness from their Lord; but they wait for the faith of the ancients to overtake them, or to be confronted with the punishment (*on Judgement Day*).

A parable can be defined as an uncomplicated short story used to illustrate a religious, moral or philosophical idea. Allah's allegories differ from that definition in one significant way; for the layperson, and even the scholar, they can be somewhat confusing. Allah's parables also tend to differ from those found in the New Testament in that the correct choice or the lesson to be learned is not always evident. His often tall tales are much like riddles which only certain people will understand, as Allah readily admits.

> 2:26 Surely Allah does not disdain to give as a parable an insect or something bigger. Those who have believed know that it is the Truth from their Lord; but those who have disbelieved say: "What does Allah mean by this parable?" By it, He leaves many in error, and guides well many others. And by it, He leaves in error only the sinners (those who disobey Allah).

> 29:43 Those are the parables We devise for mankind, and only the learned will grasp them.

Allah says His parables are also meant to make one reflect, but what is there to reflect about in inanimate objects being self-aware, such as a mountain which is simultaneously prostrate and rent asunder, not because of the weight of the Book Allah threatens to send down upon it, but out of fear of Allah. Then again, the message of such a parable may be that if Allah can scare a mountain, you should be afraid, you should be very afraid; and that is definitely something to reflect upon, something that should make everyone think twice about defying this god.

> 59:21 Had We sent down this Qur'an upon a mountain, you would have seen it bowing down and rent asunder out of the fear of Allah. Those are the parables which We Recite to mankind, that perchance they might reflect.

Allah revealed that His exhaustive supply of parables (Yusuf Ali's translation's identifies 26 altogether) are intended to make His Message easier to remember.

> 39:27 We have given mankind every kind of parable in this Qur'an, that perchance they might remember.

Allah's parables are meant to "illustrate truth and falsehood" in an often obscure sort of way.

> 13:17 He sends water from the sky making riverbeds flow, each according to its measure. Then the torrent carries along swelling foam; similar to it is the scum that comes out from that which they smelt on the fire for making ornaments or tools. Thus Allah illustrates truth and falsehood. The scum is cast away, but what profits mankind remains in the earth. Thus Allah sets forth the parables.

Allah's "every manner of parable" may also be signs which are likewise dismissed by the clueless as being falsehoods because He has sealed their hearts.

> 30:58 We have cited in this Qur'an every manner of parable; indeed were you to bring the unbelievers a sign, they would only say: "You are purveyors of falsehoods."

> 30:59 Thus Allah places a seal upon the hearts of those who do not know.

The "certitude of faith" will definitely be helpful in understanding and not questioning the seemingly unexplainable and the outwardly bizarre comparisons made by Allah.

> 30:60 Be patient then, for Allah's Promise is true; and do not be disheartened by those who lack the certitude of faith.

While you will learn something from Allah's parables, don't tell Him parables, they have nothing to teach Him.

> 16:74 Do not set forth parables for Allah. Surely Allah knows and you do not know.

The King Who Disputed With Abraham

In this parable, the Patriarch of Arabs and Jews explains to a king why Allah is more powerful. The king is dumfounded by the explanation, and with good reason.

> 2:258 Have you not considered him who disputed with Abraham regarding his Lord, because He had given him the kingdom? When Abraham said: "My Lord is He Who gives life and causes death", the other said: "I give life and cause death." Abraham [then] said: "Allah brings the sun from the East, bring it up from the West." Thereupon the unbeliever was confounded. Allah does not guide the wrongdoers.

The Traveller Who Slept for a Hundred Years

Revelation 2:259 is a parable about a man whom Allah causes to sleep for a hundred years, while keeping his food from rotting and his drink from evaporating, but perhaps not him "Look also at the bones [and see] how we have restored them, then clothed them with flesh". After a hundred years He restores him, and his ass I assume, to pristine condition and wakes him up and asks him "how long have you tarried?" When he learns how long, he quickly realises that Allah, indeed, "has power over all things."

> 2:259 Or [consider] him who, passing by a ruined city (Jerusalem) said: "How will God bring this to life after its death?" Thereupon Allah caused him to die for a hundred years, then brought him back to life. Allah asked him: "For how long have you tarried?" He said: "I tarried for a day or part of a day." Allah said: "No, you have tarried for a hundred years. Look at your food and drink; the years have not changed them. Look at your ass. With this we make of you a sign for mankind. Look also at the bones [and see] how we have restored them, then clothed them with flesh." When [all] this became clear to him, he said: "[Now] I know that Allah has power over all things."

The Good Tree and the Foul Tree

> 14:24 Do you not see how Allah sets forth as a parable that a good word is like a good tree, whose root (sic) is firm and its branches are in the sky.
>
> 14:25 It brings forth its fruit all the time, by its Lord's Leave. Allah gives parables to mankind that perchance they may be mindful.
>
> 14:26 And a foul word is like a foul tree which has been uprooted from the surface of the earth, having no stable base.

The Secure Town

> 16:112 Allah has given as a parable a town which was safe and secure, and its provision came in abundance from every side; then it denied Allah's Blessings, and so Allah made it taste the engulfing hunger and fear on account of what they used to do.
>
> 16:113 A Messenger from among them came to them, but they denounced him, and so they were smitten by our punishment for being wrongdoers.

The Two Gardens

A parable that bears some resemblance to the *Talents* parable of the New Testament.

> 18:32 And relate to them as a parable the case of two men. To one of them, We gave two gardens of vine, which we surrounded with palm trees and placed between them a cornfield.
>
> 18:33 Both gardens yielded their produce and did not waste any of it, and We caused a river to flow through them both.
>
> 18:34 And he had some fruit. So he said to his companion, while conversing with him: "I have greater wealth than you and a mightier following."

He must have been on his neighbour's or his companion's property for he then enters his garden (no it is not a typo, we started with two gardens and now it's one) and makes a comment which Allah interprets as a denial of the last Day.

> 18:35 Then he entered his garden, wronging himself. He said: "I do not think this will ever perish.
>
> 18:36 "And I do not think the hour is coming. If I am

returned to my Lord, I will surely find a place better than this."

Moududi's interpretation of the phrase "I will surely find a place better than this" is that of an unwarranted presumption, the type which gets Allah's blood boiling. His explains that the man who entered his garden assumed he was "a favourite of God" because of his prosperity and therefore will "fare even better there (Paradise) than in the present." Wrong!

> 18:37 His companion said to him, while conversing with him: "Do you disbelieve in Him Who created you from dust, then from a sperm, then fashioned you into a man?

The parable may not be about not associating other gods with Allah but why pass up the opportunity.

> 18:38 "But as for me, Allah is my Lord and I do not associate anyone with my Lord.

What the gardener should have done and said, according to his companion, and the repercussions for that dangerous oversight.

> 18:39 "If only you were to say, upon entering your garden: 'What Allah pleases [shall come to be]; there is no power save in Allah'. If you see me possessing less wealth and children than you;

> 18:40 "Perhaps, my Lord will give me a better garden than yours and will release upon yours a thunderbolt from the sky, so that it will turn into a barren wasteland.

> 18:41 "Or its water will sink into the ground, so that you will not be able to draw it."

The unpardonable sin is not ingratitude, but of associating other gods with Allah. Go figure!

> 18:42 Then, his fruit was destroyed, and so he began to wring his hands at what he had spent on it, while it had fallen down upon its trellises, and he was saying: "I wish I had not associated anyone with my Lord."

Not only that, no one came to his aid. Allah could have, but He declined for a reason that has to with the significance of the parable.

> 18:43 And he did not have a faction to help him besides Allah, nor was he able to defend himself.

The unexpected lesson to be drawn from this parable:

18:44 There, protection is from Allah, the True God. He is Best in rewarding and Best in requiting.

The Companions of the City

To confirm that the following revelations were indeed a parable and not a recollection of actual events, I consulted other translations including Yusuf Ali, who translated revelation 36:13 as: "Set forth to them, by way of a parable, the (story of) the Companions of the City. Behold!, there came apostles to it."

36:13 And relate to them the case of the people of the city, when the Messengers came thereto.

36:14 When We sent them two men, but they denounced them as liars, and so We reinforced them with a third. Then they said: "We are indeed Messengers unto you."

36:15 They said: "You are only mortals like ourselves and the All-Compassionate has not sent down anything. You are only lying."

36:16 They (the Messengers) said: "Our Lord knows that we are indeed Messengers unto you,

36:17 "And it is up to us to deliver the Manifest Message."

36:18 They said: "We augur ill of you. If you will not desist, we will stone you and a very painful punishment from us will afflict you."

36:19 The (the Messengers) said: "Your bird of omen is with you, if you are reminded, but you are an extravagant people."

36:20 Then a man came from the farthest point of the city. He said: "My people, follow the Messengers.

36:21 "Follow those who do not ask you for a wage and are rightly guided.

36:22 "And why should I not worship Him who created me and unto Him you shall be returned?

36:23 "Shall I take, apart from Him, gods whose intercession, should the All-Compassionate wish me ill, will not avail me anything and they will not deliver me?

36:24 "Then, I am truly in manifest error.

36:25 "I have believed in your Lord, so listen to me."

36:26 It was said: "Enter Paradise." He said: "I wished my own people knew;

36:27 "About my Lord's forgiving me and making me one of the favoured."

36:28 After him, We sent down no troops from heaven; nor would We ever send any down[14].

36:29 It was only one cry; and behold they were silenced.

36:30 Woe betide the servants; no Messenger comes to them but they mock him.

36:31 Have they not seen how many generations before them We destroyed and unto them they will not return?

36:32 And all of them will be brought before Us?

The Companions Tested

An allegory of sorts, which is a variation on *The Two Gardens* parable. In this garden story, a crop is destroyed as a punishment for arrogance, or to prove that, except for the punishment or the bliss, nothing is a sure thing where Allah is concerned. Glorify Him if you do not want nasty surprises like seeing your harvest disappear overnight.

68:17 We have tested you, just as We tested the Companions of the Garden when they swore to pluck its fruit in the morning.

68:18 Without any reservations.

68:19 Then a night-stalker from your Lord visited them while they were asleep.

68:20 And so it (the Garden) became black like a cropped off field.

68:21 Thereupon they called out to each other in the morning:

68:22 "Go forth to your tillage, if you would crop it off."

68:23 So, they set out whispering to each other:

---

[14] The battle of Badr (8:9, 3:124-125), the battle of Hunayn (9:26) and the invisible solders Allah sent to protect His Prophet when he hid in a cave (9:40) to avoid being captured by Meccans intent on killing him may have all been exception to this hard and fast rule.

68:24 "Let no destitute person enter it today with you around."

68:25 And they proceeded next morning angrily, fully determined.

68:26 When they saw it, they said: "We have surely gone astray.

68:27 "Rather we are dispossessed."

68:28 The most reasonable of them said: "Did I not tell you, if you only glorify."

68:29 They said: "Glory to our Lord, we were indeed wrongdoers."

68:30 Then, they turned to one another, reproaching each other.

68:31 They said: "Woe betide us; we have indeed been domineering.

68:32 "Maybe our Lord will give a better substitute for it (the Garden). We are truly turning to our Lord."

68:33 Such is the punishment; but the punishment of the Hereafter is greater, if only they knew.

68:34 Surely, for the God-fearing there are Gardens of Bliss with their Lord.

The Lesser Gods and the Fly

22:73 O People, an example has been given; so listen to it. Surely, those (gods) whom you call upon, besides Allah, will never create a fly, even if they band together. And if a fly should rob them of something, they cannot retrieve it from it. How weak is the invoker and the invoked!

22:74 They do not give Allah His True Measure. Surely, Allah is strong and mighty.

Slaves in Parables

There are at least four parables where slaves are mentioned or implied. These parables are, for some, the clearest indication that Allah approves of slavery.

The Incapable Slave and the Well-Provided-For Slave

16:75 Allah sets forth this parable. Consider an owned slave who is unable to do anything; and one for whom We have provided from Our Bounty a fair provision, and he spends from it secretly and publicly. Are they then alike? Praise be to Allah; but most of them do not know.

According to Dr. Victor A. Gunasekara, author of *Slavery and the Infidel in Islam*, this verse is "one of the clearest instances where the institution of slavery is justified in the Koran as a divine dispensation.":

> This parable contrasts two people a slave who is owned by another and is completely powerless and a freeman on whom Allah has granted 'a goodly sustenance' which he can spend openly or secretly as he pleases ... Since Allah claims for himself the position of the granter of all benefits both the freeman's fortune and the slave's misfortune are ultimately determined by Allah. By his rhetorical question 'Are the two alike?' the Prophet Muhammad is actually justifying the inequality between the slave and the freeman as if it was a natural thing ... because it is what Allah has ordained and 'all praise is due to Allah'.

The Dumb Slave and the Righteous Slave

Some choices would seem obvious, but you can never be sure, especially if you are mentally challenged.

> 16:76 And Allah sets forth the parable of two men. One of them is dumb, unable to do anything and is a burden on his master; wherever he directs him, he brings no good. Is he equal to him who enjoins justice and is upon a straight path?

The Jointly-Owned Slave

> 30:28 He gave you a parable from your own selves. Do you have among what your hands own (slaves) partners in what We provided for you, so that you are equal therein? Do your fear them as you fear each other? Thus We expound the revelations to a people who understand.

Moududi:

> The mushriks ("one who falsely associates (something) with God"), even after admitting that Allah is the Creator and Master of the earth and heavens and all that they contain, held some of His creatures as associates in His attributes and powers, and prayed to them ... they used to pronounce while going round the Ka'ba. They said: "Here I am, O Allah, here I am in Thy presence! Thou hast no partner

except the partner who is Thy own. Thou art his owner as well as owner of what he owns." ... Allah has refuted this kind of shirk (associating other gods with Allah) in this verse. The argument is to this effect: "When you do not make your own slaves partners in your wealth, how do you think and believe that Allah will make His creatures partners in His Godhead?"

The Jointly-Owned Slave and the Slave of Just One Man

> 39:29 Allah has given as a parable a man owned by partners who are at odds and a man exclusively owned by one man. Are they equal in status? Praise be to Allah, but most of them do not know.
>
> 39:30 You are mortal and they are mortal too.
>
> 39:31 Then on the Day of Resurrection, you shall appear before your Lord defending yourself.

Moududi on revelation 39:29:

> Allah in this parable has explained the difference between shirk and Tauhid (monotheism) and the impact each has on human life so clearly that it is not possible to put across such a vast theme so concisely and effectively in other words. Everyone will admit that the person who has many masters, each one pulling hire to himself, and the masters also so ill-tempered that no one spares him time in his service to obey the other, and no one rests content only with threatening and cursing him if he fails to carry out his command from among the contradictory commands of the other masters, but is bent upon punishing him, his life would certainly be in great anguish. On the contrary, the person who is the slave or servant of only one master, would be living a life of ease and comfort because he will not have to serve and seek the pleasure of another master. This is such a straightforward thing which does not need deep consideration for its understanding

Intriguing Comparisons and Mixed Metaphors

The Screamer

2:171 Those who disbelieve are like one who screams but is heard by one who hears only calling and shouting. They are deaf, dumb and blind, and so they do not understand.

Multiplication of the Grain

2:261 Those who spend their wealth in the Way of Allah are like a grain [of wheat] which grows seven ears, each carrying one hundred grains. Allah multiplies [further] to whom He wills. Allah is Munificent, All-Knowing.

Charity is Like Rain

2:264 O believers, do not render vain your charities by taunts and injuries, like him who spends his wealth for the sake of ostentation and does not believe in Allah and the Last Day. He is like a smooth rock covered by earth; when heavy rain falls on it, it leaves it completely bare. Such people get no reward for their works. Allah does not guide the unbelievers.

2:265 But those who spend their money in order to please Allah and to strengthen their souls (by having a stronger grasp of faith) are like a garden on a hill which, when heavy rain falls on it, its produce is doubled; and if no heavy rain falls on it, then a shower [suffices]. Allah is aware of what you do.

Cold Cash

3:116 As for the unbelievers, neither their riches nor their children will avail them anything against Allah. Those are the people of Hell, abiding therein forever!

3:117 That which they spend in the present life is similar to a frosty wind which smote the harvest of a people who had wronged themselves, and so destroyed it. Allah did not wrong them, but they wronged themselves!

Lost in the Dark

6:122 Is one who was dead, then We brought him back to life and gave him a light to walk among the people, like one who is in total darkness and cannot get out of it? Thus the unbeliever's evil deed is made attractive to them.

Wasted Water

13:14 To Him is the Call of Truth; and those on whom they call besides Him will not answer any of their prayers. They are like one who stretches out his hand to the water so that it might reach his mouth, but it will not reach it. The call of the unbelievers is only wasted.

The Blind Man and the Copycat Gods

13:16 Say: "Who is the Lord of the heavens and the earth?" Say: "Allah." Say: "Have you then taken, besides Him, protectors who have no power to profit or harm even themselves?" Say: "Are the blind and the man who sees alike; or are the darkness and the light alike? Or have they assigned to Allah associates who created the likeness of His Creation, so that both creations seem to them alike?" Say: "Allah is the Creator of everything and He is the One, the Almighty."

The Blind Again

13:19 Is he who knows that what is revealed to you from your Lord is the truth, like he who is blind? Indeed, only the people of understanding take heed.

Ashes in the Wind

14:18 The likeness of those of those who disbelieve in their Lord is this: their works are like ashes scattered by the wind on a stormy day, and they have no power over anything they have earned. That is truly the great perdition.

Straw in the Wind

18:45 And give them the simile of the present life; it is like the water We send down from the sky; then the vegetation of the earth is mixed in with it, and so it becomes straw which the wind scatters. Allah has power over everything.

The Rope to the Sky

22:14 Allah shall admit those who believe and do the righteous deeds into the Gardens underneath which rivers flow. Allah surely does whatever He pleases.

22:15 He who thinks that Allah will not give him support in this world or the next, let him stretch a rope to the sky then cut it up. Let him then see if his guile will remove what angers him.

22:16 That is how We revealed it (the Qur'an) as clear revelations, and Allah guides whomever He pleases.

Whose Work is like a Mirage in Level Ground or Dark Shadows on the Sea

24:36 In houses Allah allowed to be raised and His Name to be mentioned therein, He is glorified therein, mornings and evenings,

24:37 By men who are not distracted, by trading or trafficking, from mentioning Allah's Name, performing the prayer and giving the alms. They fear a Day whereon the hearts and eyesight shall be turned around;

24:38 So that Allah may reward them for their fairest works and increase them from His Bounty. Allah provides for whomever He pleases without reckoning.

24:39 As to the unbelievers, their works are like a mirage in level ground, which the thirsty supposes to be water; but when he comes close to it, he finds that it is nothing. Instead, he finds Allah there and so he pays Him his account in full. Allah is quick in reckoning.

24:40 Or like dark shadows in a turbulent sea, covered by waves upon waves, above which are clouds. Dark shadows above which are dark shadows; if he brings his hand out, he will hardly see it. He to whom Allah as not granted a light will have no light.

The House of the Spider

29:41 The case of those who took up other protectors, apart from Allah, is like that of a spider who built a house. Truly, the most brittle of houses is the house of the spider, if only they knew.

29:42 Allah knows what they call upon, apart from Him, and He is the All-Mighty, the Wise.

The Blind and Deaf

30:53 And you shall not lead the blind away from their error. You will only make those who believe in Our Signs hear. For they are submitting.

Ranking goodness

41:34 The fair and evil deeds are not equal. Respond with that which is fairer, so that he against whom you have a grudge shall be like an intimate friend.

41:35 None shall be accorded this rank except those who have stood fast, and none shall be accorded it except one blessed with great good fortune.

In Yusuf Ali's translation "rank" becomes "goodness":

> 41:35 And no one will be granted such goodness except those who exercise patience and self-restraint,- none but persons of the greatest good fortune.

You may find Moududi's explanation as confounding as the revelations.

... achieving the rank of someone who can ward of evil with good "requires a great [of] will power, resolution, courage, power of endurance and full control over one's own self", and that it "is a law of nature. Only a man of very high rank is characterised by these qualities..." which is why Allah added "persons of the greatest good fortune" to the revelation.

His Brother's Flesh

49:12 O believers, avoid much suspicion; for some suspicion is a sin. Do not spy and do not backbite one another. Does any of you wish to eat his brother's flesh dead (sic)? You would surely hate it. Fear Allah, for Allah is Truly Absolving, Merciful.

The Present Life

57:20 Know that the present life is but sport and diversion, adornment, boasting among you and rivalry in amassing wealth and children. It is like rain whose vegetation delighted the unbelievers, then it withered and you see it turning yellow and then it becomes stubble. In the Hereafter there is a terrible punishment, forgiveness from Allah and good pleasure. The present life is but the enjoyment of vanity.

Those who walk on their faces and their Creator

67:22 Is he who walks prone upon his face better guided, or he who walks a Straight Path?

67:23 Say: "It is He Who originated you and created for you hearing, sight, and hearts. How little do you give thanks?"

Then there are the obvious comparisons:

11:24 The case of the two parties (the believers and the unbelievers) is like the blind and the deaf compared with the man who sees and hears. Are they both alike? Do you not pay heed?

35:19 The blind and the seeing man are not alike.

35:20 Nor dark shadows or light;

35:21 Nor shade and torrid heat.

40:58 The blind and the seeing man are not equal; nor are those who believe and do the righteous deeds and the evil-doer. Little do you remember!

59:20 The Companions of the Fire and the Companions of Paradise are not equal. The Companions of Paradise are indeed the winners.

Then there are the apparently obvious:

35:22 Nor are the living and the dead alike. Allah makes whomever He wish to hear, but you will not make those in their graves hear.

30:52 For you cannot make the dead hear and you cannot make the deaf hear the call, if they flee turning their back.

39:9 Is he who worships devoutly in the watches of the night, prostrating himself and standing up, fears the Hereafter and hopes for the Mercy of his Lord [like unto the other]? Say: "Are those who know and those who do not know alike?" Only those possessed of understanding will remember.

Then there are the unanswered questions, such as "why should creatures that crawl die for man's sins and not the birds, the fish and the amphibians?"

35:45 Were Allah to take men to task for what they have earned, He would not have left upon the face of the earth a single creature that crawls; but He defers them unto an appointed term. Then, when their term arrives, Allah is surely fully Conversant with His servants.

Allah, Two Boys and a Dog

The following story from surah 18, *The Cave,* is somewhat typical of many of Allah's tales: simple, surreal and out-of-time. It could also be considered a parable, a long parable, a multi-verse parable with many mixed messages which serve to remind the reader what Islam is all about. The story revolves around a riddle to which only Allah has the answer.

The story about boys asleep in a cave "while their dog was stretching its paws in the yard" is the type of story that unbelieving adults might consider infantile, a childish boast. The story is reminiscent of the Rip-Van-Winkle tale, a children's fable by Washington Irving about a man who falls asleep for twenty years. In Allah's version, He causes as many as seven boys to fall asleep in a cave, leaving their dog outside, for perhaps three hundred years.

> 18:7 We have made everything on earth an adornment, in order to test them [and see] who of them is best in work.
>
> 18:8 And We shall reduce what is on it to barren dry soil.
>
> 18:9 Or did you think that the people of the Cave and al-

> Raqim (the mountain where the cave was) were the wonders of Our Signs?
>
> 18:10 When the youths took refuge in the Cave saying: "Our Lord, accord us from Yourself mercy, and guide us well in our affair."
>
> 18:11 Then We sealed their hearing in the Cave for many years.
>
> 18:12 Then We roused them to learn who of the two parties was able to calculate the time they had lingered.

A verse hinting at the compass bearing of the entrance to the cave and how Allah can be either a trusted or a duplicitous guide; and then it starts to get a little weird. I am deliberately skipping four verses here. In my opinion, the moral or point to this story can be found in verses 18:13-16 which are given at the end of this chronicle of sleeping boys and their dog.

> 18:17 And you might have seen the sun, when it rose, inclining from their Cave towards the right, and when it set, inclining to the left, while they were in an open space inside it (the Cave). That was one of Allah's Signs. He whom Allah guides is well-guided; and he whom Allah leads astray, you will not find a friend to direct him.

After Allah has turned them this way and that way, he wakes them up and asks them to guess how long they have been asleep before sending one of them out to get something to eat.

> 18:18 You would think them awake, whereas they were sleeping. We turned them over to the right, then to the left, while their dog was stretching its paws in the yard. If you looked at them, you would have turned away from them in flight, and would have been filled with fear.

If Allah won't tell the boys how long they have been asleep, revelation 18:19, He probably has a good reason.

> 18:19 Thus We roused them, that they might question each other. One of them said: "How long have you lingered?" They said: "A day or part of a day." They said: "Your Lord knows best how long you have lingered. So send someone with this silver [coin] of yours to the city, and let him see what food is purest. Then let him bring you some provision thereof, and let him be gentle and let him apprise no one about you.
>
> 18:20 "Surely, if they learn about you, they will stone you or

force you back into their religion; and then you will never prosper."

Some people who came across the unknown number of sleeping or arguing lads wanted to encase them in a shrine of some type.

> 18:21 That is how We made them known [to people] so as to know that Allah's Promise is true and the Hour is undoubted. As they were arguing among themselves concerning their affair, they said: "Build over them an edifice; their Lord knows best their condition." Then those who prevailed over them said: "Let us build over them a mosque."

Allah is not being deliberately vague in revelation 18:22 as to the number of boys because He does not know the answer. For an All-Knowing, All-Seeing All-Powerful god such as Allah this is not possible.

> 18:22 Some say: "[The sleepers were] three; their dog was the fourth of them"; and [others] say: "Five; their dog was the sixth of them", interpreting the unseen. And they say; "Seven; their dog being the eighth of them." Say (O Mohammad): "My Lord knows best their number; none knows them, save a few." Do not then, dispute concerning them, except with reference to that which is clear to you, and do not question, concerning them, any of them."

A couple of verses which may or may not have anything to do with this story:

> 18:23 And do not say of anything: "I will do that tomorrow," [unless you add]:

> 18:24 "If Allah wills." Remember your Lord, if you forget, and say: "Perhaps, my Lord will guide me to something closer to this in rectitude?"

Back to our sleepers:

> 18:25 And they lingered in their Cave three hundred years, and [some] add nine.

> 18:26 Say: "Allah knows best how long they lingered. His is the Unseen of the heavens and the earth. How clear is His Sight and His Hearing! Apart from Him, they have no protector, and He has no associates in His Sovereignty."

So, what is the moral of this story? In keeping with my understanding of the Koranic themes, it is about loyalty, keeping the faith, not mixing with those who believe in other gods; and if you do all that, Allah will look after you even if you have to seek refuge in a real or metaphorical cave. Here is what the boys and Allah had to say about the whole experience.

> 18:13 We relate to you their story in truth. They were youths who believed in their Lord and We increased them in guidance.
>
> 18:14 And We strengthened their hearts when they arose saying: "Our Lord is the Lord of the heavens and the earth. We will not call on any god besides Him. For then we would be uttering an enormity.
>
> 18:15 "These our people have taken other gods besides Him. Why do they not bring a clear authority for them? Who is, then, more unjust than he who invents lies about Allah?"
>
> 18:16 When you withdraw from them and what they worship, apart from Allah, take refuge in the Cave, and your Lord will extend to you some of His Mercy and prepare for you a suitable course in your affair.

~~~~~~~~~~~~

"A popular attraction outside of Amman is the Kahf Al-Raqim or the Cave of the Seven Sleepers... it is located outside the village of Al-Raqim, 10 km east of Amman. Persecuted by the despotic rule of Trajan for monotheism, a group of pious youths took refuge in this cave. To preserve them, God put them to sleep, and when they revived 309 solar years later, they thought that they were only asleep for a day or so. Christianity was widespread by then, and when they were discovered God put them to rest forever."

Jordan Tourism Board

Allah's Do Not Do List

Is there a better way of getting a handle on what type of god you're dealing with than getting acquainted with what they consider a damnable offence. Allah's list of sins which will get you an invite to an eternity burning in Hell is lengthy by the standards by which such list are measured, with the Ten Commandments at the more succinct end.

Grave Sins - An Introduction

The Greater Sins (or Grave Sins) are those where the Koran, or a saying of the Prophet explicitly state, or imply that those who commit these sins will go to Hell; or where there is a consensus among Islamic scholars that the sinner is going to Hell. It does not matter if the sin is committed in secret.

> 6:120 Avoid open and secret sins. Surely those who commit sin shall be punished for what they have perpetrated.

Indecency and unwarranted aggression are sins, the following revelation setting them apart notwithstanding.

> 7:33 Say: "My Lord has only forbidden open and secret indecencies, sin, unjust aggression, and your association with Allah that for which He sent down no authority, and your saying about Allah that which you do not know."

Do not worry about small indecencies.

> 53:31 And to Allah belongs whatever is in the heavens and on the earth, that He may reward the evildoers for what they did, and reward the righteous with the fairest reward;

> 53:32 Those who avoid grave sins and foul acts, except for venial ones. Your Lord's forgiveness is indeed ample. He knows you very well since He produced you from earth, and while you were still embryos in your mothers' wombs. Do not commend yourselves, He knows very well who is the God-fearing.

Make sure you know the difference between an evil deed and a grave sin!

> 4:31 If you avoid the grave sins you are forbidden, We will remit your evil deeds and let you enter into an honourable place (Paradise).

From my understanding of revelations on the subject, your "evil deeds" will be forgiven if they were committed out of ignorance, and when it became clear to you that what you did was evil, you repented immediately and not because you were threatened with death or on your death bed. Of course, an unbeliever can repent all he or she wants; it won't do him or her any good.

> 4:17 Allah has taken upon Himself to accept the repentance of those who commit evil in ignorance and then repent immediately after that. Those, He will forgive and Allah is All Knowing, Wise.

> 4:18 But not the repentance of those who commit evil deeds, and when one of them is faced with death, he says: "Now I repent"; nor the repentance of those who die as unbelievers. For these, we have prepared a very painful punishment!

The Greatest Sin of All

Considering Allah relentless invectives against would-be competitors, it should come as no surprise that worshipping other gods is the greatest sin of all and for which men, women and children have been killed in their tens of millions, with the greatest number slaughtered in the name of a pathologically jealous god being Indus, their numbers estimated at 70 million dead (K. S. Lal, Growth of Muslim Population in Medieval India, 1973).

> 17:39 That is part of what your Lord has revealed to you of wisdom. Do not set up with Allah another god, or else you will be cast in Hell, despised and rejected.

> ----

> 22:12 He calls, besides Allah, on that which neither harms nor profit him (other gods). That is the worst (the farthest from the Way) error.

> 22:13 He calls upon him whose harm is likelier than his profit. Wretched is the Master and wretched is the ally!

The Top 40

17:38 The evil of all this is hateful in the sight of your Lord.

Forty greater sins in descending order of evilness[15] for which there is a verse in the Koran or a saying of the Prophet about the sinner going to Hell with "associating other gods with Allah" being the greatest evil.

1. Shirk (polytheism), associating other gods with Allah.
2. Yās (despair), to doubt Allah's Mercy.
3. Qunut (despondence), losing hope in Allah.
4. Not fearing Allah's punishment.
5. Murder.
6. Parental disobedience.
7. Breaking up with relatives.
8. Usurping the property of orphans.
9. The charging of interest on borrowed money.
10. Fornication (adultery).
11. Sodomy.
12. Wrongfully accusing a chaste believer of adultery or homosexuality.
13. Drinking alcoholic beverages
14. Gambling,
15. To neglect an obligatory religious duty.
16. Playing musical instruments or listening to music.

---

[15] On the order of greater sins and type of sins Allah and His Messenger may have disagreed, with God prevailing of course.

Narrated Abdullah:

I asked the Prophet, "What is the greatest sin in the Sight of Allah?"

He said, "That you set up a rival unto Allah though He Alone created you."

I said, "That is indeed a great sin."

Then asked, "What is next?"

He said, "To kill your son lest he should share your food with you."

I asked, "What is next?"

He said, "To commit illegal sexual intercourse with the wife of your neighbor."

Bukhari 60.4

17. Singing.

18. Lying.

19. False oaths.

20. False testimony.

21. Concealing evidence.

22. Breaking a promise.

23. Misappropriation of property.

24. Stealing.

25. Short weighing or cheating in business.

26. Eating of what is unlawful.

27. Usurping the rights of others.

28. Avoiding Jihad.

29. Becoming A'Arāb after Hijrat, "the condition when a desert Bedouin before acquiring the necessary knowledge of religion turns back to his ignorant ways."

30. Helping the oppressors.

31. Not helping the oppressed.

32. Sorcery.

33. Extravagance e.g. wasteful expenditures.

34. Arrogance.

35. To war against Muslims.

36. Eating of carrion, pork and blood.

37. Omitting prayer intentionally.

38. Non-payment of Zakat (obligatory charity).

39. To consider the Hajj (mandatory pilgrimage) insignificant.

40. Persistence in minor sins (committing a lesser sin repeatedly).

10 Made Up Sins

Greater Sins for which there is no explicit verse or saying of the Prophet damning the sinner to an eternity roasting in Hell.

41. Backbiting.

42. Telling tales.

43. Insulting a believer.

44. Intrigue, deception and breaking covenants.

45. Hoarding and selling on the black-market.

46. Disrespect of the Qur'an.

47. Disrespect of Ka'ba.

48. Disrespect to Masajid (mosque).

49. Disrespect of the Tomb of the Prophet.

50. Disrespect to the soil of Imam Husain's Grave (Shia Islam).

Tips for Avoiding the Grave Sins

Amid all the hate and the cruelty, every now and then Allah will surprise you with the odd revelation about being kind and thoughtful, like the following which may prove helpful in navigating the mine field of grave sins.

Be kind to your parents

Considering Allah's decrees that a believer must disown a parent who will not submit to His Will the following revelations about being kind to your parents has to apply to believing parents only.

> 17:23 Your Lord has decreed that you worship none but Him and to be kind to your parents. If either of them or both reach old age with you, do not say to them "Fie", nor tell them off, but say to them kind words.

> 17:24 And lower to them the wing of humility out of mercy and say: "Lord, have mercy on them, as they took care of me when I was a child."

> 17:25 Your Lord knows best what is in your hearts. If you are righteous, He is All-Forgiving to those who repent.

Give your kinsman his due

Women are not mentioned, but Allah's heart, as it was with his revelations about being kind to your parents, is in the right place, if only in passing, so He too should be given His due.

> 17:26 And give the kinsman his due, and to the destitute and the wayfarer, and do not squander your wealth wastefully.

> 17:27 Surely the spindrifts are the brothers of the devils; and the Devil is ever ungrateful to his Lord.

If you have nothing to give, say something nice.

> 17:28 But if you turn away from them (the kinsman, the destitute and the wayfarer), seeking a mercy (because you have nothing to give and are seeking the bounty of your Lord) you expect from your Lord, then speak to them kindly.

And if you do have some wealth to spare, the ever practical Allah suggests that you don't give away so much of your wealth as to become like them; follow His example, revelation 17:30.

> 17:29 Do not keep your hand chained to your neck, nor spread it out fully, lest you sit around condemned and reduced to poverty.

> 17:30 Surely your Lord gives generously to whom He pleases, and He gives sparingly [to whom He pleases]. He knows and observes His Servants well.

Do not kill your children for fear of poverty

> 17:31 Do not kill your children for fear of poverty. We will provide for you and for them. To kill them is a great sin.

This is not a universal declaration against killing your children! Remember, not killing your children, if they decide to abandon Allah or behave in a manner He disapproves of, especially where girls and sex are concerned, is the greater sin, which may explain many of the so-called honour killings of females.

Remember the orphans

> 17:34 Do not go near the orphan's property except in the fairest way until he comes of age; and honour your pledge, because the pledge involves responsibility.

Be honest in your weights and measures

> 17:35 And give full measure when you measure, and weigh with a just balance. That is fair and better in the end.

Don't be arrogant

> 17:37 And do not walk in the land haughtily; for you certainly will not pierce the earth, nor equal the mountains in height.

Allah knows much about arrogance.

> 17:43 Glory be to Him and may He be greatly exalted above what they say.

> 17:44 The seven heavens, the earth what is in them praise Him, and there is nothing which does not celebrate His

praise; but you do not understand their praise. He is indeed Clement, All-Forgiving.

59:23 He is Allah. There is no god but He, the King, the Holy, the Peace-Giver, the Faith-Giver, the Overseer, the All-Mighty, the Overlord, the Haughty. May Allah be exalted above what they associate.

59:24 He is Allah, the Creator, the Maker, the Fashioner. His are the most Beautiful Names; whatever is in the heavens and on the earth glorifies Him. He is the All-Mighty, the Wise.

Allah and the Ptolemaic Universe

> 35:41 Allah holds the heavens and the earth firmly lest they become displaced; were they displaced, none will hold them together after Him. He is indeed Clement, All-Forgiving.

The Dark Ages is generally accepted to be the period in our history between 400 and 1000 A.D. Islam is a product of that gloomy period. For author Thomas Cahill the defining moment when civilization lost its mind and its humanity is the murder of Hypatia of Alexandria by crazed monks encouraged in their murderous enterprise by Cyril the Christian bishop of the city.

> In 415, a wild-eyed army of illiterate, black-cowled monks filled the streets of Alexandria like so many crazed bats ... Now they encountered Hypatia, a philosopher and mathematician on her way home ... She was a pagan teacher, an unescorted woman; she did not bow to their beliefs. She lured impressionable young Christians to her lectures; she consorted with Jews; she had dared speak against the patriarch ... They dragged her from her carriage and into the cathedral, where they stripped her; gauged her eyes out, skinned her alive, and tore her to pieces with jagged tiles ripped from the mosaics...

> Cahill, *Mysteries of the Middle Ages*, p. 29.

This was the same type of religious zealotry which, according to Cahill, would serve as a model for many of the clerics of the next religion to rise from the deserts of the Middle East: Islam!

With the coming of the Dark Ages more than 500 years of Greek astronomical observations were temporally lost. The Greeks had identified five planets in the night sky, not counting the Sun and Moon: Mercury, Venus, Mars, Jupiter and Saturn. The existence of these planets was documented in the summary of the Greek's astronomical discoveries and speculations on the nature of the universe in the *Almagest* (the Greatest), by mathematician, geographer and astronomer Ptolemy of Alexandria [90-169 A.D.)

Ptolemy in *The Almagest* also speculated on the circular orbits of the five known planets, the Moon and the Sun around planet Earth which was believed at the time to be the center of the universe. It was common knowledge among latter philosophers of antiquity that these five known planets, the Moon and the Sun were some distance from the earth.

In the Koran, and Islamic Traditions dating back to the Prophet Muhammad, there is no mention of these planets per se, and the Moon is believed to be above the clouds and the first level of Paradise somewhere around the orbit of this celestial body. While the Prophet and his early followers, who revelled in his illiteracy and their ignorance, would probably not have known about the Greek and Roman discoveries in astronomy, what is Allah's excuse?

Could Allah's apparent lack of knowledge about what was generally known about the earth's star-lit canopy be evidence that the Koran could not be the Word of God?

But is not Allah demonstrating a knowledge of the planets in his use of the phrase "by the alternating stars" in verses announcing the coming of Judgement Day?

> 81:14 Then each soul shall know what it had brought forth.
>
> 81:15 No, I swear by the alternating stars;
>
> 81:16 Which circle then hide;

Not really. Not if you consider the following reference to the planets as ornaments; a line of obstacles to guard against the devil.

> 37:6 We have adorned the lower sky with the ornament of the planets,
>
> 37:7 To guard against every rebellious devil.

The second line of defence, so to speak, is what science, not too long ago described as stars, just like our sun. To Allah and His Messenger, these were lamps on the perimeter of the bottom layer of heaven which could be thrown by the angels guarding heaven's borders at the devils and the jinn who got pass the planetary defences. Once thrown, these lamps became the shooting stars which followed the eavesdropper on down like a modern missile.

> 37:8 They do not listen to the Higher Assembly (the High Council of Paradise, *Moududi*) and are pelted from every side;
>
> 37:9 Expelled; and theirs is a lasting punishment.

37:10 Except for him[16] who eavesdropped once; and so a shooting star followed him.

67:5 We have adorned the lower heaven with lamps, and We turned them into missiles launched against the devils; and We have prepared for them the punishment of the Fire.

Then, there is that pesky revelation about the sun never overtaking the moon (revelation 36:40), among other things:

36:37 And as sign unto them is the night, from which We strip of the day; and lo, they are in darkness.

36:38 And the sun runs into its fixed station. That is the decree of the All-Mighty, the All-Knowing[17].

36:39 And the moon, We have determined its phases, until it became like an old twig.

36:40 The sun ought not to overtake the moon, nor the night outstrip the day; and each in its orbit is floating.

Anyone who has ever watched a solar eclipse[18] knows that the

---

[16] In Yusuf Ali's translation what Allah meant by "him" is more inclusive.

37:10 Except such as snatch away something by stealth, and they are pursued by a flaming fire, of piercing brightness.

What is "snatch away", in Muhammad Assad's translation, is "knowledge" of what Allah and His angels discuss.

37:10 but if anyone does succeed in snatching a glimpse [of such knowledge], he is [henceforth] pursued by a piercing flame.

Another explanation is that "him" is the jinn who flew up to heaven on behalf of the soothsayer in the Prophet's grand-father's employ to find out what Allah would accept in exchange for the grand-father not sacrificing Abdullah, the future father of the Prophet Muhammad, as he had promised Allah, if He gave him ten sons.

[17] Where the sun can be found at sunset:

Narrated Abu Dharr:

Once I was with the Prophet in the mosque at the time of sunset. The Prophet said, "O Abu Dharr! Do you know where the sun sets?"

I replied, "Allah and His Apostle know best."

He said, "It goes and prostrates underneath (Allah's) Throne; and that is Allah's Statement: 'And the sun runs on its fixed course for a term (decreed). And that is the decree of All-Mighty, the All-Knowing....' (36.38)

Bukhari 60.326

[18] For the Prophet, an eclipse was a "state" imposed by Allah which He could be convinced to remove thru prayer.

revelation about the sun not overtaking the moon is patently false as we understand it, and even more so when you consider that, in the earth-centered Koranic/Ptolemaic universe, the sun and the moon "float" around the earth (in the Koran, back and forth in a 180 degree arc above a flat earth).

As to the night never being longer than a day, tell that to an Inuit (Eskimo) in December, the 21st preferably, when the Arctic day is one long night, and be laughed out of his igloo into the cold dark day.

As to the floating part, I am sure you can find a scholar to say that this is Allah describing gravity. But I don't think so. Allah in the very next verse talks about a floating ship, the Ark. It's all about the push of buoyancy and not the pull of gravity.

> 36:41 And a sign unto them is that We carried their progeny in the laden Ark.

The Near-Earth Constellations

> 15:16 We have indeed set up constellations in the heavens and made them attractive to the beholders;
>
> 15:17 And guarded them against every accursed devil;
>
> 15:18 Except for him[19] who eavesdrops stealthily and was pursued by a visible flame.

In Yusuf Ali's translation constellations become signs of the zodiac.

> 15:16 It is We Who have set out the zodiacal signs in the heavens, and made them fair-seeming to (all) beholders;

In Habib Shakir's they are strongholds:

> 15:16 And certainly We have made strongholds in the heaven and We have made it fair seeming to the beholders.

Narrated Abu Bakra:

The solar eclipse occurred while we were sitting with the Prophet He got up dragging his garment (on the ground) hurriedly till he reached the mosque. The people turned (to the mosque) and he offered a two-Rak'at prayer whereupon the eclipse was over and he traced us and said, "The sun and the moon are two signs among the signs of Allah, so if you see a thing like this (eclipse) then offer the prayer and invoke Allah till He remove that state,"

Bukhari 72.676

[19] These are jinns who specialize in eavesdropping on Allah's conversations with his angels and on the angels talking among themselves. They fly as close as possible to the lowest of the seven levels of heaven dogging rocks thrown by the angels to keep them away, to find out what Allah has to say about was happening down below.

Moududi favours Shakir's interpretation, and here's why:

> "Fortified spheres" (buruj) are Signs of Allah for it is not possible to pass through one sphere of the Heaven into another, as each sphere of the space has been fortified by invisible boundaries. In this connection, it may be noted that literally the Arabic word buruj means "a fortified place" but as a technical term of ancient astronomy this stood for each of the twelve Signs of the Zodiac, which marked the sun's path through the heavens. This has led some of the commentators to form the opinion that in this verse the word buruj refers to the same.

Another revelation about constellations, revelation 25:61, and more:

> 25:58 Put your trust in the Living God who does not die and sing His Praise. He suffices as the All-Informed Knower of the sins of His servants,

> 25:59 Who created the heavens and the earth and what lies between them is six days. Then the Compassionate sat upon the Throne. So ask about Him, the Well-Informed.

> 25:60 And if it said to them: "Prostrate yourselves before the Compassionate"; they reply: "But who is the Compassionate? Shall we prostrate ourselves to what you (*Muhammad*) order us?" This only increases their aversion.

> 25:61 Blessed is He Who placed in the heaven constellations and placed in it a lamp and an illuminating moon.

> 25:62 And it is He who made the night and the day to succeed each other, for him who wants to remember or wants to give thanks.

Allah and the Shape of the Earth

Floating On A Sea of Mud

Dhul-Qarnayn, in the Koran, "is believed to be Alexander the Great" writes Fakhry. For much of what Allah has to say about the shape of the earth we have to look at what He revealed about Alexander walking a flat earth to where the sun set in a sea of mud, and then to another corner of the world where the sun rose.

> 18:83 And they ask you about Dhul-Qarnayn. Say: "I will give this account of him."
>
> 18:84 We established him firmly in the land and We gave him access to everything.
>
> 18:85 And so he followed a course;
>
> 18:86 Then, when he reached the setting-place of the sun, he found that it sets in a spring of black mud[20] and found, by it, a people. We said: "O Dhul-Qarnayn, either you punish them or show them kindness."

---

[20] The sun pauses beneath Allah's Throne, perhaps giving rise to those spectacular sunsets, before sinking in a sea of mud on which a flat earth appears to float, and re-emerging the next morning on the other side..

Narrated Abu Dhar:

The Prophet asked me at sunset, "Do you know where the sun goes [at the time of sunset]?"

I replied, "Allah and His Apostle know better."

He said, "It goes till it prostrates itself underneath the Throne and takes the permission to rise again, and it is permitted and then [a time will come when] it will be about to prostrate itself but its prostration will not be accepted, and it will ask permission to go on its course but it will not be permitted, but it will be ordered to return whence it has come and so it will rise in the west. And that is the interpretation of the Statement of Allah: And the sun runs its fixed course for a term [decreed]. That is The Decree of [Allah] The Exalted in Might, The All-Knowing."

Bukhari 54.421

This hadith would also suggest that Allah's Throne can be found in the western region of heaven.

18;87 He said: "As to the wrongdoer, we shall torture him; then he will be returned over to his Lord, Who will punish him a terrible punishment.

18:88 "But he who believes and does good deeds, he will have the fairest reward (Paradise), and we will command him to do what is easy for him."

Alexander then walked to the other end of the earth to witness the sun rise.

18:89 Then he followed [another] course.

18:90 But when he reached the rising-place of the sun, he found it rising on a people whom We have not provided with any screen against it.

18:91 So it was. We had full knowledge of what he had.

The well-travelled Alexander then headed north, assuming that the Bible and the Koran are in agreement as to the location of the mythical kingdoms of Gog and Magog.

18:92 Then he followed another course.

18:93 But when he reached the point separating the two barriers, he found beside them a people who could barely understand what is said.

18:94 They said: "O Dhul-Qarnayn, surely Gog and Magog are making mischief in the land. Shall we pay you a tribute so that you may build a barrier between us and them?"

Pointed Revelations About a Flat Earth

Paradise, in the Koran, is just above the clouds, perhaps not high enough for Allah to make out the curvature of the earth and realise that it was not level like a carpet or a couch, as more revealed truths would suggest[21], but I doubt it!

43:9 If you ask them: "Who created the heavens and the earth?", they will certainly say: "The All-Mighty, the All-Knowing created them."

---

[21] Cleric Mohammed Yusuf, the decease leader of Boko Haram, Nigeria's largest gathering of holy warriors whose designation literally means "non-Islamic education is a sin" said in a 2009 BBC interview that it was all an illusion created by Allah, that the earth is flat, just like the Koran says it is..

43:10 He who made the earth level ground for you and made for you pathways therein, that perchance you may be well-guided;

67:15 It is He Who made the earth level for you; so stroll through its regions and eat of His provisions. Unto Him is the Resurrection.

The earth is flat with a solid flat roof.

79:27 Are you, then, stronger in constitution than the heaven He has erected?

79:28 He raised its vault then levelled it off.

79:29 He dimmed its night and lighted its day.

79:30 Then, the earth, He flattened.

79:31 From it, He brought out its water and its pasture.

79:32 And the mountains, He established firmly,

79:33 As a source of enjoyment for you and your cattle.

The earth may be as flat as a couch:

2:21 O people (of Mecca), worship your Lord who has created you as well as those who came before you so that you may guard against evil;

2:22 Who has made the earth a couch for you, and the heavens a canopy, and Who sent down water from the sky, bringing forth by it a variety of fruits as a provision for you. Therefore do not knowingly set up equals to Allah.

Or even flatter:

51:48 And the earth, We have spread it out; and how excellently We smoothed it down!

~~~~~~~~~~~~~~~

Water may have existed before Allah created the heavens and the earth.

Narrated Imran bin Hussain:

While I was with the Prophet, some people from Bani Tamim came to him.

The Prophet said, "O Bani Tamim! Accept the good news!"

They said, "You have given us the good news; now give us (something)."

(After a while) some Yemenites entered, and he said to them, "O the people of Yemen! Accept the good news, as Bani Tamim have refused it."

They said, "We accept it, for we have come to you to learn the Religion. So we ask you what the beginning of this universe was."

The Prophet said "There was Allah and nothing else before Him and His Throne was over the water, and He then created the Heavens and the Earth and wrote everything in the Book."

Then a man came to me and said, "O Imran! Follow your she-camel for it has run away!"

So I set out seeking it, and behold, it was beyond the mirage! By Allah, I wished that it (my she-camel) had gone but that I had not left (the gathering)."

Bukhari 93.514

Who Stops the Sky From Falling?

Heaven is help up by invisible pillars anchored on a flat earth.

> 31:10 He created the heavens without pillars that you can see and laid down in the earth immovable mountains, lest it shake with you, and scattered throughout it every variety of beast. And We have sent down water from heaven, thereby causing it to grow in it every noble [kind of plant].
>
> 31:11 This is Allah's Creation; so show Me what those apart from Him have created. Indeed, the wrongdoers are in manifest error.

Knowing this, Allah's revelation that He keeps the sky from falling[22], revealed truth 22:65, makes sense.

---

[22] Heaven and earth are made of the same materials, which would explain the need for pillars to stop it from crashing to the ground.

> 21:30 Have the unbelievers not beheld that the heavens and the earth were a solid mass, then We separated them; and of water We produced every living thing. Will they not believe, then?
>
> 21:31 And We set up in the earth immovable mountains lest it should shake with them; and We created therein wide roads, that perchance they may be guided.

22:63 Do you not see that Allah sends down water from the sky, whereupon the earth turns green. Allah is Gracious, Well-Informed.

22:64 To Him belongs what is in the heavens and the earth and it is Allah Who is the Self-Sufficient and the Praiseworthy.

22:65 Do you not see that Allah has subjected to you what is on earth and the ships which sail in the sea at His Command? And He keeps the sky from falling to the ground, save by His Leave. Allah is Gracious and Merciful to mankind.

But is mankind grateful?

22:66 And it is He Who gives you life, then He causes you to die, then He will bring you back to life. Man, however, is truly thankless.

Full Circle in Seven Verses

15:19 As for the earth, we have spread it out, laid down upon it firm mountains and caused to grow therein all sorts of fair (sic).

15:20 And We have made in it provisions for you and for those whom you do not provide for.

15:21 There is nothing for which We do not have the storehouses and sources, and We send it down only in a well-known measure.

15:22 And We send forth the winds as fertilizer; and then We send down water from the sky and give it to you to drink. But you do not store it up.

15:23 It is We Who give life and cause to die, and We are the Inheritors.

15:24 And We know those of you who came before and those who will come later.

15:25 And surely your Lord shall gather them. He is truly Wise, All-Knowing.

21:32 And We made the sky a well-guarded canopy; and they still turn away from its signs.

Allah's Calendar

The Islamic calendar is based on a lunar cycle of twelve months (29 or 30 days) making the *Islamic* year 354 days long. Islam (610 - 632 A.D.) is a product of the Dark Ages (400 - 900 A.D.) when most of the science of the Greeks and Romans was temporarily lost. Lost to humanity perhaps, but not to God I am sure.

Why Allah chose the primitive inaccurate lunar calendar over the more accurate scientific solar calendar such as the Julian calendar introduced by Julius Caesar in 45 B.C. remains a mystery? Unlike the lunar calendar, it neatly divided a 365 day year into 12 months and added a leap day to February every four years.

The first solar calendar was probably developed by the Egyptians who, as a settled agrarian civilization, needed an accurate way of determining the end of one season and the beginning of another. It is true that being able to accurately determine the best time to plant your crops would not have been an issue for the desert dwellers of the arid Arab peninsula whose main occupation was trade and the raising of livestock; mainly sheep, goats and camels. But what about the rest of the world who would be forced to adopt the lunar calendar as Islam spread across the globe.

Allah had to know better; so why choose such an inaccurate way of measuring the passage of time and saddling humanity with it?

As a businessman who led caravans as far north as modern day Syria, God's Messenger would have travelled these long distances mainly at night because of the desert heat. On these night journeys, the moon was more of a friend than the blistering desert sun, and therefore a natural candidate for measuring the passage of time.

Could the Prophet have just chosen the lunar calendar for the same reason he chose Friday as Islam's day of worship – to further differentiate the believers from the unbelievers?

For the believers there is only one reason why God's Messenger adopted the lunar calendar, *because Allah told him so,* and if Allah chose it, then the traverse of the moon must be a better way of measuring the passage of the days, the months and the years than the traverse of the sun, as was done when the moon was a god worshipped by most of the inhabitants of the Peninsula.

> 2:189 They ask you about the crescents (the new moons), say: "They are times fixed for mankind and for the pilgrimage." It is not righteousness to enter houses from the back; but the righteous is he who fears Allah. Enter then the houses by their front doors; and fear Allah that you may prosper.

The moon's brightness is a reflection of the sun's light. Allah has reverse these in selecting the moon to measure the passage of time. Can His fondness for a former competitor in the pantheon of Arabian gods be any more evident.

> 10:5 It is He Who made the sun a bright radiance and the moon a light, and determined phases for it so that you may know the number of years and the reckoning[23]. Allah did not create that except in truth, expounding the Signs to a people who know.

> 10:6 Indeed, in the alternation of night and day and in what Allah has created in the heavens and the earth are real signs for people who are God-fearing.

The lunar calendar need not have been a calendar that needlessly complicated things by moving through the seasons if Allah had not banned the practice of adding a thirteenth month every third year or so.

It was the custom of some of the tribes that shared the Peninsula, before the Muslim conquest, to add a thirteenth month when it became obvious that the lunar calendar had lost all connection with the seasons and needed to be re-synchronized with the solar calendar. This, Allah claimed, was an attempt by the polytheists i.e. unbelievers to interfere with his sacred months and He forbade it.

> 9:36 The number of months, with Allah, is twelve months by Allah's Ordinance from the day He created the heavens and the earth. Four of these are Sacred. This is the right religion, so do not wrong yourselves during them; but fight the polytheists all together just as they fight you all together; and know that Allah is on the side of the righteous.

---

[23] In another revelation, it is the sun that Allah suggest you use to mark the passage of years and do your "reckoning".

> 17:12 We have made the night and the day two signs; then We blotted out the sign of the night and made the sign of the day luminous, that you may seek bounty from your Lord, and learn the number of years and the reckoning, and everything We have expounded clearly.

9:37 Postponing the [Sacred Month] is an added disbelief by which the unbelievers seek to mislead, allowing it one year and prohibiting it another year, so as to equal the number [of months] Allah has made sacred. Their evil deeds are made attractive to them; and Allah does not guide the unbelieving people.

~~~~~~~~~~~~~~~

A hadith where the usefulness of having a 29 day month is self-evident:

Narrated Um Salama:

The Prophet vowed to keep aloof from his wives for a period of one month, and after the completion of 29 days he went either in the morning or in the afternoon to his wives. Someone said to him "You vowed that you would not go to your wives for one month."

He replied, "The month is of 29 days."

Bukhari 31.134

The Names of the Months

The names of the months of the Islamic calendar are said to predate Islam and many reflect weather conditions on the Arabian Peninsula. Allah and His Messenger's adoption of a primitive calendar based on local weather conditions where each month begins eleven days (365 - 354) earlier every year (not counting leap years) makes for some interesting juxtapositions.

Somewhere in the world, people are freezing during *The Month of Great Heat* or seeking shelter from torrential rains during *The First Dry Month* and perhaps *The Second Dry Month*.

1 The Sacred Month
2 The Month of Travelling
3 The First Spring
4 The Second Spring
5 The First Dry Month
6 The Second Dry Month
7 The Month of Respect
8 The Dividing Month
9 The Month of Great Heat
10 The Month of Hunting

11 The Month of Rest

12 The Month of Pilgrimage.

Year Zero

In 637, Caliph Umar made the year 622, the year the Prophet fled Mecca and settled with his followers in Medina, year zero of the Islamic calendar. The year of this exodus is known as the Hijra or Hegira and is represented as 1 AH or 1 al-Hijra. The Hegira marks the alleged transition from ignorance to enlightenment.

Allah and the Beginnings of Life

6:98 And it is He Who created you from a single living soul; then [gave you] a resting place and a repository. Indeed, We have made plain Our signs for a people who understand.

13:8 Allah knows what every female bears and what the wombs carry for a shorter or a longer term; and everything with Him is by measure.

13:9 [He is] the Knower of the Unseen and the Seen, the Great, the Most High.

40:65 He is the Living One; there is no god but He. So call on Him professing sincerely the religion unto Him. Praise be to Allah, the Lord of the Worlds.

40:66 Say: "I have been forbidden to worship those you call upon, apart from Allah; since the clear proofs have come to me from my Lord and I have been commanded to submit to the Lord of the Worlds."

40:67 It is He who created you from dust, then from a sperm, then from a clot. Then He brings you out as infants; then allows you to come of age, then become old men. Some of you will pass away before that, but you will attain a fixed term, that perchance you might understand.

40:68 It is He Who brings life and causes to die. Then, if He decrees a certain matter, He only says: "Be", and it comes to be.

A Fluid Beginning

Water, or some kind fluid, is most often the base material from which Allah creates a human being in the womb with its two senses, a heart and no brain, as the heart was understood at the time of the Prophet to do much of what we know today to be the exclusive domain of the brain.

16:78 And Allah brought you of your mothers' bellies knowing nothing; and gave you hearing, sight and hearts, that perchance you may give thanks.

25:54 And it is He who created from water a human being; then he made him a kin by blood or marriage. Your Lord is All-Powerful.

77:20 Have we not created them from base water?

77:21 That We laid in a secure place;

77:22 Until an appointed term.

77:23 We determined, and what excellent determiners were We!

77:24 Woe on that Day (Judgement Day), betide those who denounce.

Yes, science tells us that life originated in the oceans and that without water life as we know it would not exist, but I do not think that it is the insight offered by Allah. What is more likely is that Allah is referring to the water released from the rupture of the amniotic sac at the onset of labour. Of course, the "flowing water" in verse 86:6 was the medium in which the embryo developed after conception; the baby was actually created from the fusion of sperm and egg[24].

THE NIGHT –VISITOR

86 At-Tariq

In the Name of Allah,
the Compassionate, the Merciful

86:1 By the heavens and the night-visitor.

86:2 If only you knew what is the night visitor,

86:3 The piecing star.

---

[24] Moududi writes that "mixed sperm" in revelation 76:2 is actually "the intermingling of the male sperm with the female ovum". This could indicate that Allah knew about the female contribution to conception although He never mentions it explicitly.

> 76:1 Has there come upon man a period of time when he was not a noteworthy thing?
> 76:2 We have indeed created man from a mixed sperm to test him; and so We made him capable of hearing and sight.
> 76:3 We have guided him upon the path, either as thankful or thankless.

86:4 Every soul has a watcher;

86:5 So let man consider what he was created from.

86:6 He was created from flowing water;

Snakes, those who "crawls on their bellies" in the following revelation are hatched from eggs, as are chickens which walk "on two feet". The list is quite extensive, as you probably know. If for Allah, the egg white in which the yolk is suspended is water, or some type of water-like liquid, then revelation 24:45 has some validity.

24:45 Allah created every beast from water. Some of them crawl on their bellies, some walk on two feet and others walk on four. Allah creates whatever He pleases. Allah, indeed, has power over everything.

Allah, as He is tends to do when describing the inner workings of the human body, is somewhat vague as to the location of the amniotic sac and the source of the liquid it contains.

86:7 Emanating from what lies between the loins and the breast-bones.

An example from the animal kingdom as to Allah's difficulties in explaining what occurs beneath the skin.

16:66 And there is, surely, a lesson for you in the cattle. We give you to drink of what is in their bellies, between the bowels and blood, pure milk which is palatable to the drinkers.

In another series of verses Allah provides a bit more information as to conception and what comes after.

75:36 Does man think that he shall be left unattended?

75:37 Was he not a drop of sperm released?

75:38 Then, he was a leech; then He created and fashioned (him);

75:39 Making of him a couple, male and female.

75:40 Is not that One Able to quicken the dead?

The previous three revealed truths bare a remote resemblance to what actually happens, if you ignore the role of a woman's egg and the fact that the sex of an individual is decided at conception.

Bones Then Flesh

Allah's understanding of what happens after conception becomes even more suspect in a verse, revelation 23:14, where He reveals the process by which He creates the baby that will eventually emerge from the birth canal. First He creates flesh which becomes bone which He then covers with flesh.

> 23:12 We have created man from an extract of clay;
>
> 23:13 Then we placed him as a sperm in a secure place;
>
> 23:14 Then we created out of the sperm a clot; then made from the clot a lump of flesh, then made the lump of flesh into bones; and then covered the bones with flesh; then fashioned him into another creation. So Blessed be Allah, the Best of Creators.
>
> 23:15 Then after that you will surely die.
>
> 23:16 Then on the Day of Resurrection you will surely be raised from the dead.

There is no such stage when bones are formed first and coated with flesh. Remember, Islam is a product of the Dark Ages when much of the scientific discoveries of the Greek and Roman civilizations were temporally lost, including medical knowledge related to conception and gestation, and replaced by superstitions and half-truths.

Beware of the Clot

In surah 96, *The Clot*, Allah reveals what Islamic scholars often point to as proof that He knew more about conception then was known at the time; that Allah was aware that babies developed from a fertilized egg, a zygote. They interpret "clot" in verse 96:2 to mean zygote.

> THE CLOT
>
> 96 Al-`Alaq
>
> *In the Name of Allah,*
> *the Compassionate, the Merciful*
>
> 96:1 Read, in the Name of your Lord, Who created:
>
> 96:2 He created man from a clot.

To back up their argument they also point to verse 22:5:

> 22:5 O people, if you are in doubt regarding the resurrection, We have indeed created you from dust, then from a sperm, then from a clot, then from a little lump of

flesh, partly formed and partly unformed, in order to show you. We deposit in the wombs whatever We please, for an appointed term; then we bring you out as infants; till you attain full strength. Some of you are made to die, and some are returned to the vilest age, so that they may not know, after having acquired some knowledge, anything. And you see the earth barren, but when We send down water upon it, it stirs and swells and produces vegetation of every pleasing variety.

22:6 That is because Allah is the Truth, and He brings the dead to life and He has power over everything.

Allah's "clot" appears to be a mutation of a man's sperm, which He has implanted in a woman's uterus (the "secure place" in verse 23:13), and from which He will fashion a fetus; bones first, sex later.

It's All About the Sperm

Sperm deposited in the water contained in the amniotic sack is all you need to create an embryo, and that is an immutable fact, as are all Allah's revealed truths.

16:3 He created the heavens and the earth in truth; may He be exalted above what they associate [with Him].

16:4 He created man from a sperm-drop and, behold, he is a professed disputant.

56:57 We have created you, if only you would believe!

56:58 Have you seen the semen you emit?

56:59 Do you create it, or are We the Creators?

80:17 May man perish! How thankless he is!

80:18 Of what did He create him?

80:19 Of a sperm, He created him and determined him.

80:20 Then He smoothed his path;

80:21 Then He caused him to die and entombed him;

80:22 Then, if He wishes He will raise him from the dead.

80:23 No indeed; he did not fulfil what He commanded him.

Early on in the Koran, in the second surah, The Cow, Allah reveals that He brought humans back to life and it wasn't Judgement Day.

> 2:28 How can you disbelieve in Allah. You were dead (being a life-germ i.e. not living yet) and He brought you back to life (as a child), then He will cause you; to die and bring you back to life again then unto Him you will return.

"Life-germ" is used by M. Shakir in his translation instead of sperm:

> 35:11 And Allah created you of dust, then of the life-germ, then He made you pairs; and no female bears, nor does she bring forth, except with His knowledge; and no one whose life is lengthened has his life lengthened, nor is aught diminished of one's life, but it is all in a book; surely this is easy to Allah.

Fakhry's translation of 35:11:

> 35:11 Allah created you from dust, then from a sperm, then made you into couples. No female bears or gives birth, save with His knowledge, and no man advances in years or his life-span is diminished, except as ordained in the Book. That indeed is an easy matter for Allah.

The sperm, or life-germ, is a living thing not a dead thing as implied by Fakhry's attempted explanation of Allah's confounding revelation that He brings people back to life twice: when they are born and on Judgement Day.

Things Which Don't Come in Pairs

> 13:3 And it is He Who spread out the earth and placed therein firm mountains and rivers; and of each kind of fruit He created two pairs (males and females). He causes the night to cover the day. Surely in that are signs for people who reflect.

> 36:36 Glory be to Him Who created all the pairs of what the earth brings forth, of their own kinds and of what they know not.

> 78:8 And created you in pairs?

What about asexual reproduction, and single-cell organisms that reproduce asexually i.e. no partners, where there is no transfer of reproductive material from a male donor to a female "receptacle"?

What about animals higher up the evolutionary ladder, such as the female whiptail lizard and other species who reproduce through pathogenesis (no males required). Science may have to revisit this entire asexual reproduction thing. And, as for living organisms that don't come in pairs, it has to be a mistake. And as to self-pollinating fruit trees, the less said the better.

Allah as Proof that Imperfection Is Pervasive

For Allah a menstruating woman is impure; the impurity being the discharge of her unfertilized eggs. If the Prophet had been aware of the role a woman's eggs and menstruation play in the reproductive cycle, would Allah have considered her contaminated during her menses thereby admitting that the reproduction cycle of which He is so proud and which He closely controls is flawed because it not only leads to the creation of new life but to impurities (the bloody discharge of unfertilized eggs) of which He is responsible, the God "Who fashioned well everything He created".

> 32:7 Who fashioned well everything He created, and originated the creation of man from clay.

> 32:8 Then He fashioned his progeny from an extract of fluid.

> 32:9 Then He shaped him well and breathed into him of His Spirit. He gave you hearing, sight and hearts. How little do you give thanks!

If genetics do influence the type of person one grows up to be, and that person turns out to be a disappointment to his or her parents and to God, it may not be all their fault if the DNA is all from the sperm.

> 36:77 Does not man see that We created him from a sperm; and behold he is a manifest trouble-maker?

Allah and the Jinn

The Myth and the Reality

Of all the inhabitants of the Koran, jinns (Allah refers to them collectively as *the jinn*) are the most fascinating. They are the most versatile and mischievous of creatures. They even have a chapter of the Koran named after them, surah 72, *The Jinn*. Pre-Islamic Arabs believed in the existence of the jinn and this may explain their significant presence in the Koran. The jinn are said to be spirits which inhabit another dimension. Allah created the jinn from fire before He created man. The caricature of the genie is undoubtedly based on this creature of the Koran.

The jinn may not be unlike humans in appearance as representation of the genie in film and literature would also suggest.

> 7:179 And We have created for Hell multitudes of jinn and men. They have hearts, but do not understand; and they have eyes, but do not see; and they have ears, but do not hear. Those are like cattle, or rather are even more misguided. Those are the heedless ones.

Like the angels, men and jinn were created to worship Allah, not to look after Him; He can feed himself, and He will feed the wrongdoers, just don't rush Him.

> 51:56 I have not created the jinn and mankind except to worship Me.

> 51:57 I do not desire provision from them, and I do not want them to feed Me.

> 51:58 Surely, Allah is the All-Provider, the Mighty One, the Strong.

> 51:59 The wrongdoers will have a portion like the portions of their fellows; so let them not rush Me.

> 51:60 Woe unto the unbelievers on that Day which they have been promised.

Allah created the jinn out of fire before he created man whom, in one version of Adam's creation, He moulded out of clay and slime.

> 15:26 And We have created man from potter's clay, moulded out of slime.

> 15:27 And the jinn We created before that from blazing fire.

> 55:15 And He created the jinn from tongues of fire.

Some people, at one point in time, worshipped the jinn instead of Allah. Allah was under the impression that these wrongly-guided individuals had worshipped His angels. On Judgement Day His angels will set Him straight.

> 34:40 On the Day that He will muster them, then say to the angels: "Are those the ones who used to worship you?"

> 34:41 They will say: "Glory be to You; You are our protector, apart from them." No, rather, they used to worship the jinn, most of them believing in them.

> 34:42 Today, none of them has the power to profit or harm the other, and We will say to the wrongdoer: "Taste the punishment of the Fire which you used to question."

There is no relationship between Allah and the jinn, no matter what they allege, and they will be treated like everybody else on Judgement Day.

> 37:158 And they alleged a kinship between Him and the jinn, whereas the jinn know very well that they will be summoned.

> 37:159 May Allah be exalted above their allegation.

> 37:160 Except for Allah's sincere servants.

> 37:161 Surely, neither you nor what you worship,

> 37:162 Against Him can ever turn anyone;

> 37:163 Except he who will be roasting in Hell.

Allah does not share power with the jinn.

> 6:100 They set up the jinn as Allah's partners, although He created them; and they falsely ascribe to Him sons and daughters without any knowledge. Glory be to Him, and highly exalted is He above what they ascribe to Him!

Bad jinns can be persuaded to do good if given the proper incentive.

Some less than cooperative jinn, with a little prodding from Allah, helped Solomon build the first temple.

> 34:12 And We subjected the wind to Solomon, blowing in the morning the space of a month and in the evening the space of a month; and We smelted for him the fount of brass. Of the jinn some worked before him, by the Leave of his Lord, and whoever of them swerved from Our Command, We shall make him taste the punishment of the blazing Fire.
>
> 34:13 To fashion for him whatever he wished of palaces, statues, basins like water-troughs and immovable cooking-pots. "Work thank-fully, O David's House; for few of My servants are truly thankful."

How the Jinn Heard About the Koran etc.

The jinn, according to Allah, had no knowledge of the Koran, or perhaps its contents. This was in spite of having eavesdropped on conversations between Allah and his angels and they talking among themselves for possibly eons. A group of the jinn did, however, become Muslim after hearing His Messenger recite verses from the Book.

THE JINN

72 Al-Jinn

In the Name of Allah,
the Compassionate, the Merciful

> 72:1 Say: "It was revealed to me that a company of jinn listened; then they said: 'We have indeed heard a wonderful Qur'an;
>
> 72:2 '"It guides to rectitude; so we believed in it, and we shall never associate anyone with our Lord;

The Koran is not clear, but the verses heard by these jinn, judging by their response, was probably about Allah denouncing those who would say he had consorted with a female or ever had a son i.e. Jesus.

> 72:3 '"And that He, may our Lord's majesty be exalted, has not taken a consort or a son;

The jinn who happened upon the Prophet reciting verses from the Koran now considered themselves Muslims; they now thought it foolish to have been disrespectful or to have believed that Allah would reveal anything but the truth.

72:4 "'And that our fools used to speak impertinently of Allah;

72:5 "'And that we thought that neither mankind nor the jinn will impute to Allah any falsehood;

From the sayings of the Prophet we get additional information about this fortuitous stealth encounter of the jinn and the Prophet.

Narrated Ibn Abbas:

The Prophet set out with the intention of going to Suq Ukaz (market of Ukaz) along with some of his companions. At the same time, a barrier was put between the devils and the news of heaven. Fire commenced to be thrown at them.

The Devils went to their people, who asked them, "What is wrong with you?"

They said, "A barrier has been placed between us and the news of heaven. And fire has been thrown at us."

They said, "The thing which has put a barrier between you and the news of heaven must be something which has happened recently. Go eastward and westward and see what has put a barrier between you and the news of heaven."

Those who went towards Tuhama came across the Prophet at a place called Nakhla and it was on the way to Suq 'Ukaz and the Prophet was offering the Fajr prayer with his companions.

When they heard the Qur'an they listened to it and said, "By Allah, this is the thing which has put a barrier between us and the news of heaven."

They went to their people and said, "O our people; verily we have heard a wonderful recital (Qur'an) which shows the true path; we believed in it and would not ascribe partners to our Lord."

Allah revealed the following verses to his Prophet (Sura Jinn 72) Say: "It has been revealed to me."

And what was revealed to him was the conversation of the jinn.

Bukhari 12.740

In another hadith, it was a tattle-tale tree which informed the Prophet about the jinn's presence, but perhaps not what Allah revealed was the impact on the jinn of hearing His Messenger recite from the Koran.

Narrated Abdur-Rahman:

I asked Masruq, "Who informed the Prophet about the Jinns at the night when they heard the Qur'an?"

He said, "Your father Abdullah informed me that a tree informed the Prophet about them."

Bukhari 58.199

Some humans sought refuge with the jinn. This, Allah may have considered an unnatural relationship considering His use of the word "perversion" in the following verse.

> 72:6 '"And that some individual humans used to seek refuge with some men of the jinn, and so they increased them in perversion;

The jinn, like the Prophet, once thought that Allah could not raise the dead.

> 72:7 '"And that they thought, as you thought, that Allah will not raise anybody from the dead;

The jinn admit that they have been eavesdropping on Paradise, that Allah is fully aware of what they have been doing, and that even bigger rocks, the comets in the following verse, will now be aimed in their direction if they persist.

> 72:8 '"And that we reached out to heaven, but we found it filled with mighty guards and comets;

> 72:9 '"And that we used to sit around it eavesdropping; but whoever listens now will find a comet in wait for him;

After listening in on Allah's conversations with his angels for who knows how long, the jinn confess to still not knowing Allah's plans for the people on earth. It did not matter whether they were good or bad jinn, both "persuasions" were clueless about what Allah intended for His earth-bound bipeds.

> 72:10 '"And that we do not know whether ill was intended for whoever is on earth, or whether their Lord intended rectitude for them;

> 72:11 '"And that some of us are righteous and some are less than that for we were of diverse persuasions;

Two verses about the believing jinn's confession-like ramblings from which you can draw your own conclusions.

> 72:12 '"And that we knew that we will not thwart Allah on earth, and that we will not thwart Him by flight;
>
> 72:13 '"And that when we heard the Guidance, we believed in it; for he who believes in his Lord need not fear to be stinted or over-burdened;

There are jinn who submit and jinn who don't.

> 72:14 "And that some us are submitting and some are diverging.' Those who have submitted have surely sought rectitude."

And just like the humans who will not submit, the bad jinn are Hell's firewood. They may have been created "from blazing fire" but that does not mean that they cannot be burnt over and over, especially when no water will be available.

> 72:15 But those who have diverged, have been firewood for Hell;
>
> 72:16 And that had they followed the Right Path, We would have given them abundant water to drink;
>
> 72:17 So as to test them thereby. He who refrains from the mention of His Lord, He will afflict him with terrible punishment;

The jinn may have wanted to intercept the Prophet when he flew up to heaven on al-Burak, taking off from "the farthest Mosque" i.e. Temple Mount in Jerusalem, to meet with Allah, and the reason they may not have done so:

> 72:18 And that mosques are Allah's; so do not call, besides Allah, upon anyone else;
>
> 72:19 And that when the Servant of Allah (the Prophet Muhammad) got up calling on Him, they almost set upon him in throngs.
>
> 72:20 Say: "I only call upon my Lord, and I do not associate with Him anyone else."
>
> 72:21 Say: "I have no power to harm or guide you rightly."

Not unlike the Christian tradition of an angel rebellion, Allah had a falling out with one of the jinn who would be the progenitor of all evil jinn.

18:50 And [remember] when we said to the angels: "Prostrate yourselves to Adam", and they all did except Satan; he was one of the jinn, then he disobeyed the Command of his Lord. Will you, then, take him and his progeny as protectors, besides Me, while they are all your enemies?" Evil is the exchange for the wrongdoers!"

Considering the importance of the jinn in the Koran it is surprising that belief in the jinn is not one of the *Pillars of Faith (Appendix Pillars of Islam)*.

Jinn and Men Together on Judgement Day

6:128 And on the Day when He shall gather them all together [saying]: "O, company of jinn, you have mislead a great many men." Their supporters among men will say: "Lord, we have profited much from each other and we have attained the term that you assigned for us." Then He will say: "The Fire is your resting-place, abiding therein forever, except as Allah wills. Your Lord is truly Wise, All-Knowing."

6:129 And thus We cause some of the evildoers to dominate the others, because of what they used to do (the evil they committed).

Messengers to the Jinn

Jinn had their own Messengers.

6:130 O company of jinn and men, did there not come Messengers from among yourselves to you, reciting to you My Revelations and warning you of seeing this Day of yours? They will say: "We bear witness against ourselves." They were deluded by the earthly life and will bear witness against themselves that they were unbelievers.

6:131 That is because your Lord would not destroy cities on account of their people's wrongdoing without warning them (by sending a Messenger to them).

Orderly processing of sinners, jinn and men, will be the order of the Day.

6:132 And to all are assigned ranks according to what they have done; and your Lord is not unaware of what they do.

Jinn and men, be advised that your All-Sufficient Merciful Lord may or may not destroy you, and that's a promise.

6:133 Your Lord is the All-Sufficient, the Merciful. If He wishes, He will destroy you and bring out after you, as successors, whomever he wishes, as He had produced you from the seed of another people.

6:134 Indeed, whatever you are promised will surely come to pass, and you are not able to escape [it].

In typical Allah fashion, He issues a warning about misbehaving after He has brought on the end-of-times. Of all the gods that exist in the past, present and future simultaneously Allah, it seems, has the most difficulties keeping his "times" straight. Then again, this may just be His Way, and His Way is, of course, the Best Way.

The Jinn and the Prophet's Grandfather

Virgil Gheorghiu in his biography of the Prophet, *La vie de Mahomet* (*The Life of Muhammad*) writes about how the Prophet's grandfather Abd al-Muttalib who, in another variation of the story of Abraham and Isaac and the thwarted immolation, had promised Allah to sacrifice his tenth son if He gave him ten male heirs.

When the time came for al-Muttalib to keep his promise, he consulted a dervish to find out if he could fulfil his promise to God in some other manner that did not involve killing his tenth son Abdullah who was destined to be God's Messenger's father. The dervish the Prophet's grandfather consulted was no ordinary soothsayer; he was a dervish with jinn in his employ, jinn who specialized in eavesdropping on Allah's conversations with his angels and on the angels talking among themselves. They would fly as close as possible to the lowest of the seven levels of heaven, the one closest to the earth, dogging rocks thrown by the angels to keep them away[25], to find out what Allah had to say about was happening down below.

To try to answer his client's question, the dervish sent his jinns to eavesdrop on God's conversation. One reported that Allah, in a conversation with an angel, had indicated that he would be happy with a sacrifice of camels. But how many camels? The dervish then threw some dice (bone fragments of some type according to Gheorghiu) to find out how many camels. The answer they gave was one hundred camels as the price of a human life. This is the price the Prophet reminded the faithful in his last sermon shortly before he died, that Allah had set as the payment to the family or clan of the

---

[25] Another pre-Islamic myth that found its way into the Koran: 67:5 We have adorned the lower heaven with lamps, and We turned them into missiles launched against the devils: and We have prepared for them the punishment of the Fire.

deceased for a non-premeditated homicide, what our legal system defines as the crime of *manslaughter*.

And intentional murder shall be punished according to talion law; where the murderess intention is not clear and the victim is killed using a club or a stone it will cost the perpetrator one hundred camels as blood money. Whoever demands more is a man from the time of ignorance.

From a translation of the Prophet's last sermon by Islamic scholar and author Dr. Muhammad Hamidullah [1908-2002]

Allah and She Who Blows in Reeds

Ali Hussain Sibat hosted a popular show broadcast in Arabic from Beirut. On his show, he offered advice on a variety of subjects and made predictions about the future. In 2008, he went on pilgrimage to Saudi Arabia, was arrested by the religious police and charged and convicted of sorcery and sentenced to be beheaded.

Every year Saudi Arabia beheads a witch or warlock or two; they do exist and they are evil as Allah will attest. Witchcraft or Sorcery is the 32nd gravest sin, sins for which death is the normative sentence under the Sharia, God's Law.

Allah first broaches the subject of witchcraft early on in His Koran, at the end of a wide ranging condemnation of the Jews for allegedly breaking their covenant with Him.

> 2:99 Indeed, we have revealed to you clear Signs (the revelations) in which only the wicked will disbelieve.

> 2:100 Will it be that every time they make a covenant, a group of them will cast it aside? Indeed, most of them do not believe.

> 2:101 And when a Messenger came to them from Allah confirming what they had, a group of those who were given the Book (the Torah) cast the Book (Qur'an) of Allah behind their backs, as if they knew nothing;

> 2:102 And they believed what the devils said about Solomon's kingdom. Not that Solomon disbelieved; but the devils did, teaching the people witchcraft and that which was revealed in Babylon to the two angels, Harut and Marut. Yet those two angels did not teach anybody without saying [to him]: "We are a temptation. So do not disbelieve." Those [who wished] learned from them what would sow discord between man and wife, but could not harm anybody with it (what they had learned), except with Allah's Permission. They learn what harms them and does not profit them. They knew that he who bought it will have no share in the Hereafter. Evil is the price for which they sold themselves, if only they knew.

In the Prophet's time witches were thought to blow into knots to cast spells; another superstition from the Dark Ages which appears to have found its way into the Koran. The second to last surah of the Koran implores Allah to protect men from the evil He admits to creating, including "those who blow into knotted reads", and "from the evil of the envious when he envies."

THE DAYBREAK
113 Al-Falaq

*In the Name of Allah,
the Compassionate, the Merciful*

113: 1 Say: "I seek refuge with the Lord of the Daybreak,

113:2 "From the evil of what He has created,

113:3 "And the evil of the darkness when it gathers,

113:4 "And the evil of those who blow into knotted reeds (witches or sorceresses),

113:5 "And from the evil of the envious when he envies."

The Prophet, if not typical of his generation, was a product of his time, as his belief in an evil eye will attest.

Narrated Um Salama:

That the Prophet saw in her house a girl whose face had a black spot. He said. "She is under the effect of an evil eye; so treat her with a Ruqya (not unlike an exorcism where repeating over and over specific verses from the Koran figure prominently)."

Bukhari 71.635

Allah and the Unseen

> 59:22 He is Allah; there is no god but He, the Knower of the Unseen and the Seen. He is the Compassionate, the Merciful.

If Allah knows the Unseen, it is because He has the keys to wherever the Unseen can be found.

> 6:59 With Him are the keys of the Unseen; only He knows them, and He knows what is on land and in the sea. Not a leaf falls but He knows it; and there is no grain in the dark bowels of the earth, nor anything green or dry, but is [recorded] in a Clear Book.

What are the keys to the Unseen you ask? A believer must have asked the Prophet that very question.

> **Narrated Ibn Umar:**
>
> Allah's Apostle said, "The keys of Unseen are five which none knows but Allah:
>
> None knows what will happen tomorrow but Allah;
>
> none knows what is in the wombs (a male child or a female) but Allah;
>
> none knows when it will rain but Allah;
>
> none knows at what place one will die;
>
> none knows when the Hour will be established but Allah." (31:34)
>
> *Bukhari 60.219*

Seeing is knowing – maybe not for you or anyone who has ever looked through a telescope in wonder, but it is Allah – whether it be what you can or cannot see!

> 64:18 Knower of the Unseen and the Seen, the All-Mighty, the Wise.

> 67:12 Indeed, those who fear their Lord unseen will be accorded forgiveness and a great reward.

Who is more fitting to sit in judgement than one who knows about the Unseen and the Seen!

> 39:46 Say: "O Allah, Creator of the heavens and the earth, Knower of the Unseen and the Seen, you shall judge between your servants regarding that whereon they used to differ."

To whom Allah discloses the Unseen and how He makes sure His message reaches its destination.

> 72:25 Say: "I do not know whether what you are promised is near, or whether my Lord shall extend it for a period.
>
> 72:26 "Knower of the Unseen, He does not disclose His Unseen to anyone."
>
> 72:27 Except for any Messenger He is well-pleased with. He then will dispatch watchmen before him and behind him;
>
> 72:28 So as to know that they have delivered the Messages of their Lord. And He encompasses whatever they have and numbers everything.

Those whom Allah has not taken into His confidence are hurled the truth about the Unseen.

> 34:48 Say: "My Lord hurls down the truth. He is the Knower of the Unseen."

Open-minded people have always speculated about what Allah warned they must not, the Unseen, which included the perplexing *Seen* for which explanations were not yet forthcoming. The worst offenders had to be the Meccans. Most being the Prophet's kin, they were the least willing to put up with his demand that they not think for themselves about matters his Mentor had decreed were off limits.

> 34:53 They have already disbelieved in Him and they speculate about the Unseen from a far-off place (Mecca, *Moududi*).
>
> 34:54 And they were barred from what they desired, as was done with their ilk before. Indeed, they were in disturbing doubt.

Allah is the inheritor of the wealth and children of unbelievers who presume too much; their suppositions Allah will write down and they will be doubly punished for their overconfidence.

19:77 Have you seen him who disbelieves in our Revelations and [yet] says: "I shall certainly be given wealth and children."[26]

19:78 Does he have knowledge of the Unseen, or did he take a pledge from the Compassionate (received permission, *Moududi*)?

19:79 No, We shall write down what he says and shall add punishment to his punishment.

19:80 And We will inherit from him what he says and he will come to Us alone.

Some blessings of Allah's may be obvious, other less so, leading to disputes about exactly what Allah is talking about, such as the "outward and inward", revelation 31:20, which, if they are the same as the "Outer and the Inner", revelation 57:3, is about the Unseen and the Seen.

31:20 Have you not seen how Allah has subjected to you whatever is in the heavens and on earth and granted you His Blessings, both outward and inward? Some people, however, continue to dispute regarding Allah, without any knowledge or guidance or an illuminating Book.

---

[26] Allah's need to communicate a revealed truth about our existence in the here-and-now or the Hereafter was often preceded by the most banal boast, even a joke, as appears to be the case here where a man promises to pay a blacksmith in the afterlife when Allah will have provided him with the means i.e. "property".

Narrated Khabbab:

I was a blacksmith and did some work for Al-'As bin Wail. When he owed me some money for my work, I went to him to ask for that amount. He said, "I will not pay you unless you disbelieve in Muhammad."

I said, "By Allah! I will never do that till you die and be resurrected."

He said, "Will I be dead and then resurrected after my death?"

I said, "Yes."

He said, "There I will have property and offspring and then I will pay you your due."

Then Allah revealed. 'Have you seen him who disbelieved in Our signs, and yet says: I will be given property and offspring?'

Bukhari 36.475

IRON

57 Al-Hadîd

*In the Name of Allah,
the Compassionate, the Merciful*

57:1 Whatever is in the heavens and the earth glorifies Allah. He is the All-Mighty, the Wise.

57:2 To Him belongs the dominion of the heavens and the earth. He bring to life and causes to die, and He has power over everything.

57:3 He is the First and the Last, the Outer and the Inner, and He has knowledge of everything.

57:4 It is He Who created the heavens and the earth in six days; then He sat upon the Throne. He knows what penetrates into the earth and what comes out of it; what comes down from heaven and ascends to it. He is with you, wherever you are: Allah perceives whatever you do.

57:5 To him belongs the dominion of the heavens and the earth, and unto Allah all matters are ultimately referred.

57:6 He causes the night to phase into the day and the day to phase into the night, and He knows the secrets within the breasts.

Today, much of the *Unseen* in the Koran and in the Sayings of God's Messenger is now the *Seen*, the most obvious being the sex of a developing embryo. I suspect that God's admonition about speculating about the *Unseen* may have had more to do with His Messenger not having a ready plausible response to a question from a member of his audience.

God's Messenger was very much a prophet who knew his limitations, confining most of his observations to apocryphal explanations about things that had already happened such as the destruction caused by conflicts barely remembered and natural phenomena; wanton devastation which he attributed to the work of a thin-skinned deity cleansing the world of unbelievers.

Muhammad the merchant's prophet credentials come mainly from a prediction that has been a staple of people who claimed to have the gift since time immemorial and that is the coming of Judgement Day. A prudent prophet, he also admonished his followers not to write down anything he said, whether it was from him or from Allah, lest he be caught out, perhaps.

Self-Sufficient Heart Reader

Allah is All-Sufficient. You need Him, He does not need you, especially if you don't believe. He could annihilate you at any time and it would not bother Him one bit.

> 4:132 To Allah belongs what is in the heavens and on earth, and Allah suffices as Guardian!
>
> 4:133 If Allah wants, O people, He would annihilate you and replace you by others. Allah has the power to do that.
>
> 4:134 Whoever desires the reward of this world, [let him know that] with Allah is the reward of this world and the next. Allah is All-Hearing, All-Seeing!

> 29:5 He who expects to encounter Allah, surely Allah's Term shall come; and He is the All-Hearing, the All-Knowing.
>
> 29:6 He who strives only strives for himself. Allah is All-Sufficient, in need of no being.
>
> 29:7 And those who believe and do the righteous deeds, We shall remit their sins, and We shall reward them with the best of what they used to do.

If He does not need you because you do not believe in Him, why does He not leave you alone to live your life in peace, and quit smiting you all the time? The fact is, He does need you, He feeds on your praise and your fear; and in that He is very much your typical god even though He would like you to think otherwise.

> 35:15 O people, it is you who have need of Allah, whereas Allah is the All-Sufficient, Praiseworthy One.
>
> 35:16 If He wishes, He will annihilate you and bring forth a new creation.
>
> 35:17 That for Allah is not a grave matter.

31:24 We allow them to indulge themselves a little, then We will compel them to taste a harsh punishment.

31:25 And if you ask them: "Who created the heavens and the earth", they will certainly say: "Allah." Say: "Praise be to Allah." However, most of them to not know.

31:26 To Allah belongs what is the heavens and the earth. Allah, is indeed, the All-Sufficient, the Praiseworthy.

Unfortunately, Allah constantly monitors your brain waves, He knows what is on your mind, your heart in the Koran, for the heart, not the brain when Allah commutated His immutable eternal facts to a mortal during the depth of the Dark Ages was thought to do what is the brain's raison d'être.

39:7 If you disbelieve, Allah does not need you, although He does not approve disbelief in His servants. However, if you give thanks, He will approve that in you. No sinning soul shall bear the burden of another. Then unto your Lord is your return and He will tell you what you used to do. He knows the secrets within the breasts.

31:23 Whoever disbelieves, let not his disbelief sadden you. Unto us is their return and then We will tell them what they did. Allah knows well the secret of the breasts.

35:38 Surely Allah knows the Unseen of the heavens and the earth. He knows fully the secrets within the breasts.

An actual revelation about thoughts emanating from where they have no business originating from, revealed truth 64:4!

MUTUAL EXCHANGE

64 At-Taghâbun

*In the Name of Allah,
the Compassionate, the Merciful*

64:1 Everything in the heavens and on the earth glorifies Allah. His is the sovereignty and His is the praise, and He has power over everything.

64:2 It is He Who created you. Some of you are unbelievers, and some believers; and Allah perceives what you do.

64:3 He created the heavens and the earth in truth, and He fashioned you and shaped well your forms. Unto Him is the ultimate resort.

64:4 He knows what is the heavens and on the earth, and He knows what you conceal and what your reveal. Allah knows well the thoughts hidden in the breasts.

Allah's Bounties

The Prophet said that surah 55, *The All Compassionate,* was "the adornment of the Qur'an". This is why the surah is often referred to as "The Beauty of the Qur'an". As they say, beauty is in the eye of the beholder, or perhaps, in this case, the eye of the believer.

THE ALL-COMPASSIONATE

55 Ar-Rahmân

*In the Name of Allah,
the Compassionate, the Merciful*

55:1 The Compassionate,

55:2 Has taught the Qur'an.

55:3 He created man;

55:4 And taught him elocution.

55:5 The sun and the moon move according to a plan.

55:6 And the shrubs (or stars) and the trees prostrate themselves.

55:7 And the sky, He raised and He set up the balance;

55:8 That you may not transgress in the balance.

55:9 Conduct your weighing with equity and do not stint the balance.

55:10 And the earth, He set up for all mankind.

55:11 In it are fruit and palm trees in buds;

55:12 And grain in blades and fragrant plants.

Part of the attraction of surah 55 has to be the refrain which we first encounter at revelation 55:13:

55:13 So, which of your Lord's Bounties do you, both (jinn and humans) deny?

The Bounties are said to be Allah's Grace and Mercy. In surah 55, Allah repeatedly challenges the jinn and humans to deny His

Bounties after enumerating one or more things He has done for them, or after, what you should have come to expect no matter what the topic, expounding on His own Magnificence.

Angels are strangely absent from the alleged most beautiful surah in the Koran; yet believing in angels is one of the six (or seven) Pillars of Faith (*Appendix -Pillars of Islam*). The fact that the jinn is included in His challenge, and not his angels, should not come as surprise. This pervasive and enigmatic creature of the Koran, is, after all, part of the Koran's trinity of intelligent beings (angels, jinn and humans). The jinn's importance in Allah's revelations should have made it a shoo-in for what Muslims must believe to be considered a "Muslim".

The jinn can be described as the ghosts of the Koran. Was believing in ghosts stretching credibility one belief too far for those who, early on, based on Allah's revelations, came up with the *Pillars of Faith*? The genesis of both man and jinn is mentioned in many surahs, as they are in surah 55, a testament to their respective importance in the Koran.

> 55:14 He created man from hard clay, like bricks.

> 55:15 And He created the jinn from tongues of fire.

> 55:16 So, which of your Lord's Bounties do you both (jinn and humans) deny?

The question about which bounty is to be denied is addressed to both jinn and man, therefore, Allah bragging in revelation 55:17 about being "The Lord of the two Easts and the two Wests" may be a reference to the sunrise and the sunset in their respective spatial and/or temporal dimension.

> 55:17 The Lord of the two Easts and the two Wests.

> 55:18 So, which of your Lord's Bounties do you both (jinn and humans) deny?

Two revelations that, together, are held to be a miracle of the Koran; that Allah knew about the phenomenon (the barrier in revelation 55:20) where the water from one sea, as it merges with another sea, loses its distinctive characteristic e.g. salinity.

> 55:19 He unleashed the two seas so as to merge together.

> 55:20 Between them is a barrier which they do not overstep[27].

---

[27] As mentioned in a previous footnote, this is undoubtedly a reference to the fresh water Black Sea and the salty Marmara in which it flows. There is of course nothing

55:21 So, which of your Lord's Bounties do you both (jinn and humans) deny?

Yes, there is such a thing as fresh water coral and fresh water pearls.

55:22 From them both come out pearls and coral.

55:23 So, which of your Lord's Bounties do you both (jinn and humans) deny?

Desert nomads and merchants were obviously impressed by large seaworthy boats when their travels took them to the coast, for Allah to claim ownership.

55:24 To Him belong the seagoing ships towering upon the sea like mountains.

55:25 So, which of your Lord's Bounties do you both (jinn and humans) deny?

Allah will maintain His composure, even in the midst of chaos and death of which He is the author and which He considers a Bounty?

55:26 Everyone upon it (the earth) is perishing;

55:27 But the Face of Your Lord, full of majesty and nobility, shall abide.

55:28 So, which of your Lord's Bounties do you both (jinn and humans) deny?

Allah is a busy god; which makes you wonder why, when everything is pre-ordained, He has such a hectic schedule.

55:29 Whatever is in the heavens or on the earth petitions Him, and every day He is attending to some new matter.

55:30 So, which of your Lord's Bounties do you both (jinn and human) deny?

---

to stop fresh water and salt water from mixing as they do in the Sea of Marmara leading to the sea being one third less salty than the oceans.

In another revelation about the two seas, Allah is unambiguous about what the barrier separates.

25:53 And it is He Who mixed the two sea, this one sweet and pure and that one salty and bitter; and He set up between them a barrier and a firm prohibition.

From the ostensibly profound to the patently obvious:

35:12 The two seas are not the same; one is sweet, clear and delectable to drink and the other is salty and bitter. Yet from both you eat tender flesh and extract ornaments which you wear, and you see ships cruising therein, that you may seek His bounty, and that perchance you may be thankful.

For Allah, the jinn are a race on an equal footing with the human race. Race, in the Koran, is based on the material used in the creation of the first progenitor.

> 55:31 We shall attend to you, O two races (jinn and humans)?

> 55:32 So, which of your Lord's Bounties do you both (jinn and humans) deny?

It will definitely be easier for the jinn to accept Allah's challenge in verse 55:33, as they are able to fly above the clouds all the way to the first level of heaven. But should they, or the "human folk" for that matter, attempt to get into heaven without first getting an okay from Allah, they will be met with fire and melted brass (verse 55:35). Where is the beauty, or Bounty in that?

> 55:33 O jinn and human folk, if you can pass through the bounds of the heavens and the earth, pass through them. You will not pass through without some authority.

> 55:34 So, which of your Lord's Bounties do you both (jinn and humans) deny?

> 55:35 A flame of fire and brass will be loosed (sic) upon you, so that you will not receive any support.

> 55:36 So, which of your Lord's Bounties do you both (jinn and humans) deny?

Another favourite topic of Allah is *Judgement Day*, whatever is being revealed.

> 55:37 When the heaven shall be rent asunder and turned red like pigment.

> 55:38 So, which of your Lord's Bounties do you both (jinn and humans) deny?

> 55:39 On that day, none shall be questioned about his sin, whether a man or a jinn.

> 55:40 So, which of your Lord's Bounties do you both (jinn and humans) deny?

Another favourite topic of Allah is *Hell*, whatever is being revealed. Revelation 55:41 begs the question: how will bald forelockless (sic) criminals be manhandled into Hell?

> 55:41 The criminals shall be known by their marks; then they shall be seized by their forelocks and their feet.

55:42 So, which of your Lord's Bounties do you both (jinn and humans) deny?

55:43 This is Hell, which the criminals deny.

55:44 They circle between it and between a hot-water caldron.

55:45 So, which of your Lord's Bounties do you both (jinn and humans) deny?

Paradise is also a favourite topic of Allah, whatever is being revealed.

55:46 But, for him who fears his Lord two gardens [are reserved].

55:47 So, which of your Lord's Bounties do you both (jinn and humans) deny?

55:48 They have numerous branches.

55:49 So, which of your Lord's Bounties do you both (jinn and humans) deny?

55:50 And there are therein two flowing springs.

55:51 So, which of your Lord's Bounties do you both (jinn and humans) deny?

55:52 Therein is a pair of every fruit.

55:53 So, which of your Lord's Bounties do you both (jinn and humans) deny?

55:54 Reclining upon couches whose linings are of brocade and the fruits of the two gardens are near at hand.

55:55 So, which of your Lord's Bounties do you both (jinn and humans) deny?

The remaining revelations (55-56:78) in the surah *The Compassionate* can be found in the chapter that is all about Allah's hedonistic utopia in the sky: *Heaven* of *Pain, Pleasure and Prejudice*.

The Rainmaker

An illiterate's fascination with books and the written word is evident in much of what Allah reveals in His Koran; another, is a desert dweller's captivation with gardens and the precipitation which makes them bloom. The references to earthly gardens are not nearly as frequent as those to Paradise – oases, by any other name, which do not require rain with rivers running beneath, a necessary component for the earthly variety. So rare and so welcomed by the desert dwellers of the Prophet's time that rain was thought to be the spit angels.

Spit or not, Allah never tires of reminding the sun-drenched inhabitants of the Hijaz (the so-called holy land of Islam. The area comprises most of the western part of modern-day Saudi Arabia and is centered on Mecca and Medina) who were the first to benefit from His transmitted wisdom, that He is the Rainmaker and therefore responsible for everything good that comes from the water He sends down from "the sky". A short illustrative selection:

> 2:266 Does any one of you wish to have a garden of palms and vines, under which rivers flow and from which he gets all kinds of fruit; and when he gets old and has weak offspring a whirlwind with fire hits the garden and burns it down? Thus Allah makes clear to you His Revelations so that you may reflect.

> 6:99 And it is He who sends down water from the sky. With it We bring forth all kinds of vegetation. From it We bring forth greenery, and clustered grains; and from the date-palm shoots come clusters of dates within reach. And [We bring forth] gardens of grapes, olives and pomegranates alike and unlike. Behold their fruits, when they bear fruit and their ripening, surely there are signs in that for a people who believe.

> 6:141 It is He who created gardens, trellised and untrellised (sic); palms and crops of diverse produce; and olives and

pomegranates, both like and unlike. Eat of their fruits when they bear fruit, and pay their due on the day of harvesting them. And do not be prodigal; [for] He does not like the prodigals.

7:57 It is He Who sends forth the winds bearing good news of His Mercy; so that when they bear heavy clouds, We drive them towards some dead land upon which We send down water. With it We bring forth every variety of fruit. Thus We bring out the dead, so that you may take heed.

7:58 Good land produces vegetation by the Will of its Lord; but that which has gone bad will not produce vegetation except with difficulty. Thus We make plain the revelations to a people who give thanks.

13:4 And in the earth are plots adjoining each other and gardens of vines, tillage and palm trees, from one or different roots, which are irrigated by the same water; yet, We prefer some of them over the others in produce. Surely in that are signs for a people who understand.

14:32 [It is Allah] Who created the heavens and the earth and sends down water from the sky, bringing forth fruits for sustenance. He has made the ships subservient to you so as to sail in the sea at His Behest and He has subjected to you the rivers.

16:65 It is Allah who sends down water from the sky reviving thereby the earth after its death. Surely, there is in that a sign to a people who listen.

24:42 To Allah belongs the dominion of the heavens and the earth and unto Allah is the ultimate return.

24:43 Have you not seen that Allah drives the cloud, then brings them together, then piles them into a heap, from which you see rain coming. He brings mountains of hail from the sky, with which He smites whomever He pleases and diverts it from whomever He pleases. The gleam of its lighting almost blinds the eyes.

30:48 It is Allah Who sends forth the winds, which stir up the clouds. Then He spreads them out in the sky, as He pleases, and causes them to breakup into pieces; and you see the rain issuing from their midst. Then, when He allows the rain to reach whomever He wishes of His servants, behold, they rejoice.

30:49 Whereas they were, before that, despondent.

30:50 Behold, then, the marks of Allah's Mercy, how He revives the earth after it was dead. He, indeed, is the One Who revives the dead and He has power over everything.

35:9 It is Allah Who looses (sic) the wind, so as to stir up clouds; then We drive them towards a dead land, reviving the earth therewith after it was dead. Such is the Resurrection!

36:33 A sign unto them is the dead land, that We revived and brought out of it grain, from which they eat.

36:34 And We caused to grow in it gardens of palms and vines, and caused springs to gush forth therewith.

36:35 That they might eat from its fruit, although their hands brought it not out. Will they not, then, give thanks?

39:21 Have you not seen that Allah has sent down water from heaven, then treaded it as springs in the ground. Then He brings out vegetation of various hues through it. Then it withers, and you see it looking yellow; then He turns it into scraps. In that, there surely is a Reminder to people of understanding.

41:39 And of His Signs is that you see the earth desolate but when We send down water upon it, it quivers and swells. Indeed, He who revived it shall revive the dead. Truly He has power over everything.

42:28 It is He Who sends the rain down, after they have despaired, and spreads out His Mercy. He is the Protector, the Praiseworthy.

THE KNEELING ONE

45 Al-Jâthiyah

*In the Name of Allah,
the Compassionate, the Merciful*

45:1 Ha - Mim.

45:2 This is the revelation of the Book from Allah, the All-Mighty, All-Wise.

45:3 Surely, in the heavens and the earth there are signs for the believers.

45:4 And in your creation and the beasts scattered abroad, there are signs for people who are of certain faith.

45:5 And in the alternation of the night and the day and in what Allah has sent down from heaven as provision (*water*), reviving thereby the earth after it was dead and in the disposition of the wind – there are signs for people who understand.

45:6 Those are the Signs of Allah which We recite to you in truth. In what discourse other than Allah's and His Signs, then, will they believe?

45:12 It is Allah who subjected the sea to you, so that ships might sail in at His Command, and that you might seek some of His Bounty, and that perchance you might give thanks.

45:13 And He subjected to you what is in the heavens and the earth all together[as a grace] from Him. There are in that signs for a people who reflect.

50:7 And the earth We have spread out and set in it immovable mountains; and We cause to grow in it every delightful variety;

50:8 As a guidance and reminder to every penitent servant.

50:9 And We brought down from heaven blessed water and caused thereby gardens to grow and harvest grain;

50:10 And tall palm trees with clusters well-knit,

50:11 As provision for the servants; and We have revived thereby a dead town. Thus will the Resurrection be.

57:17 Know that Allah revives the earth after it is dead. We have expounded the Signs clearly for you, that perchance you might understand.

78:14 And brought down from the rain-clouds abundant water?

78:15 To bring forth thereby grain and vegetation?

78:16 And luxurious gardens?

80:24 Let man consider his nourishment.

80:25 We have poured the water abundantly;

80:26 Then, We split the earth wide open;

80:27 Then caused the grain to grow therein,

80:28 Together with vines and green vegetation;

80:29 And olives and palm trees;

80:30 And gardens with dense trees,

80:31 And fruits and grass,

80:32 For your enjoyment and that of your cattle.

THE MOST HIGH
87 Al-A`la

*In the Name of Allah,
the Compassionate, the Merciful*

87:1 Glorify the name of your Lord, the Most High;

87:2 Who created and fashioned well;

87:3 And Who fore-ordained and guided rightly;

87:4 And Who brought out the pasture;

87:5 Then turned it into greenish-black straw.

Today we know that most of the precipitation that falls from the sky comes from the surface evaporation of the oceans. Evaporation followed by condensation tends to create a clear, tasteless H2O. Changing the water cycle so as to make rainwater bitter, as Allah threatens to do in revelation 56:70, would have presented some serious challenges unless the water supply is up there with You and You are its custodian[28].

56:68 Or have you seen the water that you drink?

56:69 Have you brought it down from the clouds or did We sent it down?

56:70 Had We wished, We would have made it bitter; if only you would give thanks.

---

[28] A revelation quoted elsewhere: 23:18 And We send down water from heaven in measure, then lodge it in the ground, although we are Able to allow it to drain away.

Allah on the Present Life

87:14 He who cleanses himself shall prosper;

87:15 Remembering your Lord's Name and praying.

87:16 No, you prefer the present life;

87:17 Whereas the Hereafter is better and more lasting.

87:18 That, indeed, is in the ancients scrolls,

87:19 The scrolls of Abraham and Moses.

There is no humor in Islam. There is no fun in Islam. There can be no fun and joy in whatever is serious.
Ayatollah Khomeini

Allah never misses an opportunity to remind people how life is better in the Hereafter. In one of more than a dozen revelations about a God who provides for whomever He pleases in whatever quantity He pleases, He makes a rare admission about life in the here-and-now being pleasurable, if only for a short time

13:26 Allah enlarges and restricts the provision to whom He pleases. They rejoice at this worldly life, but worldly life is nothing but a fleeting pleasure compared with the life to come.

Enjoying living in the here-and-now is a sin, as benefits a religion which often takes on many of the trappings associated with death cults, the suicide bomber being its most violent manifestation.

16:107 That is because they love the present life more than the Hereafter, and because Allah does not guide the unbelievers.

16:108 They are those whose hearts, ears and eyes Allah has sealed; and those are the heedless.

Hell awaits those who prefer living in the here-and-now; those who have a *passion* for life as opposed to a yearning for death.

79:34 Then when the Great Calamity (*Judgement Day*) shall come;

79:35 On the Day that man will remember what he has done;

79:36 And Hell shall be exhibited to whoever can see.

79:37 Then, as to him who has transgressed,

79:38 And preferred the present life;

79:39 Hell, indeed, is the refuge.

79:40 But as to him who fears the station of his Lord, and forbids his soul from passion;

79:41 Then, Paradise is the refuge.

Signs, Signs, Everywhere Signs

> "Sign, sign, everywhere a sign ... Do this, don't do that, can't you read the sign ... If God was here, He'd tell you to your face, man, you're some kinda sinner."

Allah's Signs are not at all like the signs the *Five Man Electrical Band* ranted against – except perhaps for the Koran which is one big written sign with many "Do this, don't do that" – but, the sentiments expressed in the selected lyrics are, oh, so appropriate.

People wanted signs that were out of the ordinary for them to believe, such as having angels descend from heaven, or the dead come to life to say a few words on Allah's behalf ... but such sign were out of the question. Allah kept those to himself. His rational being that they would still not believe unless He allowed them too, something He was also not prepared to do.

> 6:109 They swear by Allah most solemnly that, were a sign to come to them, they would surely believe in it. Say: "Signs are only with Allah"; but how do you know that, if those signs come, they will still not believe?

> 6:110 And We will divert their hearts and their sights [from the truth], as they failed at first to believe in it; and We shall leave them dumbfounded in their wrongdoing.

> 6:111 Even if We send the angels to them and the dead speak to them, and if We bring everything before them, they would not believe, unless Allah wills; but most of them are ignorant.

Allah's Signs are, for the most part, naturally occurring phenomena, circadian rhythms which He professes to manipulate and calibrate and genocidal acts of wanton destruction for which He claims authorship – the exception being the claim of creating heaven and earth and everything in between, Judgement Day and the existence of the Hereafter.

Allah making you die for a short period every night by taking away your soul is a Sign for thinking people.

6:60 And it is He Who makes you die at night and knows what you do by day. He raises you up in it, until a fixed term is fulfilled; then onto him is your ultimate return. He will declare to you what you used to do.

39:42 Allah carries off the souls of men upon their death and the souls of those who are not dead in their sleep. He then holds back those whose death He has decreed and releases the others till an appointed term. Surely, there are in that signs for a people who reflect.

It is Allah Who creates night and day and the sun, the moon and the stars as a means of finding your way, and those too are Signs.

6:96 [He is] the Cleaver of the dawn; and He made the night a time of rest, and the sun and the moon a means of reckoning. Such is the ordering of Allah, the Mighty, the All-Knowing.

6:97 And it is He Who created the stars for you so as to be guided by them in the dark depths of the land and sea. We have made plain the signs for a people who know.

40:61 It is Allah Who made the night for you, to rest in it, and the day to see your way. Allah is truly Bountiful to mankind, but most people do not give thanks.

40:62 That for you is Allah your Lord, Creator of everything. There is no god but He. How then are you perverted?

40:63 Thus as those who used to repudiate Allah's Signs were perverted too.

In addition to His signs, Allah sends down provisions which should be an even greater incentive to call on him even if it displeases the less credulous.

40:13 It is He who shows you His Signs and sends down from heaven provision for you; but only he who repents will remember.

40:14 So, call on Allah professing religion sincerely unto Him, even if the unbelievers should resent it.

Well-fed and starving people are also signs from Allah.

39:52 Did they not know that Allah expands the provision to whomever He wishes and constricts it? Surely, there are in that signs to a people who believe.

Allah will drown those who don't believe in His Signs, such as making sailing ships stop and go.

> 30:46 And of His Signs is sending forth the wind bearing good news and to let you taste part of His Mercy, and that the ships may sail at His Command, and that you might seek part of His Bounty; that perchance you may give thanks.
>
> ...
>
> 42:32 And of His Signs are ships sailing in the sea like high mountains.
>
> 42:33 If he wishes, He will calm the wind, and then they will remain motionless upon its surface. In that are signs to every steadfast and thankful person;
>
> 42:34 Or destroy them for what they (the passengers) have earned, while pardoning many;
>
> 42:35 That those who dispute concerning Our Signs might know that they have no escape.

Allah, the wind beneath the wings is another sign.

> 16:79 Do they not see the birds subservient in the vault of the sky, nothing holding them aloft but Allah? Surely, there is in that signs for a people who believe.
>
> 67:19 Have they not considered the birds above them spreading their wings and folding them? They are only held up by the Compassionate. He is the Perceiver of everything.

Signs within signs:

> 31:31 Have you not seen that ships cruise upon the sea by Allah's Grace, to show you some of His Signs. There are in that signs for every steadfast, thankful one.

Only ungrateful traitors repudiate Allah Signs.

> 31:32 And if waves cover them like a canopy, they call upon Allah, professing religion sincerely to Him; but when He delivers them to the dry land, some of them are lukewarm. Yet none repudiate Our Signs except every ungrateful traitor.

What will happen to the *ungrateful traitors!*

> 34:4 Those who have believed and did the righteous deeds those shall receive forgiveness and a generous provision.

34:5 But those who go around striving to rebut Our Signs those shall have the punishment of a very painful scourge.

34:38 But those who go around challenging Our Signs those will be summoned to the punishment.

Five signs in a row:

30:21 And of His Signs is that He created for you, from yourselves, spouses to settle down with and He established friendship and mercy between you. There are in all that signs for a people who reflect.

30:22 And of His Signs is the creation of the heavens and the earth and the diversity of your tongues and colours. Indeed, there are in that signs for those who know.

30:23 And of His Signs is your sleeping by night and day and your seeking some of His Bounty. There are in that signs for people who hear.

30:24 And of His Signs is showing you the lighting, to fear and to hope; and He brings down from the sky water with which He revives the earth after it was dead. There are in that signs for a people who understand.

30:25 And of His Signs is that the heavens and the earth shall arise at His Command. Then, if He summons you once, behold, you shall be brought out of the earth.

30:26 And to Him belongs whoever is in the heavens or on earth. They are all submitting to Him.

30:27 It is He Who originates the creation, then brings it back again; and that is easier for Him. He is the loftiest exemplar in the heavens and on earth, and He is the All-Mighty, the Wise.

Genocide as a Sign!

32:23 We have, indeed, given Moses the Book; so do not be in doubt concerning his encounter, and We made it a guidance to the Children of Israel.

32:24 And We appointed some of them as leaders guiding by Our Command, when they stood fast and believed firmly in Our Signs.

> 32:25 It is your Lord Who will judge between them on the Day of Resurrection, regarding that whereof they used to differ.
>
> 32:26 Was it not shown to them how many generations We have destroyed before them, while they were strolling in their dwellings? Surely, there are signs in that; do they not hear?

Allah says punishment a lot, and it most often has to do with not believing or making fun of His Signs and believing in other gods.

> 45:7 Woe unto every sinful liar;
>
> 45:8 He hears Allah's Signs recited to him, then perseveres in his arrogance as though he did not hear them. Announce to him, then, the good news of a painful punishment.
>
> 45:9 And if he learns about any of Our Signs, he takes them in jest. Such people shall have a demeaning punishment.
>
> 45:10 Behind them is Hell and what they earned will not profit them a whit, nor what they have taken, apart from Allah, as protectors; and they will have a terrible punishment.
>
> 45:11 This is true guidance, and those who have disbelieved in the Signs of their Lord will have the punishment of a painful scourge.

Not Doing What is Being Asked as a Sign

A sign from Allah can also be <u>not</u> doing what He is asked to do, for example *not dropping* a peace of heaven, revelation 34:9, on those who do not believe in the Hereafter to prove the existence of Paradise[29].

---

[29] Remember, Paradise, in the Koran, was once part of the earth and only invisible pillars stop it from crashing to the ground, giving Allah the ultimate vantage point and plenty of handy materials to drop on the fools below who refuse to believe in His Signs.

> 21:30 Have the unbelievers not beheld that the heavens and the earth were a solid mass, then We separated them; and of water We produced every living thing. Will they not believe, then?
>
> ----
>
> 31:10 He created the heavens without pillars that you can see and laid down in the earth immovable mountains, lest it shake with you, and scattered throughout it every variety of beast. And We have sent down water from heaven, thereby causing it to grow in it every noble [kind of plant].

34:7 The unbelievers say: "Shall we show you a man who will tell you that, once you have been torn to pieces, you shall become again a new creation?

34:8 "Does he impute falsehood to Allah or is he possessed?" No, those who do not believe in the Hereafter will undergo the punishment and are in grave error.

34:9 Have they not looked at what is in front of them and behind them of the heavens and the earth? Had We wished, we would have caused the earth to cave in under them, or dropped fragments from heaven upon them. Surely, in that is a sign to every repenting servant.

Why No Signs for the Messenger

It's not that the Prophet's audience did not want to believe that Muhammad was the latest spokesperson for the Almighty; if only Allah would give them a sign.

2:118 Those who do not know say: "If only Allah would speak to us (tell us that you are His Messenger), or a sign come to us." Thus said those who came before them (to their Prophets). Their hearts are all alike. Indeed, We have made clear the signs for people who firmly believe.

Instead of sending a sign, Allah tells His Messenger not to answer questions about Hell, at this time – those answers will come later – followed by a warning about abandoning the new religion.

2:119 We have sent you with the Truth as a bearer of good tidings and as a warner. You are not to be questioned about the people of Hell.

2:120 Neither the Jews nor the Christians will be pleased with you until you follow their religion. Say: "Allah's Guidance is the [only] Guidance." And were you to follow their desires after the Knowledge that came down to you, you will have no guardian or helper [to save you] from Allah.

2:121 Those to whom We have given the Book recite it as it ought to be recited. Those [people] believe in it; but those who disbelieve are the losers.

Those who believe don't need signs!

13:27 And the unbelievers say: "If only a sign were sent down to him by His Lord!" Say: "Allah leads astray whomever He pleases and guides to himself those who repent,

13:28 Those who believe and whose hearts find comfort in remembering Allah." Indeed, in remembering Allah the hearts find comfort.

13:29 May those who believe and do the good works be blessed and have a happy homecoming!

The never-seen Book should be sign enough!

29:50 They said: "If only signs from his Lord were sent down on him (Muhammad)." Say: "Signs are only with Allah, and I am only a manifest warner."

29:51 Does it not suffice them that We have sent down on you the Book which is recited to them? There is, indeed, in that a mercy and a reminder to a believing people.

29:52 Say: "Allah suffices as a witness between you and me. He knows what is in the heavens and on the earth; and those who have believed in falsehood and disbelieved in Allah – those are the losers."

Are you a pervert?

40:69 Have you not observed those who dispute regarding Allah's Signs, how they are perverted?

A soul's lament!

39:56 "Lest any soul should say: 'Woe betide me for what I have neglected of my duty to Allah and for having been one of the scoffers.'

39:57 "Or it should say: 'Had Allah guided me, I would have been one of the God-fearing.'

39:58 "Or it should say, when it sees the punishment: 'If only I had a second chance, then I would be one of the beneficent'."

39:59 Yes indeed! My signs came to you, but you denounced them as lies and waxed proud and were one of the unbelievers.

Allah the Eternal Adolescent

Allah's unsophisticated, often confusing parables, His arrogance, His juvenile insistence that He be praised for whatever He does or doesn't do, His love of charades e.g. having Zachary and Mary perform pantomimes as a sign that He has done them a favour (see Shared Prophets), His vivid imagination e.g. sending an angel with a flying horse to fetch His Messenger etc. are all indications of both an immature mind and a volatile personality. But, it is in the-god-who-never-grew-up's self-bravado, His love of violence and His insensitivity to the pain He causes others – an insensitivity that borders, if not embraces sadism – that the eternal adolescent finds its fullest expression.

Allah is a god you don't mess with! Pharaoh learnt this the hard way, over and over again. You believe in His Revelations or He will get you in this world and the next; His vengeance will be merciless, never ending and often original. Allah is a god who is much given to puerile challenges and boasts about committing the most adult of atrocities.

The question "Are your unbelievers better than all those" in revelation 54:43 refers to Noah's people, the people of 'Ad and Thamud, the people of Lot, and undoubtedly many other communities whom Allah bragged about obliterating in surah 54, *The Moon*.

> 54:41 The warnings also came to Pharaoh's folk.

> 54:42 They denounced all Our Signs as lies; so We seized them in the manner of One Who is Mighty and Strong.

> 54:43 Are your unbelievers better than all those; or have you been exonerated in the Scriptures?

> 54:44 Or do you say: "We are a band which will conquer."

> 54:45 The host *(Pharaoh's army)* will certainly be routed and turn theirs back in flight.

Judgement Day will be particularly painful for these "criminals"!

> 54:46 No, the Hour shall be their appointment; and the Hour is very grievous and bitter.

54:47 The criminals are indeed in error and blazes;

54:48 The day they will be dragged upon their faces into the Fire: "Taste now the touch of Saqar (another name for Hell)."

A not unexpected boast about creating everything, some of it in the wink of an eye, followed by another somewhat childish challenge from the most powerful god ever, about having taken down opponents as powerful as Pharaoh. Don't you remember?

54:49 Indeed, We have created everything in measure.

54:50 Our Command is like one word, like twinkling of an eye.

54:51 We have destroyed your likes; is there anyone who will remember?

In the following revelation Allah may be confusing the book of good and bad deeds, which will be given to believers and unbelievers alike on Judgement Day, with the Scriptures; or He is still talking about Pharaoh Rameses II, who ruled Egypt during the alleged biblical Exodus and whose purported role is recorded in the Torah.

54:52 Everything they have done is recorded in the Scriptures.

54:53 Everything, small or big, is written down.

Pharaoh and his people will definitely not be joining the God-fearing on a "seat of truth" in Paradise next to the pitiless pathologically punitive slaughterer of those who dare not submit to His Terror, including the innocent who have yet to know fear like this God wants them to know fear, their children.

54:54 The God-fearing are, indeed, amid gardens and rivers.

54:55 Upon a seat of truth in the presence of an Omnipotent King.

Doomed Children at Play

Even in revelations about the cities He has destroyed you can hear the boy in Allah talking. During a normal day i.e. morning or afternoon, even in the Prophet's time, children played and adults worked, or were busy with more important things, from making love to making war. Yet, it is people at play that Allah brags about killing; and like children might say or do, He schemed to make their obliteration come about. An omnipotent, omnipresent god does not need to scheme to get His way, but a child often does.

> 7:97 Did the people of the cities feel assured that Our punishment would not come upon them at night while they were sleeping?
>
> 7:98 Or did the people of the cities feel assured that Our punishment would not come upon them during the day while they were playing?
>
> 7:99 Or did they feel secure against Allah's Scheming? For none feels secure from Allah's Scheming save the losing people.

The earth may not be completely devoid of intelligent life after all the people have returned to Allah. He may repopulate it with more action figures (angels or jinn perhaps?) who, like their human predecessors, will have to play by His Rules if they know what's good for them.

> 7:100 It is not clear to those who inherit the earth after its people [are gone] that if We will, We can smite them for their sins and seal their hearts so that they cannot hear.

Allah's scheming included making the unbelievers still not believe in what they had not believed. Yes, it does not make much sense, except perhaps to a child-like mind.

> 7:101 Those cities, We relate to you some of their tales; their Messengers came to them with clear signs; but they would not believe in what they had denied earlier. Thus Allah seals the hearts of the unbelievers.

The cities which ran the greatest risk of being annihilated were those which did not have a covenant, an agreement between supplicants and a god, or a covenant that they did not keep.

> 7:102 And We have not found among most of them any who honours a covenant; but We found most of them evildoers.

The Responsible Adult vs. The Adolescent:

Would the persona of Allah the teenager, like His Messenger, if He had married and started accumulating partners in intimacy have favoured the playful as opposed to the responsible?

> **Narrated Jabir bin Abdullah:**
>
> I was with the Prophet in a Ghazwa (Military Expedition) and my camel was slow and exhausted. The Prophet came up to me and said, "O Jabir."

I replied, "Yes?"

He said, "What is the matter with you?"

I replied, "My camel is slow and tired, so I am left behind."

So, he got down and poked the camel with his stick and then ordered me to ride.

I rode the camel and it became so fast that I had to hold it from going ahead of Allah's Apostle. He then asked me, have you got married?"

I replied in the affirmative.

He asked, "A virgin or a matron?"

I replied, "I married a matron."

The Prophet said, "Why have you not married a virgin, so that you may play with her and she may play with you?"

Jabir replied, "I have sisters (young in age) so I liked to marry a matron who could collect them all and comb their hair and look after them."

Bukhari 34.310

In slightly different variation of the same story by the same narrator, we are informed of a preference for a hairless vagina.

Narrated Jabir bin Abdullah:

While we were returning from a Ghazwa (Holy Battle) with the Prophet, I started driving my camel fast, as it was a lazy camel. A rider came behind me and pricked my camel with a spear he had with him, and then my camel started running as fast as the best camel you may see. Behold! The rider was the Prophet himself.

He said, "What makes you in such a hurry?"

I replied, "I am newly married."

He said, "Did you marry a virgin or a matron?"

I replied, "A matron."

He said, "Why didn't you marry a young girl so that you may play with her and she with you?"

When we were about to enter (Medina), the Prophet said, "Wait so that you may enter (Medina) at night so that the lady of unkempt hair may comb her hair and the one whose husband has been absent may shave her pubic region."

Bukhari 62.16

More Destruction, Less Creation

The Prophet had many abilities, but painting or sculpture where not among them. Like an adolescent, and like His Mentor, he was more into destruction than creation, a phase which he may never have outgrown while he grew to despise those who could do what he could not, associating this with a prohibition from Allah.

Then again, like most gods, Allah is somewhat insecure in His omnipotence, the most visible manifestation being his obsessions with what they worship apart from Him, the so-called idols from which we get Islam's prohibition against sculptures.

The reason for the prohibition against representations of the human or animal form on canvas or frescos is less obvious. Arguments advanced include that Allah is concerned that the artist will want to worship his or her creation and entice others to do the same – to worship a work of art instead of His All-Powerfulness. Some believers, Sunnis mostly, even consider photographs prohibited.

Another, is that the depiction of the human or animal form in any medium is "an act of creation" therefore an infringement on Allah's domain, which, like the almost two-thousand years old Bamiyan Buddhas, and the more recent Islamic State inspired destruction of treasures of antiquity, must be obliterated at the earliest opportunity. Since the Prophet's sayings and example is the law if the Koran does not offer a contrary opinion, the prohibition against images may have more to do with something God's Messenger said about painters and paintings.

Narrated Aisha:

I bought a cushion with pictures on it. When Allah's Apostle saw it, he kept standing at the door and did not enter the house. I noticed the sign of disgust on his face, so I said, "O Allah's Apostle! I repent to Allah and H is Apostle. (Please let me know) what sin I have done."

Allah's Apostle said, "What about this cushion?"

I replied, "I bought it for you to sit and recline on."

Allah's Apostle said, "The painters (i.e. owners) of these pictures will be punished on the Day of Resurrection. It will be said to them, 'Put life in what you have created (i.e. painted).'"

The Prophet added, "The angels do not enter a house where there are pictures."

Bukhari 34.318

Narrated Abu Talha:

I heard Allah's Apostle saying; "Angels (of Mercy) do not enter a house wherein there is a dog or a picture of a living creature (a human being or an animal)."

Bukhari 54.448

Playing With Toys

The Koran's prohibition is unequivocal. No statues of people or animals – what Allah calls idols!

Does this prohibition against statues, paintings and drawings of animals and people extend to children's toys such as dolls and stuffed animals? Is Allah concerned that children who play with dolls and stuffed animals will end up worshipping them instead of Him? If Allah is anything like His Messenger, toys in the hands of children or adults playing with their children playing with toys are not on His prohibited list.

> Said the Prophet's wife Aishah (may Allah be pleased with her): I used to play with dolls in the house of the Messenger of Allah (peace and blessings be on him) and my friends would come over to play with me.
>
> They would hide when they saw the Messenger of Allah (peace and blessings be upon him) approaching, but he was in fact very happy to see them with me, and so we played together.
>
> *Reported by al-Bukhari and Muslim*

Aisha also reported:

One day the Messenger of Allah (peace and blessings be upon him) asked me, "What are these?"

"My dolls," I replied.

"What is this in the middle?" he asked.

"A horse," I replied.

"And what are these things on it?" he asked.

"Wings," I said.

"A horse with wings?" he asked.

"Have not you heard that Solomon, the son of David, had horses with wings?" I said.

Thereupon the Messenger of Allah (peace and blessings be upon him) laughed so heartily that I could see his molars."

Reported by Abu Dawud

Hooked On Praise

Allah, the Prophet let it be known, is addicted to praise; He cannot get enough of it.

Narrated Abdullah bin Mas'ud:

Allah's Apostle said, "None has more sense of ghaira (self-respect, also spelled ghira) than Allah, and for this He has forbidden shameful sins whether committed openly or secretly, and none loves to be praised more than Allah does, and this is why He Praises Himself."

Bukhari 60.161

No mainstream god expects his everyday minions to spend so much time in worship, praise's ultimate paranoid expression, than Allah. The incessant tribute to a god possibly insecure in His omnipotence, which the adolescent-like need to be praised may betray, becomes a form of collective brainwashing which leaves no room for an appraisal as to whether the boundless accolades are always warranted. You question this praise-worthiness at your risk and peril, one reason why Islam has endured and continues to prosper.

The narcissism reflected in the ad nausea self-glorification makes a reading of the Koran an even more maddening tedious read than it needs to be. This inane need for acclaim, whether it be self-congratulation or demanded of His admirers, is also reflected in the five daily prayers which consist mainly of verses from the Koran; the tenants of Islam, the so-called Five Pillars ; the rituals e.g. the greater and lesser pilgrimages, the Hajj and the Umrah respectively; the obligation that is the month of fasting and praying i.e. Ramadan ...

I AM THE GREATEST!

WORSHIP ME!

Prayers

One-on-One With Allah

The third holiest site in Islam is a rock underneath the *Dome of the Rock,* which is part of the *Al-Aqsa* Mosque complex on *Temple Mount* in Jerusalem. Muslims believe that this is the rock from which the Prophet ascended to heaven on a magical night in 621 on the back of a winged-horse named Al-Burak.

The Prophet had just finished his late-night prayers when the angel Gabriel appeared accompanied by Al-Burak. He got on the horse and flew off to Jerusalem where he met with the spirits of lesser, dead prophets and led them in prayer. He may even have taken the opportunity to ask them the all-important question about Allah's obsession, the alleged other gods, revelation 43:45, before getting back on his horse for the next leg of his journey – the flight to heaven.

> 43:44 And it (the Qur'an) is surely a Reminder to you and to your people; and you shall be questioned.
>
> 43:45 Ask those of Our Messengers We sent before you: "Have We ever set up, apart from the All-Compassionate, any other gods to be worshipped?"

The Koran refers to this one-on-one meeting with Allah as the flight between two mosques: the makeshift mosque in Mecca (Islam was still in its infancy and confined mainly to Mecca and its surroundings) and what most commentators believe is Jerusalem. The city surrendered to the Muslims in 638 A.D., six years after the death of God's Messenger i.e. "His servant". Therefore, there could not have been a mosque there, in the conventional sense, during the events described in verse 17:1.

THE NIGHT JOURNEY

17 Al-Isrâ'

In the Name of Allah,
the Compassionate, the Merciful

> 17:1 Glory be to Him Who caused His servant to travel by night from the Sacred Mosque to the farthest Mosque,

whose precincts We have blessed, in order to show him some of Our Signs. He is indeed the All-Hearing, the All-Seeing.

The trip to heaven was not without its perils, with the jinn intercepting the Prophet on his way up. Allah had already informed His Messenger as to what to say to be allowed to pass.

> 72:19 And that when the Servant of Allah (the Prophet Muhammad) got up calling on Him, they almost set upon him in throngs.
>
> 72:20 Say: "I only call upon my Lord, and I do not associate with Him anyone else."
>
> 72:21 Say: "I have no power to harm or guide you rightly."
>
> 72:22 Say: "No one shall protect me from Allah, and I will not find apart from Him any refuge;
>
> 72:23 "Except for a proclamation from Allah and His Messages. He who disobeys Allah and His Messenger, for him the Fire of Hell is in store. Therein they shall dwell forever."
>
> 72:24 Until, when they see what they are promised, they will then know certainly who is weaker in supporters and is fewer in numbers.

There were no witnesses to the departure from Mecca, the landing in Jerusalem, the takeoff for heaven or the landing in Mecca the following morning. When the Prophet described this journey to the Meccans the next day, many believed he had gone insane. It was only after he described seeing a caravan from the air (which shortly arrived in Mecca) that some of the accusations of insanity were withdrawn.

Negotiating the Prayers

During his short stay in Paradise, the Prophet met with Allah and more deceased Messengers, the most important being Moses[30]. It was

---

[30] During his ascent and descent from Paradise the Prophet encountered with many figures from the Bible, such as Jesus and Moses, whose appearance he describes in hadiths such as the following; but nowhere could I find a description God with whom he spent the most time with.

Narrated Ibn Abbas:

The Prophet said, "On the night of my ascent to the Heaven, I saw Moses who was a tall brown curly-haired man as if he was one of the men of Shan'awa tribe, and I saw Jesus, a man of medium height and

during this face-to-face meeting with God that the number of daily prayers that a believer must perform every day was established.

Allah in His Koran may be short on specifics, but not the Prophet, who must have delighted his listeners with his swashbuckling tale of flying to heaven on a Pegasus-like horse from Greek mythology to meet with God for so many to recall, with slight variations, his account of his journey. The following hadith is from the Sahih Muslim collection; it is, to my knowledge, the only recollections where the narrator remembers God's Messenger mentioning his stopover in Jerusalem:

> It is narrated on the authority of Anas b. Malik that the Messenger of Allah (may peace be upon him) said: I was brought al-Buraq Who is an animal white and long, larger than a donkey but smaller than a mule, who would place his hoof a distance equal to the range of version.
>
> I mounted it and came to the Temple (Bait Maqdis in Jerusalem), then tethered it to the ring used by the prophets.
>
> I entered the mosque and prayed two rak'ahs in it, and then came out and Gabriel brought me a vessel of wine and a vessel of milk. I chose the milk, and Gabriel said: You have chosen the natural thing. Then he took me to heaven.
>
> Gabriel then asked the (gate of heaven) to be opened and he was asked who he was. He replied: Gabriel.
>
> He was again asked: Who is with you?
>
> He (Gabriel) said: Muhammad.
>
> It was said: Has he been sent for?
>
> Gabriel replied: He has indeed been sent for. And (the door of the heaven) was opened for us and lo! we saw Adam. He welcomed me and prayed for my good.
>
> Then we ascended to the second heaven. Gabriel (peace be upon him) (asked the door of heaven to be opened), and he was asked who he was.
>
> He answered: Gabriel; and was again asked: Who is with you?
>
> He replied: Muhammad.

---

moderate complexion inclined to the red and white colors and of lank hair ..."

Bukhari 54.462

It was said: Has he been sent for?

He replied: He has indeed been sent for. The gate was opened.

When I entered Isa b. Maryam and Yahya b. Zakariya (peace be upon both of them), cousins from the maternal side, welcomed me and prayed for my good.

Then I was taken to the third heaven and Gabriel asked for the opening (of the door).

He was asked: Who are you?

He replied: Gabriel.

He was (again) asked: Who is with you?

He replied Muhammad (may peace be upon him).

It was said: Has he been sent for?

He replied He has indeed been sent for. (The gate) was opened for us and I saw Yusuf (peace of Allah be upon him) who had been given half of (world) beauty. He welcomed me prayed for my well-being. Then he ascended with us to the fourth heaven.

Gabriel (peace be upon him) asked for the (gate) to be opened, and it was said: Who is he?

He replied: Gabriel.

It was (again) said: Who is with you?

He said: Muhammad.

It was said: Has he been sent for?

He replied: He has indeed been sent for.

The (gate) was opened for us, and lo! Idris was there. He welcomed me and prayed for my well-being (About him) Allah, the Exalted and the Glorious, has said:" We elevated him (Idris) to the exalted position" (Qur'an 19:57).

Then he ascended with us to the fifth heaven and Gabriel asked for the (gate) to be opened.

It was said: Who is he?

He replied Gabriel.

It was (again) said: Who is with thee?

He replied: Muhammad.

It was said Has he been sent for?

He replied: He has indeed been sent for. (The gate) was opened for us and then I was with Harun (Aaron-peace of Allah be upon him). He welcomed me prayed for my well-being. Then I was taken to the sixth heaven.

Gabriel (peace be upon him) asked for the door to be opened.

It was said: Who is he?

He replied: Gabriel.

It was said: Who is with thee?

He replied: Muhammad.

It was said: Has he been sent for?

He replied: He has indeed been sent for. (The gate) was opened for us and there I was with Musa (Moses peace be upon him) He welcomed me and prayed for my well-being.

Then I was taken up to the seventh heaven.

Gabriel asked the (gate) to be opened.

It was said: Who is he?

He said: Gabriel

It was said. Who is with thee?

He replied: Muhammad (may peace be upon him.)

It was said: Has he been sent for?

He replied: He has indeed been sent for. (The gate) was opened for us and there I found Ibrahim (Abraham peace be upon him) reclining against the Bait-ul-Ma'mur and there enter into it seventy thousand angels every day, never to visit (this place) again.

Then I was taken to Sidrat-ul-Muntaha whose leaves were like elephant ears and its fruit like big earthenware vessels. And when it was covered by the Command of Allah, it underwent such a change that none amongst the creation has the power to praise its beauty.

Then Allah revealed to me a revelation and He made obligatory for me fifty prayers every day and night.

Then I went down to Moses (peace be upon him) and he said: What has your Lord enjoined upon your Ummah?

I said: Fifty prayers.

He said: Return to thy Lord and beg for reduction (in the number of prayers), for your community shall not be able to bear this burden. as I have put to test the children of Israel and tried them (and found them too weak to bear such a heavy burden).

He (the Holy Prophet) said: I went back to my Lord and said: My Lord, make things lighter for my Ummah.

(The Lord) reduced five prayers for me. I went down to Moses and said. (The Lord) reduced five (prayers) for me, He said: Verily thy Ummah shall not be able to bear this burden; return to thy Lord and ask Him to make things lighter.

I then kept going back and forth between my Lord Blessed and Exalted and Moses, till He said: There are five prayers every day and night. O Muhammad, each being credited as ten, so that makes fifty prayers. He who intends to do a good deed and does not do it will have a good deed recorded for him; and if he does it, it will be recorded for him as ten; whereas he who intends to do an evil deed and does not do, it will not be recorded for him; and if he does it, only one evil deed will be recorded.

I then came down and when I came to Moses and informed him, he said: Go back to thy Lord and ask Him to make things lighter.

Upon this the Messenger of Allah remarked: I returned to my Lord until I felt ashamed before Him.

Sahih Muslim book 1 hadith 309

In another remembrance of this legendary journey, this one from the Bukhari collection, there is more back and forth negotiations to get Allah down to five daily prayers (Shi'ites only perform three daily prayers, combining the second and third prayer, and the fourth with the fifth).

We take up this narrative at the point where God's Messenger is being shown, by the angel Gabriel, the Al-Bait-ul-Ma'mura, a replica in the sky of the Ka'ba in Mecca situated directly above it. Like Muslims on earth, angels, as mentioned in the Sahih Muslim hadith, are required to make a pilgrimage to this Ka'ba in the sky at least once in their lifetime as immortals, and seventy thousand angels do so every day.

Narrated Abbas bin Malik:

...

Then Al-Bait-ul-Ma'mur (i.e. the Sacred House was shown to me and a container full of wine and another full of milk and a third full of honey were brought to me. I took the milk. Gabriel remarked, 'This is the Islamic religion which you and your followers are following.' Then the prayers were enjoined on me: They were fifty prayers a day.

When I returned, I passed by Moses who asked (me), "What have you been ordered to do?"

I replied, "I have been ordered to offer fifty prayers a day."

Moses said, "Your followers cannot bear fifty prayers a day, and by Allah, I have tested people before you, and I have tried my level best with Bani (*Children of*) Israel (in vain). Go back to your Lord and ask for reduction to lessen your followers' burden."

So I went back, and Allah reduced ten prayers for me. Then again I came to Moses, but he repeated the same as he had said before. Then again I went back to Allah and He reduced ten more prayers.

When I came back to Moses he said the same, I went back to Allah and He ordered me to observe ten prayers a day.

When I came back to Moses, he repeated the same advice, so I went back to Allah and was ordered to observe five prayers a day.

When I came back to Moses, he said, "What have you been ordered?"

I replied, "I have been ordered to observe five prayers a day."

He said, "Your followers cannot bear five prayers a day, and no doubt, I have got an experience of the people before you, and I have tried my level best with Bani Israel, so go back to your Lord and ask for reduction to lessen your follower's burden."

I said, "I have requested so much of my Lord that I feel ashamed, but I am satisfied now and surrender to Allah's Order."

> When I left, I heard a voice saying, "I have passed My Order and have lessened the burden of My Worshipers."
>
> *Bukhari 58.227*

Revelations pertaining to the five prayers are scattered throughout the Koran, no one verse mentioning all five prayers negotiated by the Prophet. For example, revelation 33:41-42 could lead a believer to assume that Allah only wants to be glorified through prayer only twice a day.

> 33:41 O believers, remember Allah often;
>
> 33:42 And glorify Him morning and evening.

Revelation 24:58 mentions three prayers: the Dawn Prayer, the Noon Prayer and the Sunset Prayer.

> 24:58 O believers, let those your right hands possess (slaves and maid-servants) and those who have not reached the age of puberty ask your leave three times: (to attend to you or approach you) before the dawn prayer, when you put off your clothes at noon and after the evening prayer. These are three occasions of nudity for you; after which you are or they are not at fault, if you approach each other. That is how Allah makes clear His signs to you. Allah is All-Knowing, Wise.

In an earlier surah, there is no mention of the noon prayer.

> 11:114 And perform the prayer at the two ends of the day and [the first] watches of the night. Surely the good deeds will wipe out the evil deeds; that is a reminder for those who remember.

Another reference to the sunset prayer and how you can make the dawn prayer memorable.

> 17:78 Perform the prayer at the declining of the sun till darkness of the night and recite the Qur'an at dawn. Surely the recital of the Qur'an at dawn is memorable.

The night prayer:

> 17:79 And during the latter part of the night, pray as an additional observance. For your Lord may raise you to a praiseworthy position.

An ambiguous reference to the afternoon prayer:

2:238 Attend regularly to the prayers including the middle prayer (probably the afternoon prayer), standing up in devotion to Allah.

If you are already in Paradise praying to Allah may be a way of achieving a better position in heaven.

30:17 So, glorify Allah in the evening and in the morning.

30:18 He is the praise in the heavens and on earth at sunset and at noontide.

You would think that after spending a good part of the night negotiating the daily prayers with His Messenger, Allah would be more specific about the result of these negotiations and that the time and the number of prayers would be, if not in the same verse, in the same surah.

Considering Allah's observation as to when people pray, imposing even five prayers a day may not be much of a hardship.

41:49 Man does not tire of praying for good, but when evil touches him he becomes downcast and despondent.

41:50 And if We let him taste a mercy from Us after some adversity that has visited him, he will say: "This is mine and do not believe the Hour is coming. If I am returned to my Lord, I will surely have the fairest reward." We shall, then, inform the unbelievers about the things they did and will make them taste an awful punishment.

41:51 If We are gracious to man, he slinks away and turns aside; and if an evil touches him, he is given to constant prayer.

The Call to Prayer

7:29 Say: "My Lord commands justice. Set your faces straight at every place of prayer and call on Him in true devotion. As He originated you, you shall return."

3:76 Yea, whoever fulfills his pledge and is pious – truly Allah loves the pious.

As the Muslim community of Medina grew in number, it became apparent that some way had to be devised so that everyone in town or working in the vast orchards of Medina performed the prayers at the correct and at the same time. A means had to be found and it had to be different than other religion. Muhammad Mojlum Khan in *The Muslim 100 - The Lives, Thoughts and Achievements of the Most*

Influential Muslims in History describes the origin of the call to prayer this way:

> ... the Muslims were aware that the Christians used bells to call their people to the church and the Jews blew a horn to summon their people to religious service, a number of companions suggested that they, too, should devise a method for calling the faithful to the five daily prayers. The Prophet thought that this was a good idea, but he was keen to devise a system which would differentiate the Muslims from the Christian and Jewish practices. Some companions suggested that they should kindle a fire before every prayer, while others that they could clap two pieces of wood to signal the start of the prayer time. However, none of these suggestions appealed to the Prophet.
>
> Then, one day, a companion called Abdullah ibn Zaid appeared before the Prophet and said he saw in a dream where a person was calling all the Muslims to prayer from the roof of the mosque. Subsequently, Umar appeared and confirmed that he had had a similar dream. The Prophet and his companions liked the idea. The *adhan* (or "call to prayer") was thus instituted by the Prophet.

This is what Sunnis believe; Shi'ites on the other hand believe that the call to prayer was Allah's idea which he transmitted to His Messenger in the usual manner. The call to prayer for both Sunnis and Shi'ites are almost identical except for the line "Prayer is better than sleep" which is part of the dawn call to prayer and only said by Sunnis and the declaration about Ali, the Prophet's son-in-law.

Sunni version:

> The God is the greatest/most great
> I testify that there is no deity except for The God
> I testify that Muhammad is a Messenger of The God
> Make haste towards the prayer
> Make haste towards success
> Prayer is better than sleep
> The God is the greatest!
> There is no deity except for The God

Shi'ite version:

> The God is greater than any description
> I testify that there is no deity except for The God
> I testify that Muhammad is a Messenger of The God
> I testify that Ali is the vicegerent of The God
> Make haste towards the prayer

> Make haste towards the worship
> The God is the greatest!
> There is no deity except for The God

The call to prayer in Islam, unlike the method used by Christians and Jews to remind their believers that it is time to worship their Lord or to gather for a special religious occasion, is also a reminder, five times a day, for everyone within ear-shot as to what are a Muslim's core beliefs.

A central belief of Shi'ites is that Ali, the Prophet's son-in-law and his progeny were the rightful successors of the Prophet. This is why Shi'ites are invited to add the declaration "I testify that Ali is the vicegerent of The God" after re-asserting their belief that "Muhammad was the Messenger of God."

~~~~~~~~~~~~~~~

If you know what is good for you, you won't let commerce or sport interfere with the Friday call to prayer.

> 62:9 O believers, when the call for prayer on the Day of Congregation (or Friday) is sounded, then hasten to the mention of Allah and leave off trading. That is far better for you, if only you knew.
>
> 62:10 Then, when prayer is over, spread out throughout the land and seek some of Allah's Bounty, and remember Allah often, that perchance you might prosper.
>
> 62:11 However, when they see trading or sport, they scramble towards it and leave you standing up. Say: "What Allah has in store is far better than sport or trading; and Allah is the Best of Providers."

The call to prayer was not always taken seriously by many when it was first introduced.

> 5:58 And when you call to prayer, they take it as a mockery and a sport; that is because they are a people who do not understand.

Prayers in War and Peace

The Koran may be all over the place when it comes to the daily prayers but it is clear on what you have to do beforehand. Then there are the exceptions to the rule, war being the reason for many of the dispensations. For example, if your manifest enemy is in the vicinity, a quick prayer will suffice.

> 4:101 And when you journey in the land, you are not at fault if you shorten the prayer for fear that the unbelievers will harm you. The unbelievers are your manifest enemy.

The revelations as to the prayers were received during the time when Muslims were in danger of being wiped out by their Arab brothers for denying the faith of their fathers. Allah's warning to keep your weapons at the ready and in good working order, even while praising Him for his compassion and mercy, was probably good advice then and for the wars of conquest that followed the Prophet's takeover of the Arabian Peninsula.

> 4:102 When you (Muhammad) are among them (the faithful), conducting the prayer for them, let a group of them rise with you and let them take their weapons; but when they have prostrated themselves, let them withdraw to the rear; and let another party who had not prayed come forward and pray with you, taking their precaution and carrying their weapons. The unbelievers wish that you would neglect your arms and your equipment, so that they may swoop down on you in a united attack. You are not at fault, however, if you lay aside your weapons in case you are hampered by rain or are sick; but take heed. Allah has prepared for the unbelievers a demeaning punishment.

> 4:103 When you have completed the prayer, remember Allah standing, sitting and reclining. Once you feel secure, then perform the prayer; for prayer is enjoined on the believers at fixed times.

Prayers could also be performed while walking or riding if it was too dangerous to perform the prayers as prescribed.

> 2:239 If you are in danger, then (perform the prayers) on foot or on horseback, when you feel secure remember Allah, just as He has taught you what you did not know.

Don't let the performance of the mandatory prayers weaken your resolve to defeat your enemy.

> 4:104 Do not be weak-hearted in pursuing the enemy. If you are suffering they are suffering too; but you hope from Allah what they cannot hope. Allah is All-Knowing, Wise.

The following is addressed to the Prophet, like much of the Koran; nonetheless, the believers are expected to do what Allah demands of His Messenger and not ask Him to forgive the transgressions of others, or to plead for mercy or compassion for anyone but themselves.

> 4:105 We have revealed the Book to you in truth, so as to judge between people in accordance with what Allah has shown you. And do not be an advocate of the treacherous.
>
> 4:106 And ask Allah's forgiveness; Allah is indeed All-Forgiving, Merciful!
>
> 4:107 And do not plead on behalf of those who betray themselves; for Allah does not like the treacherous or sinful.
>
> 4:108 They seek to hide themselves from men, but they cannot hide themselves from Allah; for He is with them while they secretly contemplate words that do not please Him. And Allah is fully aware of what they do!
>
> 4:109 There you are, you have pleaded on their behalf in the present world; who then will plead with Allah on their behalf on the Day of Resurrection, or who will their guardian?

Nobody, that's who! But it does not mean that Allah will not listen to a personal plea for forgiveness from a believer who has sinned, in the here-and now.

> 4:110 But he, who does evils or wrongs himself, then asks Allah's forgiveness, will find Allah All-Forgiving, Merciful.

You should not attend prayer services if you are drunk.

> 4:43 O believers, do not approach prayer while you are drunk, until you know what you say; nor when you are unclean – unless you are on a journey – until you have washed yourselves. And if you are sick or on a journey, or if anyone of you has relieved himself, or you have touched women and could not find water, you might rub yourself with clean earth, wiping you faces and hands with it. Allah indeed is Pardoning, All-Forgiving!

Cleanliness is next to godliness.

> 5:6 O believers, if you rise to pray, wash your faces and your hands up to the elbows and wipe your heads and your feet up to the ankles. If you are unclean, then cleanse yourself; and if you are sick or on a journey, and if one of you has come from the rest-room, or if you have touched women and cannot find any water, then take some clean earth and wipe your faces and hands with it. Allah does not wish to burden you, but to purify you and complete His Grace upon you, that you may be thankful.

> 5:7 And remember Allah's Grace upon you and His Covenant (*with Adam's progeny*) with which he bound you, when you said: "We hear and we obey." Fear Allah; Allah indeed knows well the thoughts in the hearts[31]!

In peace, but perhaps not in war, you should wear nice clothes when performing the prayers.

> 7:31 O Children of Adam, put on you finery at every place of prayer. Eat and drink, but do not be prodigal, He does not like the prodigals.

Morning and evening prayers should be subdued i.e. not too loud.

> 7:204 When the Qur'an is recited, listen to it and pay attention, that perchance you may receive mercy.

> 7:205 And remember your Lord within yourself, in humility and awe and without raising your voice in the morning and evening; and do not be one of the heedless.

> 7:206 Indeed, those (the angels) who are with your Lord are not too proud to worship Him, and they glorify Him and prostrate themselves before Him.

Don't shout, but pray loud enough to be heard.

> 17:110 Say: "Call on Allah or the Compassionate. By whatever name you call [Him], His are the Most Beautiful Names." And pray neither with a loud nor with a low voice, but follow a middle course.

Adding, during your prayer, that Allah has not taken a son (as the Christians claim) etc. is a nice touch; as to why He would need a "supporter to protect Him from humiliation" is anyone's guess.

> 17:111 And say: "Praise be to Allah Who has not taken a son to Himself, and Who has no partner in sovereignty and no supporter to protect Him from humiliation. And proclaim His greatness."

An Answer to a Prayer

> 3:190 There are in the creation of the heavens and the earth and the alternation of night and day real signs for people of understanding.

> 3:191 Those who remember Allah while standing, sitting or

---

[31] Like many classical philosophers, including Aristotle, Allah considered the heart the seat of reason, not the head, nor the brain contained within.

> lying on their sides, reflecting upon the creation of the heavens and the earth [saying]: "Our Lord You did not create this in vain. Glory be to You! Save us from the torment of the Fire.
>
> 3:192 "Our Lord, he whom you throw into the Fire will be disgraced by you." The evildoers shall have no supporters.
>
> 3:193 "Our Lord, we have heard a caller summoning to belief, saying: 'Believe in your Lord'; and so we have believed. Lord, forgive us our sins and acquit us of our evil deeds and cause us to die with the pious.
>
> 3:194 "Lord, and give us what You promised us through the Messengers, and do not disgrace us on the Day of Resurrection. Surely, You will not break a Promise."
>
> 3:195 And so their Lord answered them saying: "Indeed, I will not cause the loss of the work and any worker among you, whether male or female; you come one from the other." ...

Packaged with the answer to the prayer is an assurance for the persecuted Muslims, Meccans who emigrated to Medina, that their sins will be forgiven and that they will be admitted into Paradise, followed by revelations, which may or may not be related to the subject at hand depending on your point of view.

> 3:195 ... Those who have emigrated (the Meccan Muslims who, because of persecution, emigrated to Medina) and were driven out of their homes, were persecuted for My Sake, fought and were killed, I will forgive their sins and will admit them into Gardens, beneath which rivers flow, as a reward from Allah. With Allah is the best reward!
>
> 3:196 Do not be deceived by the wanderings (for business purposes) of those who disbelieved in the land;
>
> 3:197 A little enjoyment, and then their abode is Hell; and what a wretched resting place!
>
> 3:198 However, those who fear their Lord will have Gardens, beneath which rivers flow, abiding therein forever, as a Bounty from Allah. What Allah has is far better for the righteous.

The Night too is for Praying

According to Moududi "their sides shun their bed" in revelation 32:16 means "They worship their Lord instead of enjoying sensuous pleasures at night."

> 32:15 Yet those believe in Our Signs who, when reminded of them, fall down prostrate in celebrate the praise of their Lord, and they are not overbearing.
>
> 32:16 Their sides shun their couches as they call on their Lord in fear and hope, and of what We have provided [them with, they give in charity].
>
> 32:17 No soul knows what was laid up for them secretly of joyful relief, as a reward for what they used to do.

The Prayer of the People of Paradise

The prayer of the people of Paradise, revelation 10:10, is sandwiched between revelations about those "who do not hope to meet Us".

> 10:7 Those who do not hope to meet Us and are content with the present life and are at ease in it, and those who pay no heed to our signs;
>
> 10:8 Their refuge is the Fire, on account of [what] they used to do.
>
> 10:9 Surely, those who believe and do the good, their Lord shall guide them for their belief; beneath them rivers will flow in the Gardens of Bliss.
>
> 10:10 Their prayer therein shall be: "Glory be to you, O Allah"; and their greeting in it shall be: "Peace!" and they conclude their prayer by saying: "Praise belongs to Allah, the Lord of the Worlds."
>
> 10:11 And were Allah to hasten the evil for mankind (hasten mankind's punishment) just as they would hasten the good for themselves (from God), their term would have been fulfilled. Then We would leave those who do not hope to meet Us in their arrogance wandering aimlessly.

Pilgrimages – The Hajj and the Umrah

22:67 To every nation, We have given a sacred rite which they observe. So do not let them dispute with you in this matter. Call them to your Lord, for you are on a straight course.

22:68 And if they dispute with you, say: "Allah knows best what you are doing."

22:69 Allah will judge between you on the Day of Resurrection, regarding what you disagree about.

22:70 Do you not know that Allah knows what is in the heavens and on earth. All that is in a Book; and that is an easy matter for Allah.

22:71 And they worship, besides Allah, that concerning which He did not send down any authority, and of which they have no knowledge. The wrongdoers shall have no supporter.

22:72 And when Our Clear revelations are recited to them, you will recognize in the face of the unbelievers the denial. They will almost fall upon those who recite to them Our Revelations. Say: "Shall I tell you about what is worse than that? It is the Fire which Allah has promised the unbelievers; and what a wretched fate!"

Christianity has its *Ten Commandments*; Islam its *Five Pillars*, four of which are about worshipping Allah. A Muslim who fails to observe even one of these pillars in the prescribed manner dramatically increases his or her chances of spending an eternity on fire in Hell.

Apart from demanding a day of rest, the Christian God is quite flexible about how He should be worshipped. Not Allah. For Allah, you worship only who He reveals you can worship (revelation 22:71), and that is Him exclusively, and there is only one right way, and that is His Way, with input from His Messenger. His Way includes a mandatory pilgrimage to Mecca i.e. the Hajj, the fifth of the Five

Pillars (the other pillars are *Shahadah*, declaring allegiance to God; *Salat*, daily prayers; *Zakat*, annual charity; *Saum*, month-long fasting).

The Importance of Mecca

> 42:7 And so, We revealed to you an Arabic Qur'an in order to warn the Mother of the Cities (Mecca) and those around it and to warn of the Day of Forgathering which is undoubted, whereon a group shall be in Paradise and a group shall be in Hell.

Every able-bodied, financially capable Muslim adult must perform the Hajj at least once during his or her lifetime thereby making the Saudis the custodian of the metaphorical gold mine which never runs out of gold[32].

Why Mecca? Mecca is not only the birth place of the Prophet Muhammad but also the place where Abraham is said to have built the first shrine to the one true god, Allah.

> 5:97 Allah has made the Ka'ba, the Sacred House, a foundation of religion for all mankind, together with the Sacred Month and the sacrificial offerings and their garlands, so that you may know that Allah knows what is the heavens and on the earth, and that Allah knows everything very well.

At the center of town is a cube made of bricks and covered by a thick black cloth, the Ka'ba (also spelled Ka'ba). Inside you will find a black stone, a meteorite about the size of a basketball, which is said to have been part of the original shrine built by Abraham. In one tradition it is the stone that Adam grabbed just before he and Eve were literally flung out of Paradise; Adam landing somewhere in present day Sri Lanka on a mountain aptly named Adam's Peak, and Eve near present day Mecca. Mecca, in Islam, is the center of the universe.

> 2:150 From whatever place you come out, turn your faces towards the Sacred Mosque. And wherever you all are, turn your faces towards it, lest people should have cause to argue with you, except for the evil-doers among them. Do not fear them, but fear Me so that I may complete My Grace upon you, and that you may be rightly guided.

The importance of Mecca for Muslims cannot be overstated. It's also not a safe place for those who don't believe. An unbeliever caught in or around Mecca must usually convert on the spot or face summary

---

[32] Less than 300 meters from the Ka'ba is the Abraj Al Bait Complex with its five stories, 4000 stores shopping mall.

execution. A few verses confirming Mecca's honoured status among cities and as the site of the pilgrimage and the Ka'ba.

3:96 The first House founded for mankind is truly that at Bakka (Mecca), blessed and a guidance to all the nations.

3:97 Therein are clear signs and the sacred site of Abraham. Whoever enters it will be secure. It is the duty to Allah incumbent on those who can, to make the pilgrimage to the House. But with respect to those who disbelieve, Allah has no need of all mankind.

22:26 And [remember] when We appointed for Abraham the site of the (Sacred) House [saying]: "You shall not associate with Me anything and purify My House for those who circle around, those who stand up, those who kneel and those who prostrate themselves;"

22:27 And proclaim the pilgrimage to the people, and then they will come on foot or on every lean mount, coming from every deep ravine,

22:28 To witness benefits of theirs, and mention Allah's name, during certain numbered days, over such beast of the flocks as He has provided them with. Eat, then, from them and feed the wretched poor.

22:29 Then, let them complete their self-cleansing and fulfill their vows and circle round the Ancient House (the Ka'ba).

22:30 All that; and whoever venerates the sacred things of Allah, it shall be well for him with His Lord. Cattle have been made lawful to you, except what is recited to you [to avoid]: so shun the abomination of idols, and shun false testimony.

22:31 Remain true to Allah, associating no gods with Him. He who associates anything with Allah is like one who has fallen from the sky and is snatched by the birds, or the wind hurls him down a very steep place.

22:32 All that; and he who venerates the sacred rites of Allah – it is the fruit of the piety of the hearts.

22:33 You have some benefit therefrom, for an appointed term; then their place of sacrifice is the Ancient House[33].

22:34 And to every nation, We have appointed a holy rite, so that they might mention Allah's Name over whatever He has provided them with of the beasts of the flock. For your God is one God. Submit to Him and announce the good news to the humble;

22:35 Those who, when Allah is mentioned, their hearts tremble, and those who endure what befalls them, and those who perform the prayer and spend from what We have provided them with.

22:36 And the camels We have made for you as parts of the sacred rites of Allah. You have some good therein; so mention Allah's Name over them as they stand in line. When their sides fall to the ground, eat of them and feed the contented and the beggar. That is how We subjected them to you, that perchance you may be thankful.[34]

22:37 Their flesh and blood will not reach Allah, but your piety will reach Him. Thus He subjected them to you, so

---

[33] Revelation 22:33 applies to all animals destined for sacrifice, not only cows, and was revealed, according to Moududi, to clear up a misunderstanding.

This is to remove the misunderstanding about getting any benefit from the animals dedicated for sacrifice as they were also included in the "Symbols of Allah. This was necessitated because the Arabs believed that it was unlawful to get any benefit from them. One could neither ride on them nor carry any load on them nor consume their milk, after they had been dedicated for sacrifice during Hajj. In this verse that misunderstanding has been removed. Hadrat Abu Hurairah and Anas have reported that the Holy Prophet saw a tnan walking in a miserable condition on foot leading his camel by the nose-string. When the Holy Prophet asked him to ride on it, he replied that it was his sacrificial offering. The Holy Prophet again urged him to ride on his camel.

[34] Animal cruelty was not always part of the god worshipping rituals practiced by the pre-Islamic Arabs:

Narrated Said bin Al-Musaiyab:

Al-Bahira was an animal whose milk was spared for the idols and other dieties, and so nobody was allowed to milk it.

As-Saiba was an animal which they (i.e. infidels) used to set free in the names of their gods so that it would not be used for carrying anything.

Abu Huraira said, "The Prophet said, 'I saw Amr bin 'Amir bin Luhai Al-Khuzai dragging his intestines in the (Hell) Fire, for he was the first man who started the custom of releasing animals (for the sake of false gods).'"

Bukhari 76.723

that you may glorify Allah for guiding you. And announce the good news to the beneficent.

Other verses pertaining to the pilgrimages and the penance for not being able to complete them as prescribed can be found in chapter 2, *The Cow*. In these revelations, Allah again leaves nothing to chance. The "proper pilgrimage" in revelation 2:196 is the Hajj, the "lesser pilgrimage" is the Umrah, which is not compulsory but highly recommended.

> 2:196 Perform the proper pilgrimage and the lesser pilgrimage for the sake of Allah. But if you are prevented, then make whatever offering (a sheep) is available; then do not shave your heads until the offering reaches its destination (where it can be slaughtered). Whoever of you is sick or has an injury in the head can atone for it by fasting, giving alms or sacrificing. When you are secure, whoever combines the lesser pilgrimage and the proper pilgrimage, should make whatever offering is available. But if he cannot, then let him fast for three days during the pilgrimage and seven days when he returns. That is a total of ten full days. This is incumbent on him whose family is not present at the Sacred Mosque. Fear Allah and know that His retribution is severe.

No sex please, we are on pilgrimage.

> 2:197 Pilgrimage is [during] the appointed months. He who determines to perform the pilgrimage during them, shall abstain from intercourse, debauchery and acrimonious quarrel. And whatever good you do, Allah knows it. Make provision (for your journey). The best provision, however, is the fear of Allah. So fear Me, O people of understanding.

Safa and Marwa

Safa and Marwa are the names of the two mountains near Mecca between which Hagar frantically ran looking for water after being abandoned there by Abraham with their son Isma`il. Today they are part of the Hajj ritual with pilgrims re-creating Hagar's frantic search for water by running seven times between the two mountains (hills really).

The Prophet had ordered the destruction of idols, including one on each of Safa and Marwa. The believers feared being near the tainted mountains because of the previous presence of the idols. Not to worry says Allah; believers commit no sin if they go around them.

2:158 Surely Safa and Marwa are beacons of Allah (His Religion). He who performs the proper or the lesser pilgrimage commits no sin if he goes around them. And those who volunteer to do a good deed will find Allah Rewarding, All-Knowing.

Deaths, Molestations and Managing the Hajj

Permission must be obtained beforehand to perform the Hajj. More than two million Muslims every year obtain this permission from the Saudis and travel to the city at the center of Allah's Universe during the last month of the Islamic calendar for the Hajj. The Hajj consist of four major rituals, the most important being the mandatory seven circles around the Ka'ba followed by the re-enactment of Hagar's frantic search for water[35], Abraham's stoning of the devil and ending with the slow ritual bleeding to death of tens of thousands of animals, goats mostly, camels, the favoured offering of the Prophet having fallen into disfavour for both logistical and practical reasons.

The steady increase in the number of converts making the major pilgrimage has presented some serious problems for the Saudis. Problems that cannot easily be solved as no solution can interfere with the meticulous rituals of the Hajj as prescribed by God and His Messenger. This problem is bound to get worse (Islam is the world's fastest growing religion).

While the Saudis have made constant progress in safeguarding the lives of pilgrims during the Hajj, disasters still occur on a recurring basis. The latest, at this writing, the death of more than a

---

[35] After Abraham's wife Sarah became pregnant, he was told by Allah to take Hagar and their son Isma`il (Islam considers Hagar a legitimate wife of Abraham and Isma`il, not Isaac, the Patriarchs' first born son) from their home in Palestine to the desert wilderness of Arabia and leave them there. When their water ran out, Hagar ran frantically between the hills of Safa and Marwa until she collapsed next to her son who struck his foot on the ground causing a spring to gush forth, the famous well of Zam Zam

What Hagar did after Isma'il (also spelled Ishmael) caused the well of Zam Zam to gush forth may have done more than simply altered the course of scriptural history.

Narrated Ibn Abbas:

The Prophet said, "May Allah be merciful to the mother of Ishmael! If she had left the water of Zam-Zam (fountain) as it was, (without constructing a basin for keeping the water), (or said, "If she had not taken handfuls of its water"), it would have been a flowing stream.

Jurhum (an Arab tribe) came and asked her, 'May we settle at your dwelling?' She said, 'Yes, but you have no right to possess the water.'

They agreed."

Bukhari 40.556

thousand pilgrims in 2015, most trampled to death during the stoning of the devil ritual. This ritual is probably the most difficult to manage because Abraham stoned the devil, not once, not twice, but three times with seven stones reaching their target on each occasion[36] as must the stones of the pilgrims who launch their pebbles at pillars representing the devil.

Muslims make up approximately 25 percent of the world population of about 7 billion (United States Census Bureau 2011). Converting only 10% of the world's current population of unbelievers to Islam could present the Saudis with insurmountable obstacles to staying within God's instructions and His Messenger's example for the Hajj[37].

A problem that the Saudis have not been able to solve, with only an estimated billion and a half believers, country quotas[38] and a large if finite area around the Ka'ba which the believers must circle while rhythmically bowing and praying, is the groping that women and girls must endure. It is next to impossible to segregate the sexes during the Hajj, therefore, women and girls must silently submit, less they be accused of arousing the males next to them, to the probing hands of men and boys whose religion does not allow them to get as close to the opposite sex as during the Hajj until they are married, and who seek to understand with their hands what their religion has denied their eyes until their wedding night[39].

---

[36] "When he [Abraham] left Mina and was brought down to (the defile called) al-Aqaba, the Devil appeared to him at Stone-Heap of the Defile. Gabriel said to him: 'Pelt him!' so Abraham threw seven stones at him so that he disappeared from him. Then he appeared to him at the Middle Stone-Heap. Gabriel said to him: 'Pelt him!' so he pelted him with seven stones so that he disappeared from him. Then he appeared to him at the Little Stone-Heap. Gabriel said to him: 'Pelt him!' so he pelted him with seven stones like the little stones for throwing with a sling. So the Devil withdrew from him." *Al-Azraqi*

[37] The Saudis by being in charge of Mecca are literally in possession of an inexhaustible gold mine whose output increases as converts to Islam increase. Could Saudi funding of madrassas around the world which have become a breeding ground for terrorists e.g. Pakistan be the House of Saud's way of funding their lifestyle when the oil runs out?

[38] Women who cannot get a close male relative or their husband to accompany them are no longer required to perform the Hajj.

[39] A young woman I had coffee with years ago described her experience of the Hajj this way:

"I spent the entire time with a least one man's hand on my ass." She half got up from her chair, leaned forward mimicking the bowing motion, lowered her head and raised her hands. "As my hands went up," she said, "two hands would go down to grab my butt, but of course, you don't dare complain."

I would not fully understand what she meant by her statement "you don't dare complain", until years later when I read an article by Syed Shahabuddin writing in the

Safely accommodating millions more pilgrims at the Hajj

Two million is about the maximum number of pilgrims that can be accommodated for the Hajj; that is 140 million worshippers over a seventy years lifespan.

Even if the Muslim population remained at its current level, more than 80 percent of believers will not be able to fulfill a central requirement of their Faith because of the limitations of accommodating a greater number in the finite space that is the Ka'ba and its surrounding and the mandatory rituals of having two million people throw stones at pillars representing the devil and two million people running back and forth between two hills in a recreation of Hagar's frantic search for water, the two rituals most responsible for deaths at the Hajj.

You would think that God would have anticipated these problems when He made the Hajj mandatory lest a believer spend an eternity in Hell for missing it; unless it was a clever scheme to get more firewood for His Hell, but I don't think so.

Except for an entrance and an exit door, Bait-ul-Ma'mur is almost an exact replica of the Ka'ba in Mecca and is situated directly above it, somewhere above the clouds. Like Muslims on earth, angels are required to make a pilgrimage to this Ka'ba in the sky at least once in their lifetime as immortals, and seventy thousand angels do so every day, according to God's Messenger (*Sahih Muslim, book 1 hadith 309*), entering by one door and exiting by the other.

The Hajj could safely welcome millions more pilgrims if it did away with the add-ons: the Hagar search for water re-enactment and the stoning of the devil ritual[40]. And still more millions could be

---

Milli Gazette, Indian Muslim's leading English newspaper, in which he objected to the stoning of women for adultery (emphasis mine).

Apart from the brutality of the 'Rajm' (stoning), repugnant to conscience, here is an element of gender injustice in the operation of the traditional law which allows the male partner to get off scot-free, even if he has coerced and raped the female. If the woman lodges a complaint, her complaint is taken as a testimony against herself and, therefore, amounts to admission and requires no further evidence while it is necessary to get four witnesses against the man.

The young woman whose experience is recounted here was accompanied by her father. He was not aware of what happened to his daughter until after, even thought he was close to her at all times, trapped like her in a swirling mass of humanity grinding its way around the shrouded cube that is the Ka'ba.

[40] Dry, sun-baked Mecca's main claim to fame, before the Prophet did away with them, were the idols which brought pilgrims from all over the Middle East to Mecca and were central to the city's economic well-being.

Narrated Abdullah bin Masud:

The Prophet entered Mecca and (at that time) there were three hundred-and-sixty idols around the Ka'ba. He started stabbing the idols with a stick he had

accommodated if the ritual of the Hajj on earth mimicked that of the Ka'ba in the sky. This would require modifications to the Ka'ba which God's Messenger at one time considered. Perhaps it is time to revisit the concept, now that the age of ignorance, a time before Islam, is a distant memory.

> **Narrated Aswad:**
>
> Ibn Az-Zubair said to me, "Aisha used to tell you secretly a number of things. What did she tell you about the Ka'ba?"
>
> I replied, "She told me that once the Prophet said, 'O Aisha! Had not your people been still close to the pre-Islamic period of ignorance! I would have dismantled the Ka'ba and would have made two doors in it; one for entrance and the other for exit."
>
> *Bukhari 3:128*

The modifications suggested here will become even more pressing should intelligent life out there come to the same conclusion as intelligent life here, that there is only one god, and He is Allah, and that you must honour Him by making a pilgrimage to the place He designated as the center of His universe from wherever you are at least once in your lifetime, whatever that lifetime is.

The Anthropological Impact of the Hajj

In response to criticism, by believers, of the Catholic Church for such things as The Inquisition and The Crusades, a writer in Le Figaro defined the problem for those who would deny the cause-and-effect of the terrible violence done in Allah's Name. The following is my translation of pertinent parts of his article. Any misunderstandings or misinterpretations are of course my responsibility.

> The Catholic Church is not without its faults. Its history is filled with dark pages it regrets ... However, what differentiates Christianity from Islam is that Christians can always return to the values in the Gospels and to the gentle person of Jesus and ignore a Church which has lost its way.

---

in his hand and reciting: "Truth (Islam) has come and Falsehood (disbelief) has vanished." *Bukhari 43.658*

The merchant in the Messenger may have been concerned that without a multi-day pilgrimage to rival the old pagan multi-faith festival his hometown Mecca might suffer economically, the reason perhaps for the add-ons. Today, with the number of pilgrims and oil revenue, economics are no longer an issue, and these banal rituals could be reschedule so as not to coincide with Koran mandated rituals of the Hajj, which could be completed in a day or less.

> ... Jesus is nonviolent. A return [to the teachings] of Jesus is the remedy for the excesses of religious institutions. Looking to the Prophet[/Koran] for guidance, on the other hand, only reinforces the hate and the violence.
>
> Islam is a religion which in both its sacred text (Koran and Book of Hadiths) and in banal rituals promotes hatred and violence.
>
> The ritual stoning of Satan every year at Mecca is not simply a re-enactment of a superstition... Its impact is anthropological. It is a ceremony to which every Muslim is encourage to participate, and which sanctifies and encourages violence...

But the greatest impact on the pilgrims psyche may not be the banal rituals, but the slow painful public way Allah want the animals sacrificed to His Magnificence be put to death, revelation, 22:36; a way His Messenger obviously enjoyed.

> ... The Prophet slaughtered seven Budn (camel) with his own hands while the camels were standing. He also sacrificed two horned rams (black and white in color) at Medina.
>
> *Bukhari 26.772*

A calf slaughtered the ritual way may take up to eleven minutes to die: eleven agonizing minutes during which it is fully aware. In its March 8, 2012 edition, Le Point, the popular mainstream French (France) weekly published excerpts from a confidential government report prepared by Le Conseil général de alimentation, de l'agriculture et des espaces ruraux on La protection animale en abattoir; la question particulière de l'abattoir rituel (Animal protection in slaughterhouses; the question of ritual slaughter, my translation).

The excerpts reveals that during 2010, 2,068,439 cattle, 382,460 calves, 2,568,444 sheep and 35,713 goats were ritually slaughtered i.e. the animal was not rendered unconscious before being bled to death. The longest time reported for an animal to die while fully conscious was six minutes for cattle, almost twice that time for calves at eleven minutes, and five minutes for sheep. No time was available for goats or camels. The report goes on to describe in great detail the pain and suffering of animals killed the way Allah prefers and which His Messenger demonstrated at every opportunity.

The mass slaughter of animals that occurs during the Hajj and the one day Festival of Sacrifice, celebrated over all the Muslim world, has to have a conditioning effect on witnesses to the slaughter, especially young men and boys, making them immune to the pain and suffering experienced by living things cruelly put to death; even kindling a love of killing in the most cruel way whether it be an animal or an unbeliever, and they have the example of Allah to fall back on.

Narrated Abu Huraira:

The Prophet said, "On the Day of Resurrection Abraham will meet his father Azar whose face will be dark and covered with dust. (The Prophet Abraham will say to him): 'Didn't I tell you not to disobey me?'

His father will reply: 'Today I will not disobey you.'

Abraham will say: 'O Lord! You promised me not to disgrace me on the Day of Resurrection; and what will be more disgraceful to me than cursing and dishonoring my father?'

Then Allah will say (to him):' 'I have forbidden Paradise for the disbelievers."

Then he will be addressed, 'O Abraham! Look! What is underneath your feet?'

He will look and there he will see a Dhabh (an animal,) blood-stained, which will be caught by the legs and thrown in the (Hell) Fire."

Bukhari 55.569

Post Pilgrimage Rituals and Early Departures

What you can do on the way back from the pilgrimage:

2:198 It is no offence to seek a bounty from your Lord. So when you take off from 'Arafat, remember Allah (pray to Him) at the sacred monument (a mountain near Muzdalafa, where pilgrims stop for the night on their journey back from 'Arafat). Remember Him as He guided you, although you were, before that, among those in error.

2:199 Then take off from where people take off and ask Allah's forgiveness. Surely Allah is All-Forgiving, Merciful.

2:200 Once you have performed your rites, remember Allah as you remember your fathers, or even with greater glorification. Some people say: "Our Lord, give us a [a share] in this world." And yet they have no share in the Hereafter."

> 2:201 Other say: "Our Lord, give us a bounty in this world and a bounty in the Hereafter, and protect us from the torment of the Fire."
>
> 2:202 Those have a share (reward) of what they have earned (the good they did). Allah is quick in retribution.

If you have to leave early:

> 2:203 And remember Allah during appointed days (the three days following the day of sacrifice); but he who hastens making them two (the reference here is to who departs on the second day) incurs no sin, if he fears Allah. So fear Allah and know that you will surely be gathered together before Him.

Al Akhnas, like Abu Lahab, is another contemporary of the Prophet whose appearance in the Koran seems only to be a form of payback. Al-Akhnas allegedly refused to offer his protection to Muhammad after the Prophet's uncle Abd al-Muttalib died. Al-Akhnas must have at one time perform the Hajj. What he did after he departed did not go unnoticed.

> 2:204 [You will find] among the people a person whose discourse about life in this world pleases you, and who calls Allah to vouch for what is in his heart, although he is your worst enemy (Al-Akhnas Ibn Shurayq).
>
> 2:205 And when he departs, he roams the land sowing corruption therein and destroying crops and livestock; but Allah does not like corruption.
>
> 2:206 And if it is said to him: "Fear Allah", he is seized with pride in sin. Hell shall be sufficient for him and what a miserable resting-place!

Of course, not all people are like Akhnas

> 2:207 And some people sell themselves[41] for the sake of Allah's Favour. Allah is kind to [His] servants.

---

[41] 2:207 And there is the type of man who gives his life to earn the pleasure of Allah. And Allah is full of kindness to (His) devotees. *Yusuf Ali*

Ramadan

2:183 O you who believe, fasting is prescribed for you as it was prescribed for those before you, so that you may be God-fearing;

2:184 For a fixed number of days. If any of you is sick or on a journey, then [an equal] number of other days. And those who find it extremely difficult (to fast) should, as a penance, feed a poor man. He who spontaneously does more good (increases the penance), it is for his own good. To fast is better for you, if only you knew. [42]

2:185 The month of Ramadan is the month in which the Qur'an was revealed, providing guidance for mankind, with clear verses to guide and to distinguish right from wrong. He who witnesses that month should fast it. But if anyone is sick or on a journey, [he ought to fast] a number of other days. Allah desires ease and does not desire hardship for you, that you may complete the total number (of fasting days); glorify Allah for His Guidance, and that you may be thankful.

The Koran is very much all over the place as to when it was revealed. There is the month of Ramadan; in two revealed truth, revelations 44:3 and 97:1, Allah insists it was all sent down in one night, the "blessed night" and the "night of power" respectively; and in still another immutable fact communicated to a mortal by a god, revealed truth 17:106, it was sent down "piecemeal". He even threatens in revelation 25:34 to muster "on their faces in Hell" those who, in revelation 24:32, would like it sent down all at once.

44:3 We have sent it down on a blessed night. We were then admonishing.

97:1 We have sent it (the Qur'an) down on the night of Power.

---

[42] It is clear that Allah values fasting above all other form of penance or glorification, even doing good.

17:106 It is a Qur'an which we have divided into parts that you may recite it with deliberation, and We revealed it piecemeal.

25:32 The unbelievers say: "If only this Qur'an had been sent down on him all at once." That is how We wanted to strengthen your heart with it and We have revealed it in stages.

25:33 They never bring you any simile but We bring you the truth and a better exposition.

25:34 Those who are mustered on their faces in Hell; those are in a worse position and are more wayward.

Nowhere in His Book does Allah mention revealing what He revealed in dreams. Yet, this is how the Prophet's companions remember God's Messenger receiving many of God's communications.

Narrated Safwan bin Ya'la bin Umaiya from his father who said:

A man came to the Prophet while he was at Ji'rana. The man was wearing a cloak which had traces of Khaluq or Sufra (a kind of perfume).

The man asked (the Prophet), "What do you order me to perform in my Umra (the lesser pilgrimage)?"

So, Allah inspired the Prophet divinely and he was screened by a place of cloth.

I wished to see the Prophet being divinely inspired.

Umar said to me, "Come! Will you be pleased to look at the Prophet while Allah is inspiring him?"

I replied in the affirmative.

Umar lifted one corner of the cloth and I looked at the Prophet who was snoring. (The sub-narrator thought that he said: The snoring was like that of a camel).

When that state was over, the Prophet asked, "Where is the questioner who asked about Umra? Put off your cloak and wash away the traces of Khaluq from your body and clean the Sufra (yellow color) and perform in your Umra what you perform in your Hajj (i.e. the Tawaf round the Ka'ba and the Sa'i between Safa and Marwa)."

Bukhari 27.17

None dared wake up the Prophet less he interrupt a transmission from Paradise.

Narrated Imran:

Once we were traveling with the Prophet and we carried on traveling till the last part of the night and then we (halted at a place) and slept (deeply). There is nothing sweeter than sleep for a traveler in the last part of the night. So it was only the heat of the sun that made us to wake up and the first to wake up was so and so, then so and so and then so and so (the narrator Auf said that Abu Raja had told him their names but he had forgotten them) and the fourth person to wake up was Umar bin Al-Khattab.

And whenever the Prophet used to sleep, nobody would wake him up till he himself used to get up as we did not know what was happening (being revealed) to him in his sleep ...

Bukhari 7.340

For more accounts from the Prophet, his wives and companions as to how the Koran was communicated please read *1,001 Sayings and Deeds of the Prophet Muhammad, Boreal Books, 2014*.

Ramadan in the Land of the Midnight Sun

What are Muslims who live above the Arctic circle to do when the fast of Ramadan coincides with a period when the sun does not set? Allah is unequivocal about fasting during the month of Ramadan, granting only an exception for the believers who are too ill or those fighting in His cause during the holiest month in His calendar.

The Prophet Muhammad, who may not have been aware of the sun not setting above the Arctic Circle and below the Antarctic Circle during their respective summers, has nothing to say on the matter, leaving Islamic scholars to sort it out for themselves.

Some scholars have "suggested fasting by the clock instead of by the sun, using the sunrise and sunset times of the holy city of Mecca as opposed to local time". This could contravene the Koran. Allah in a revelation about when you can have sex during the month of Ramadan is clear about night and day.

> 2:187 It has been made lawful to you on the night of fasting to approach your wives; they are a raiment for you, and you are a raiment for them. Allah knows that you used to betray yourselves, but He accepted your repentance and pardoned you. So now get to them (the wives) and seek what Allah has ordained for you. Eat and drink until you can discern the white thread from the black thread of dawn. Then complete the fast till nightfall. But do not approach them (the wives) while you are in devotion at the mosque. Those are the bounds of Allah; do not approach them. Thus Allah makes clear his revelations to mankind, that they may fear Him.

To avoid contradicting God, other scholars have suggested that "those who live close to the Arctic Circle, where they have continual night or continual day for several months, should look to the closest city to them where night and day are distinct." That last suggestion, in Canada would still make for more than twenty-three hours without food if the closest city is Inuvik, Yellowknife or Whitehorse.

The issue as to when to eat and when not to eat, when to have sex and when not to have sex, when to pray becomes even more confusing when Ramadan falls in the period when the night can last for months on end in the far northern and southern latitudes.

IF TRUTH BE TOLD

Allah Does Not Care for Homosexuals

29:44 Allah created the heavens and the earth in truth. Surely there is in that a sign for those who believe.

29:45 Recite what has been revealed to you of the Book and perform the prayer. Prayer surely forbids the foul act and abomination. Allah's remembrance is greater and Allah knows what you do.

In Paradise, the grateful male dead will be reclining on couches, in a hedonistic-like setting, indulging in the pleasures of Dionysus with the vast majority being tended to by purified wives, virtuous blushing maidens and voluptuous easily aroused houris. Men who prefer boys to wait on them will not be disappointed – immortal boys with alabaster-like skin "as if they were hidden pearls" will be at their beck and call.

52:17 The God-fearing are indeed in gardens and bliss,

52:18: Rejoicing in what their Lord has given them; and their Lord shall guard them against the punishment of Hell. [saying]:

52:19 "Eat and drink merrily, for what you used to do."

52:20 Reclining on ranged couches, and We shall wed them to wide-eyed houris.

52:21 And those who have believed and their progeny followed them in belief, We shall join their progeny to them. We shall not deprive them of any of their work; every man shall be bound by what he has earned.

52:22 And We shall supply them with fruit and meat, such as they desire.

52:23 They will exchange therein a cup of wherein there is no idle talk or vilification.

52:24 And boys of their own will go around them, as if they were hidden pearls.

76:19 And there go round them immortal boys; when you see them, you will think that they are scattered pearls.

Verse 52:24 and 76:19 could be interpreted as male pedophiliac relationships i.e. adult with boys, including perhaps sodomy[43], will be permitted in Paradise; but male same sex intimacy is definitely out. Allah will remind the believers about what He thinks about homosexual relationships in at least four retellings of the story of Lot, in four different surahs no less. In one retelling, He even includes Abraham. Can His feelings on this matter be made any clearer!

Surah 7, The Ramparts

Before the people of Lot, homosexuality was unknown in the ancient world.

> 7:80 And [remember] Lot when he said to his people: "Do you commit indecencies which no one in the whole world committed before you?"
>
> 7:81 "You approach men instead of women lustfully; you are rather a people given to excess."
>
> 7:82 His people's response was simply to say: "Expel them (Lot and his people) from your city; for they are men who wish to remain chaste."

Surah 26, The Poets

> 26:160 The people of Lot denounced the Messengers as liars.
>
> 26:161 When their brother Lot said to them; "Do you not fear God?
>
> 26:162 "I am a faithful Messenger to you;
>
> 26:163 "So, fear Allah and obey me.
>
> 26:164 "I do not ask you any wage for this; my wage is with the Lord of the Worlds.

---

[43] This possibly tenuous conclusion is based on an observation made by Khomeini in *The Tahrirolvasyleh*, better known as *The Political, Philosophical, Social and Religious Principles of Ayatollah Khomeini* on sodomizing baby girls:

> A man can have sexual pleasure from a child as young as a baby. However he should not penetrate, sodomizing the child is OK. If the man penetrates and damages the child then he should be responsible for her subsistence all her life. This girl however does not count as one of his four permanent wives. The man will not be eligible to marry the girl's sister.

26:165 "Do you approach the males from all of mankind;

26:166 "And leave the wives that your Lord created for you? No, you are a transgressing people."

26:167 They said: "If you will not desist, O Lot, you will certainly be one of those expelled."

26:168 He said: "I am a detester of your deed.

26:169 "Lord, save me and my family from what they do."

26:170 So, We delivered him and his family, all together.

26:171 Except for an old woman who was one of those who lingered behind.

26:172 Then, we destroyed the others.

26:173 And We loosed on them a rain. Wretched is the rain of those forewarned!

26:174 There is in that a sign, but more of them were not believers.

26:175 Truly, your Lord is the Almighty, the Merciful.

Surah 27, The Ants

27:53 And We delivered those who believed and were God-fearing.

27:54 And Lot, when he said to his people: "Do you commit the foul act, while you perceive?

27:55 "What then, do you approach men lustfully, instead of women? No, you are an ignorant people."

27:56 The only response of his people was to say: "Drive the family of Lot out of your city. They are a people who keep themselves clean."

27:57 We delivered him and his family, except for his wife; We decreed that she should stay behind.

Surah 29, The Spider

Further confirmation that, before the people of Lot did it, sodomy was unknown in the ancient world.

29:28 And (remember) Lot, when he said to his people: "You are committing the foul act (sodomy) which no one in the whole world ever committed before you."

> 29:29 "You approach men and waylay the traveler and commit in your gatherings reprehensible acts." To which the only reply of his people was: "Bring upon us Allah's punishment, if you are truthful."
>
> 29:30 He said: "Lord, support me against the workers of corruption."
>
> 29:31 When Our Emissaries (the angels) brought Abraham the good news, they said: "We are going to destroy the inhabitants of this city. Its inhabitants have indeed been wrongdoers."
>
> 29:32 He said: "Lot is in it"; they said: "We know better who is in it. We shall deliver him and his household, except for his wife; for she is one of those who will stay behind."

The woman left behind obviously fascinates Allah. In *The Spider* He mentions her not once, but twice. The second time:

> 29:33 Then, when our Emissaries came to Lot, he was troubled and distressed on their account, and they said: "Do not fear and do not grieve; and we shall deliver you and your household, except for your wife; she is one of those who will stay behind."
>
> 29:34 We are sending down upon the inhabitants of the city a scourge from heaven, because of their sins.
>
> 29:35 And We have left as vestige of it a clear sign to a people who understand.

Crime and Punishment

> Since sodomy is a greater crime than adultery and its evils are worse, the punishment for sodomy is also more severe than that of adultery according to the Islamic law. Islam prescribes capital punishment for the active as well as the passive partner in the crime. If both are major and sane, both of them have to be killed. The active partner is beheaded with the sword or killed by stoning or burnt alive or thrown from a height with the hands and the legs tied. These are the ways prescribed for punishing the criminal, but it is at the discretion of the Judge to determine the method.
>
> Similarly, the method adopted for the death of the passive partner is also determined by the Qazi (the judge). According to Amir ul-Mu'minīn 'Ali (a.s.), a person who

has committed this sin must also be burnt after being killed.

Ayatollah Husayn Dastaghaib Shirazi. Greater Sins, the Complete Book

If a person kisses a young man with passion, on the Day of the Judgement, Allah shall tie a rein of fire on his mouth.

al-Kāfi

Allah shall punish for a thousand years in Hell, the man who kisses a boy with passion.

Mustadrak ul-Wasa'il

What is worse than looking at female children with lust in your heart:

> Refrain from looking lustfully at the children of rich people and slaves, especially those who have yet no beard. Because the mischief that is possible by such glances is greater than mischief of glancing at young girls, who are in veil.

Wasa'il ul-Shia

Where Homosexuals Go When They Die

Allahu Akbar! I have heard the Holy Prophet (S) saying that, 'Whosoever from my Umma commits the act of the Umma of Lut and dies before repenting for it shall not remain in the grave for more than three days. The earth will suck him inside and he shall reach the place of the dead of Lut. Where destiny annihilated them. Then that person will also be counted among them'.

Kitab Mualim-uz-zalfa

The Prophet is also alleged to have said:

> ... the person who allows another to mount him from behind to commit sodomy, then Allah puts him on the fringe of Hell (in extreme heat) and keeps him there till He completes the reckoning of all the people. Then He orders him to be put into Hell. One by one he is made to suffer all the punishments of Hell till he reaches the lowest stage. Then he never comes out from there.

Wasa'il ul-Shia

Allah Despises the Riba-Eaters

Narrated Samura bin Jundab:

The Prophet said: "This night I dreamt that two men came and took me to a Holy land whence we proceeded on till we reached a river of blood, where a man was standing, and on its bank was standing another man with stones in his hands. The man in the middle of the river tried to come out, but the other threw a stone in his mouth and forced him to go back to his original place. So, whenever he tried to come out, the other man would throw a stone in his mouth and force him to go back to his former place."

I asked, "Who is this?"

I was told, "The person in the river was a Riba-eater (a lender who insist on charging interest on borrowed money)."

Bukhari 34.298

Jesus of Nazareth stormed the Temple to rid it of the money changers. Allah would do Jesus one better. It is not clear, in the intervention by Jesus, as to whether he was for or against the charging of interest on borrowed money or simply against money changers using the Temple to do their business. Interest is only mentioned once directly in the New Testament in the parable of the talents (Matthew 25:14-30). Some Christians maintain this parable allows for the charging of interest while others say no. Those who say no would argue that Jesus, in the parable of the talents, is demonstrating that seeking to gain interest from money is the sign of a hard man, not a loving man, therefore not an example to follow.

Allah and His Messenger are not given to "splitting hairs" on practices they consider a sin. As you will be able to judge for yourselves, the verses pertaining to the charging of interest are unequivocal and the punishment they foretell for a believer who charges interest on money lent for whatever purpose, in whatever amount, is of the most brutal kind.

Usury is normally defined as "the act of lending money at an exorbitant rate of interest." Usury is the word used in Fakhry's interpretation of the Koran when referring to any moneys earned from the "rental" of money. I have seen the word "interest" used in other interpretations of Allah's revelations. Interest may be a more accurate word than usury when referring to Allah's prohibition against charging a fee for the use of your money by another person or organization. For Allah earning even a penny's worth of interest is a sin. In the Koran, interest and usury are synonymous which is not the case for unbelievers and anyone who has ever obtained a mortgage from a reputable bank.

Allah even makes a distinction between simple and compound interest. Both types are forbidden.

> 2:276 Allah prohibits usury and does not bless it; but He compounds alms. And Allah does not like a vicious unbeliever.

> 2:277 Verily, those who believe, do good works, perform the prayers and give the alms-tax, shall find their reward with their Lord. They have nothing to fear, and they shall not grieve.

> 3:130 O believers, do not devour usury, double and redoubled, and fear Allah that you may prosper!

> 30:39 And what you give in usury, so as to multiply people's wealth, will not multiply in Allah's Sight; but what you give in alms, desiring thereby Allah's Face. Such are the real multipliers.

Perhaps to emphasize how serious He is about His proscription against the believer making any money from money, Allah promises an all-out war, with His Messenger at His side, against those who would dare to do so.

> 2:278 O believers, fear Allah and forgo what is still due from usury, if you are [true] believers.

> 2:279 But if you fail to do that, take note of a war [waged] by Allah and His Messenger. But if you repent you will have your capital, neither wronging (sic) nor being wronged.

To be safe, make a charitable donation of moneys owing.

> 2:280 If he [the debtor] is in straights, then allow days of grace until he is at ease. But to remit [the debt] as alms is better for you, if only you knew.
>
> 2:281 Fear a Day when you will return to Allah; then each soul will be rewarded fully for what it has earned (the good works it has done); and none shall be wronged.

Some of the believers may have been confused as to the difference between increasing their wealth through strictly monetary transactions or by trade. Why was one type of transaction a sin, and the other not? While Allah uncharacteristically does not go into details in the following revelation, He informs the believers that one is not like the other, and that they better know the difference if they don't want to burn in Hell for an eternity.

> 2:275 Those who take usury will not rise up (On the Day of Resurrection) except like those maddened by Satan's touch. For they claim that trading is like usury, whereas Allah has made trading lawful and prohibited usury. Hence, he who has received an admonition from his Lord and desisted can keep what he has taken (prior to the prohibition) and his fate is to be left to Allah. But those who revert [to it (taking usury)] – those are the people of the Fire in which they shall abide forever.

A loan to Allah does not appear to be subjected to the same conditions as a loan to mortals.

> 57:18 Surely, the men and women who give in charity and who have lent Allah a fair loan will receive its double and they will have a generous wage.

The prohibition against charging interest may also have been Allah's way of getting back at the Jews.

> 4:160 And it was on account of the wrongdoing of the Jews that We forbade them certain good things which had been lawful to them; as well as on account of their frequent debarring [of people] from Allah's path;
>
> 4:161 Their taking usury, although they had been forbidden from doing it and their devouring other people's wealth unjustly. We have prepared for the unbelievers among them a very painful punishment!
>
> 4:162 But those firmly rooted in knowledge among them and the believers do believe in what was revealed to you (*Muhammad*) and what was revealed before you. Those who

perform the prayers, give the alms and believe in Allah and the Last Day – to these We shall grant a great reward!

The Prophet as Borrower

Judging from the Prophet's experience as a borrower, it is not inconceivable that, if it could have been done, he would have suggested to Allah that He not only prohibit the charging of interest, but loans altogether; that loans be considered gifts from Him.

God's Messenger owed much of his success as a merchant to Khadijah, a wealthy older Meccan woman who hired the good-looking, and later married the allegedly illiterate young man, to accompany her caravans to and from Damascus. After discovering Islam some fifteen years later, the now forty-something Muhammad, God's latest and greatest Messenger would spend all of his, and his wife's wealth, on the promotion of his new religion. It was not enough and hewas forced to borrow money to simply survive. His main source of borrowed funds was his uncle Abbas.

According to Gheorghiu, Abbas' nephew still owed his uncle the equivalent of twenty ounces of gold, including interest, when he abandoned Mecca for Medina. The Prophet's uncle Abbas was one of the seventy Meccans captured at the famous battle of Badr.

After much discussion as to whether they should be burnt alive or decapitated by a close Muslim relative to avoid having to pay blood money to the family of the prematurely deceased, the merchant in the Prophet decided, after seeking the angel Gabriel's advice, that the prisoners, or their family, could pay a ransom to obtain their freedom. To obtain his freedom, Abbas proposed to his nephew that his ransom be considered the substantial amount of money the Prophet stilled owed him.

God's Messenger would have none of it. He told his uncle, that he will have to do better than that because, "those twenty ounces of gold, was something of yours that the mighty and powerful Allah, gave to me." The kin whose money kept his nephew's dream alive after Khadijah's ran out, paid the additional ransom, and wisely forgot all about the loan.

Allah Loves His Messenger Perhaps More Than He Loves Orphans

> 2:220 ... And they ask you about the orphans, say: "To improve their condition is better for them. And if you associate with them, they are your brethren." Allah knows the dishonest and the honest. And if Allah wills, He would overburden you with restrictions. Allah is Mighty, Wise.

Orphaned boys were almost unknown in the Arab world until Allah changed their status so that His Messenger could marry his adopted son's wife.

The Prophet walked in on his daughter-in-law Zaynab when she was almost naked and "was troubled by her beauty" and he just had to have her. Zaynab was the daughter of the Prophet's paternal aunt Omayma. It was God's Messenger himself who insisted she be given in marriage to Zayd his adopted son.

Marrying your son's former wife was taboo. It did not matter if he was adopted, the same ethical and moral restrictions applied as to a natural born son. Before Allah changed the status of adopted sons from sons to "brothers in religion", revelation 33:5, Arab fathers made no distinction between adopted sons and those they had fathered.

> 33:4 Allah did not create two hearts within the breast of any man; and He did not make your wives, whom you compare to your mothers' backs; and He did not make your [adopted] sons your sons in fact. That is your own claim, by your words of mouth. Allah speaks the truth and He guides to the Right Path.

> 33:5 Assign them to their own fathers. That is more equitable in the sight of Allah; but if you do not know their real fathers, then they are your brothers in religion, your adopted fellow Muslims. You are not at fault if you err therein; but only in what your hearts intend. Allah is ever All-Forgiving, All-Merciful.

Demoting adopted sons to "brothers in religion" not only made their wives, upon divorce, eligible to be taken in marriage by your "adoptive" father; but, also disinherited them as confirmed by the following hadith:

Narrated Aisha:

Abu Hudhaifa, one of those who fought the battle of Badr with Allah's Apostle, adopted Salim as his son and married his niece Hind bint Al-Wahd bin Utba to him and Salim was a freed slave of an Ansari woman.

Allah's Apostle also adopted Zaid as his son.

In the Pre-Islamic period of ignorance the custom was that, if one adopted a son, the people would call him by the name of the adopted-father [from] whom he would inherit as well, till Allah revealed: "Call them (adopted sons) By (the names of) their fathers." (33:5)

Bukhari 59.335

The revelation changing the relationship between adopted sons and their surrogate parent so that God's Messenger could add to his collection of wives, concubines and slave-girls his former daughter-in-law have been interpreted to mean that Islam is against Western style adoption, resulting in an untold number of children in the Islamic world who have no one to call father.

Allah Loves His Cattle; Dogs, Not So Much

Cattle, in the Koran, are mentioned more often, usually in conjunction with something Allah has done for men, than any other animal, even the camel. It is obvious that Allah is extremely proud, if not mesmerized by this four-legged versatile creation of His.

An Ode to Cattle

> 16:5 And the cattle He created for you. Therein are warmth and other advantages, and from them you eat.

> 16:6 An in them you witness beauty, when you bring them back [home], and when you drive them out for pasture.

> 16:7 And they carry your burdens[44] to a distant land which you could only reach with great hardship. Surely your Lord is Clement and Merciful.

Domesticated in Paradise

Cattle were probably domesticated in heaven by Allah or His angels; my understanding of "subdued" in revelation 36:72:

> 36:71 Have they not seen that We have created for them, of Our Handiwork, cattle whereof they are now the owners?

---

[44] Some cattle may not have appreciated being beasts of burden.

Narrated Abu Huraira:

I heard Allah's Apostle saying, "While a shepherd was amongst his sheep, a wolf attacked them and took away one sheep. When the shepherd chased the wolf, the wolf turned towards him and said, 'Who will be its guard on the day of wild animals when nobody except I will be its shepherd.'

And while a man was driving a cow with a load on it, it turned towards him and spoke to him saying, 'I have not been created for this purpose, but for ploughing.'"

The people said, "Glorified be Allah."

The Prophet said, "But I believe in it and so does Abu Bakr and Umar."

Bukhari 57.15

> 36:72 And We subdued them to them, so that of some are their mounts and of some they eat.
>
> 36:73 And from them they have many benefits and beverages. Will they not, then, give thanks.

He sent a small herd of sixteen of the ruminants down from Paradise (eight males and eight females) after He created Adam and his wife. A sensible thing to do, cattle being so versatile.

One interpretation of "the three shadows of darkness" in revelation 39:6 (also translated as "veils of darkness") is 1) the anterior abdominal wall, 2) the uterine wall, and 3) the amniochorionic membrane. The idea that Allah knew so much about embryology is considered another miracle of the Koran.

> 39:6 He created you from a single soul; then, out of it, He made its mate, and brought down for you of the cattle eight pairs. He creates you in your mothers' bellies, one creation after another, in three shadows of darkness. That indeed is Allah, your Lord. His is the dominion; there is no god but He. How, then, are your diverted?

Allah confirming that, like Adam and his wife, He sent down His cattle in pairs, revelation 42:11.

> 42:10 Whatever you disagree upon, unto Allah is the decision thereof. That, then, is Allah, my Lord. In Him I have put my trust, and unto Him I repent.
>
> 42:11 Creator of the heavens and earth. Of yourselves He has made couples and of the cattle pairs, multiplying you thereby. Nothing is like unto Him; He is the All-Hearing, the All-Seeing.
>
> 42:12 To Him belong the keys of the heavens and the earth. He expends the provision to whom He wishes or constricts it. Indeed, He has knowledge of everything.

Domesticated or not, Allah does not give names to cattle.

> 5:103 Allah has not prescribed the designation of Bahirah, Sa'ibah, Wasilah or Hami (cattle sacrificed to idols at the Ka'ba); but the unbelievers impute falsehood to Allah, and most of them do not understand.

Water, Men and Cattle

Often, when water is mentioned it is so that Allah's cattle will have something to drink and something to eat – as will the men of course.

The first mention of water and cattle includes a warning about a god who strikes when you least expect it.

> 10:24 The present life is like water We send down from the sky, causing the vegetation of the earth, from which people and cattle eat, to grow luxuriant. But when the earth puts on its ornamental garb and is adorned, and the people think they are able to get what they want from it, Our Retribution comes upon it day or night, making it produce like a cropped harvest, as if it had never flourished before. Thus We expound Our Revelations to people who reflect.

A trio of revelations about water, vegetation, cattle and their owners which end in a revelation not unlike the "dust to dust" verse of Genesis 3:19.

> 20:53 He who made the earth a bed for you, and opened routes for you in it, and sent down water from the sky; from it we bring forth diverse pairs of plants.

> 20:54 Eat and pasture your cattle. In that there are signs for people of understanding.

> 20:55 From it We have created you, and into it We shall return you, and from it We shall raise you a second time.

Water brought an unnamed dead town back to life, revelation 25:49. Must have been early on after Allah's creation of cattle and man for one town's water supply to be sufficient to quench the thirst of all then living humans and livestock.

> 25:48 And it is He Who sent the wind as good news before His Mercy; and We have sent down from heaven pure water,

> 25:49 To bring to life thereby a dead town, and give it to drink to such numerous cattle and humans as We have created.

> 25:50 And We have alternated it among them, so that they may remember. However, most men have refused all but thanklessness.

Water brings forth vegetation for cattle and folks.

> 32:27 Do they not see that We conduct the water unto the barren land, bringing forth thereby vegetation, from which their cattle and their own folk eat? Do they not see, then?

Allah on the Versatility of His Cattle

You can ride them, you can use them to carry your stuff, you can eat them, some you can drink what "is in their bellies", with their hides you can make tents and from their "fur?", "wool?" and hair you can make furnishings.

> 6:142 Of cattle there are some for burden and some for slaughter. Eat of what we provided for you and do not follow in the footsteps of the Devil. Surely he is a manifest enemy of yours.
>
> ----
>
> 16:80 Allah has made of your homes places for you to dwell in, and has made for you from the hides of cattle light houses to carry on the day of moving and on the day of settling down. And from their wools and their furs and their hair He [has made for you] furnishings and means of enjoyment for a while.
>
> ----
>
> 23:21 And surely in the cattle you have a lesson. We give you to drink what is in their bellies, and you have therein many uses, and from them you eat.
>
> 23:22 And on them and on the ships you are borne.
>
> ----
>
> 40:79 It is Allah Who created for you the cattle, so that some you may ride[45] and some you may eat.
>
> 40:80 And in them, you have other benefits as well; and upon them you may attain any need within your breasts. And upon them and upon the ships you may be borne along.

Cattle and ships you can mount. This dead town must have been brought back to life much later after the creation of man and cattle for ships to have made their appearance.

> 43:11 And Who sent down water from heaven in set measure; and so We revived therewith a dead town. Thus you shall be brought forth;

---

[45] 16:8 And horses, mules and asses [He created] for you to mount, and as an adornment; and He creates what you do not know.

> 43:12 And Who created all the pairs and made for you such ships and cattle as you can mount.
>
> 43:13 That you might sit upon their backs, then remember the Grace of your Lord when you are seated thereon and say: "Glory be to Him Who subjected this to us, whereas we were not equal to it.
>
> 43:14 "And, surely, unto our Lord we shall return."

More stuff, some of which may be made from cattle and for which people are still ungrateful.

> 16:81 Allah has made for you from what He created, sunshades, and from the mountains, places of retreats, and has given you garments to protect you from the heat and coats of mail to protect you while fighting. Thus he perfects His blessings to you so that you may submit.
>
> 16:82 Then, if they turn away, your duty is to deliver the clear Message.
>
> 16:83 They know Allah's Blessing, then they deny it; and most of them are ungrateful.

Slicing the Ears of Cattle

Herdsmen, at the time of the Prophet, marked livestock that was no longer suitable for breeding purposes, by slicing an ear. Some would do this as a living offering to their god. Allah said that this was all the devil's doing, revelation 4:119. The revelation about cutting off cattle's ears as being part of the devil's plan to lead Allah's servant's astray is enclosed in still another vehement denunciation of those who would associate other gods with Allah.

> 4:116 Allah will not forgive associating [any other god] with Him, but will forgive anything less than that, to whomever He wills. He who associates [any other god] with Allah, has really gone very far astray!
>
> 4:117 Apart from Him, they only invoke (worship) the goddesses of Quraysh (*al-Lat, al-Uzza and Manat*); they only invoke a rebellious devil,
>
> 4:118 Cursed by Allah. For he (the Devil) said: "I shall take from your servants for myself a fixed number,
>
> 4:119 "And I will lead them astray, will raise their expectations and order them to cut off the cattle's ears. I will order them to alter Allah's creation." Whoever takes

the Devil for companion, instead of Allah, has incurred a great loss!

4:120 He promises them and raises their expectations; but the Devil promises them nothing but illusion.

4:121 Those people, their shelter shall be Hell and they shall find no escape from it.

4:122 But those who have believed and done the good deeds, We shall admit them into Gardens beneath which rivers flow, dwelling therein forever. This is Allah's True Promise; and who is more truthful in speech than Allah?

Scholars have interpreted Allah's revelation about cutting cattle's ears as a decree against cruelty to animals[46].

Still others claim that revelation 4:119 is another miracle of the Koran; that Allah was warning against cloning His creation i.e. genetic engineering. They base their claim on the fact that "cloning experiments are often done with cells taken from an animal's ear." The miracle of the Koran may be the miracles it inspires.

Dogs in a Cattle World

The Prophet was not a fan of man's best friend. In a hadith he said that unless a dog was kept for guarding a farm or cattle a large portion of the credit its owner gets from Allah for a good deed was deducted.

---

[46] If that was the case, then Allah would not allow His beloved cattle to suffer because of the way they are ritually slaughtered in His Name. In its March 8, 2012 edition, *Le Point*, the popular mainstream French (France) weekly published excerpts from a confidential government report prepared by *Le Conseil général de alimentation, de l'agriculture et des espaces ruraux* on *La protection animale en abattoir; la question particulière de l'abattoir rituel* (**Animal protection in slaughterhouses; the question of ritual slaughter**, *my translation*). Government investigators reported that the longest time it took for an animal to bleed to death while fully conscious after having its throat slit was six minutes for cattle, almost twice that time for calves at eleven minutes, and five minutes for sheep. No time was available for goats.

To prevent the pain and suffering of the animal during the bleeding which is necessary to prevent meat spoilage during butchering, non-ritual slaughtering methods used by most modern humane slaughterhouses render the animal unconscious prior to slaughter using was is called a captive bolt pistol to induce unconsciousness. A method I am sure Allah would approve as there are no verses in the Koran which demands that an animal destined for a believers table be made to suffer before it is put to death.

> **Narrated Abu Huraira:**
>
> Allah's Apostle said, "Whoever keeps a dog, one Qirat[47] of the reward of his good deeds is deducted daily, unless the dog is used for guarding a farm or cattle."
>
> *Bukhari 39.515*

In another narration from the same Abu Huraira, the Prophet extended a dogs use to "guarding sheep or farms, or for hunting."

Before he found a use for dogs, God's Messenger decreed that they be wiped out. This almost led to the extinction of the graceful Saluki, one of the oldest known breeds of domesticated dog. God's Messenger later amended his decree to limit the slaughter to black dogs.

> Abd Allah B. Mughaffal reported the apostle of Allah as saying: "Were dogs not a species of creature I should command that they all be killed; but kill every pure black one."
>
> *Abu Dawud*

And still later, only black dogs with white spots over their eyes.

> Abu Zubair heard Jabir Abdullah saying: Allah's messenger ordered us to kill dogs and we carried out this order so much so that we also killed the dog roaming with a woman from the desert. Then Allah's apostle forbade their killing. He said: "It is your duty to kill the jet-black (dog) having two spots (on the eyes) for it is a devil."
>
> *Sahih Muslim*

The reason God's Messenger ordered the killing of all dogs was because he blamed a puppy for the angel Gabriel not showing up when he was supposed to.

---

[47] What is a Qirat? The beginning of an answer can be found in another hadith recorded by Bukhari:

> **Narrated Abu Huraira:**
>
> The Messenger of Allah said, "Whoever follows the funeral procession and offers the funeral prayer for it, will get a reward equal to one Qirat, and whoever attends it till burial, will get a reward equal to two Qirat."
>
> It was asked, "What are two Qirat?"
>
> He replied, "Equal to two huge mountains."
>
> *Bukhari 23.410*

Maimuna (another of the Prophet's wives) reported that one morning Allah's Messenger was silent with grief.

Maimuna said: "Allah's Messenger, I find a change in your mood today."

Allah's Messenger said: "Gabriel had promised me that he would meet me tonight, but he did not meet me. By Allah, he never broke his promises," and Allah's Messenger spent the day in this sad mood.

Then it occurred to him that there had been a puppy under their cot. He commanded and it was turned out. He then took some water in his hand and sprinkled it at that place.

When it was evening Gabriel met him and he said to him: "You promised me that you would meet me the previous night."

He said: "Yes, but we do not enter a house in which there is a dog or a picture."

Then on that very morning he commanded the killing of the dogs until he announced that the dog kept for the orchards should also be killed, but he spared the dog meant for the protection of extensive fields or big gardens.

Sahih Muslim

Allah's Charity Is Not All It Seems

Charity (Zakat) is the only one of the Five Pillars of Islam that has nothing, or next to nothing to do with worshipping Allah except in an indirect sort way, and for which you will be rewarded.

Allah does not expect His proudest creation to do the right thing unless a reward is in the offing. Altruism, in the Koran, is never assumed, even where charity is concerned; expect something in return from Allah for spending for His Sake, whether it be to expand His Kingdom on earth or to help a wayfarer.

> 2:272 You (*Muhammad*) are not responsible for guiding them. Allah guides whom He wills. And whatever good you spend is for yourselves; for you do not spend except for Allah's Sake. And whatever you spend will yield good returns (it will be fully rewarded). And you shall not be wronged.

Cynics might argue that Allah instinctively appreciated the strategic value of helping people in need in recruiting for His Cause. An understanding of the persuasive power of giving that was not lost on the Islamists who, during the catastrophic flooding in Pakistan in 2010 disrupted aid from Western Countries while facilitating the distribution of the inadequate contributions from Islamic regimes; or in Somalia, where Allah's militants stopped food shipments from Western nations from reaching famine ravaged portions of the country.

How not to spend your wealth in the Way of Allah.

> 2:262 Those who spend their wealth in the Way of Allah, and then do not follow what they spend with taunts and injury, their reward is with their Lord. They shall have nothing to fear and shall not grieve.

What is better than charity.

> 2:263 A kind word and forgiveness are better than charity followed by injury. Allah is Self-Sufficient and Forbearing.

How not to do charity.

> 2:267 O believers, spend (as charity) of the good things you have earned and from what We bring out of the earth for you. Do not turn to the vile and spend from it. For you, yourselves, would not accept it except indulgently. Know that Allah is Self-Sufficient, Praiseworthy.

M. Pickthall is clearer on the concept:

> 2:267 O ye who believe! Spend of the good things which ye have earned, and of that which We bring forth from the earth for you, and seek not the bad (with intent) to spend thereof (in charity) when ye would not take it for yourselves save with disdain; and know that Allah is Absolute, Owner of Praise.

Private vs. Public Charity

Charity is charity, the more the better. A rich man making a public donation usually encourages other wealthy individuals to do the same, and therefore it is considered a good thing by most people. This begs the questions as to why Allah condemns those who don't keep their donations secret.

> 2:270 And whatever expense you spend and whatever vow you vow are known to Allah. The evil-doers shall have no supporters.

> 2:271 To give alms publically is commendable; but to keep it secret and give it to the poor is better for you, and will atone for some of your sins. Allah has knowledge of what you do.

Is Allah, perhaps inadvertently, by his condemnation of public alms in revelation 2:271, making it easier for the rich to say they have given in private when they have done no such thing? Then again, in another reveal truth, He expresses no qualms about public donations.

> 2:274 Those who spend their wealth day and night, in private and in public, will be rewarded by their Lord. They have nothing to fear and they shall not grieve.

Alms were part of the war effort, and those most entitled to your charitable donations in this regard were the poor fighting to extend Allah's Dominion.

> 2:273 [Alms is] for the poor who are held up [fighting] in the Way of Allah, and thus cannot travel in the land. The ignorant think they are rich because they are too proud [to beg]. But you can recognize them by their mark. They do

not importune people for alms. Whatever good you spend is known to Allah.

You will not be reprieved to perform charity after you are dead. Allah does not grant reprieves.

63:10 Spend freely from what We have provided for you, before death overtakes each one of you. Then he will say: "Lord, if only you would reprieve me for a short period, so that I may give in charity and be one of the righteous."

63:11 Allah will not reprieve a single soul when its term comes. Allah is Fully Aware of what you do.

Oaths Can Be Broken

What may have been one of the first revelation to the people of Medina is about homage and oaths.

> 48:7 To Allah belongs the hosts of the heavens and the earth, and Allah is All-Mighty and Wise.
>
> 48:8 Indeed, We have sent you forth as a witness, a bearer of good news and a warner;
>
> 48:9 That you (people of Medina) may believe in Allah and His Messenger, to honour, revere and glorify Him, morning and evening.
>
> 48:10 Those who pay you (the Prophet) homage are actually paying Allah homage. Allah's Hand is above their hands; so he who breaks his oath only breaks it to his loss, and he who fulfills what he has pledge unto Allah, He will grant him a great wage.

Those who honour their oaths will inherit Paradise.

> 23:8 Those who honour their trusts and promises;
>
> 23:9 And observe their prayers;
>
> 23:10 Those are the inheritors,
>
> 23:11 Who will inherit Paradise wherein they will dwell forever.

If an oath prevents you from doing good, break it[48]:

---

[48] "Authentic Traditions indicate that if a person takes a vow and discovers later that righteousness and common good are best served by breaking that vow then he should do so." *Moududi*

The example of the Prophet:

Narrated Zahdam:

... Once I went to Allah's Apostle with a group of Al-Ash'ariyin, and met him while he was angry, distributing some camels of Rakat. We asked for mounts but he took an oath that he would not give us any mounts, and added, "I have nothing to mount you on."

> 2:224 Do not make Allah in your oaths (when you swear by Allah) a hindrance to doing good, to fearing Allah and to making peace between people. Allah is All-Hearing, All-Knowing.

Thoughtless oaths are forgiven.

> 2:225 Allah will not take you to task for what is not meant [to be said] in your oaths; but He will take you to task for what you mean in your hearts. Allah is Forgiving, Clement.[49]

Oaths are not for sale!

> 3:77 Those who sell the covenant of Allah and their own oaths for a small price will have no share in the life to come; Allah will neither speak to them nor look at them nor purify them on the Day of Resurrection. A painful punishment is in store for them![50]

> In the meantime some camels of booty were brought to Allah's Apostle and he asked twice, "Where are Al-Ash'ariyin?" So he gave us five white camels with big humps.
>
> We stayed for a short while (after we had covered a little distance), and then I said to my companions, "Allah's Apostle has forgotten his oath. By Allah, if we do not remind Allah's Apostle of his oath, we will never be successful."
>
> So we returned to the Prophet and said, "O Allah's Apostle! We asked you for mounts, but you took an oath that you would not give us any mounts; we think that you have forgotten your oath."
>
> He said, "It is Allah Who has given you mounts. By Allah, and Allah willing, if I take an oath and later find something else better than, then I do what is better and expiate my oath."
>
> *Bukhari 67.427*

[49] 2:225 "Allah will not call you to account for thoughtlessness in your oaths, but for the intention in your hearts; and He is Oft-forgiving, Most Forbearing." *Yusuf Ali*

[50] When and why this revelation was sent:

Narrated Abdullah bin Mas'ud:

> Allah's Apostle said, "Whoever takes a false oath so as to take the property of a Muslim (illegally) will meet Allah while He will be angry with him."
>
> Al-Ash'ath said: "By Allah, that saying concerned me. I had common land with a Jew, and the Jew later on denied my ownership, so I took him to the Prophet who asked me whether I had a proof of my ownership. When I replied in the negative, the Prophet asked the Jew to take an oath."
>
> I said, "O Allah's Apostle! He will take an oath and deprive me of my property."
>
> So, Allah revealed the following verse: "Verily! Those who purchase a little gain at the cost of Allah's covenant and their oaths." (3.77)
>
> *Bukhari 41.599*

A parable about oaths:

> 16:91 Fulfil the Covenant of Allah when you make a covenant [with Him], and do not break the oats after you solemnly affirmed them, taking Allah as witness. Surely Allah knows what you do.
>
> 16:92 And do not be like her who unravels her yarn after she has spun it first; taking your oaths as means of deception among you, because one party is more numerous than another. Allah only tries you by this, and He will certainly may clear to you on the Day of Resurrection that whereon you differ.

The parable about the yarn spinner, according to Moududi, is supposed to be a warning to the Jews about breaking their oaths to Arabs; which brings up the next verse where Allah reveals that if He had been in the mood, He would have made Jews and Arabs "one nation".

> 16:93 Had Allah pleased, He would have made you one nation, but He leads whom He pleases astray and guides whom He pleases. And you will surely be questioned about what you did.

A warning for the believers about using oaths to deceive:

> 16:94 And do not make your oaths as means of deception among you, lest a foot should slip (lest your faith be shaken) after being firm, and lest you should taste evil on account of debarring others from Allah's Path. Grievous will be your punishment!

As a warning about obeying some who swear oaths, Allah gives the example of one of the two most detested kinsman and enemy of the Prophet (the other being Abu Lahab) to warrant a personal rancorous condemnation on His part.

> 68:7 Surely, your Lord knows better who has strayed from His Path and He knows better the well-guided.
>
> 68:8 So do not obey the unbelievers.
>
> 68:9 They wished that you would dissimulate, so that they might dissimulate too.
>
> 68:10 And do not obey every lowly swearer of oaths;
>
> 68:11 Backbiter, going around, bearing calumny;
>
> 68:12 Hinderer of good, aggressor, wicked;

68:13 Coarse, on top of that, and quarrelsome;

68:14 Because he (al-Walid Ibn al-Mughirah) has wealth and children.

More about al-Mughirah in *From Merchant to Messenger - The Prophet Muhammad's struggle for legitimacy as revealed in the Koran*, Boreal Books, 2012.

Immutable Truths About Slavery

Sometimes it is difficult to ascertain the moral or ethical imperative on which Allah bases His instructions. For example, His condoning slavery and condemning the practice of lending money at interest. Both convey an economic advantage to the slave-owner and the money-lender respectively. The transaction involving only money however, can be to the benefit of both contracting parties. The transaction in humanity, on the other hand, usually benefits only the title-holder while confining the *other* (the slave) to a life of miserable servitude.

A God's Dilemma

In 2002, the United Nations reported that the number of people forced into slavery around the world had risen to an estimated twenty-seven million. Irshad Manji, the aforementioned author of *The Trouble with Islam, A Wake-up Call For Honesty and Change* mentions the resurgence of the slave trade in African countries that have adopted the Koran as the equivalent of their constitution. Countries such as her native Uganda, Mali, Mauritania "where little boys are seduced into slavery by Muslim hustlers" to the Sudan where "Khartoum's onslaught has rekindled the trade in black slaves" to Nigeria "where Islamic governments encourage the enslavement of Christians."

The young Muhammad celebrated his marriage to the twice widowed Khadijah "by giving Barakak (the slave girl he had inherited from his father) her freedom. For her part, Khadijah gave her new husband a fifteen-year-old male slave named Zayd as a wedding gift." This marriage of the future Prophet, his first, took place more than twenty years before Allah would confirm the righteousness of both transactions in humanity in His Koran.

Allah is of two minds when it comes to slavery. His instructions concerning slavery exhibit this dichotomy. The most prominent is in revelations dealing with the treatment of female slaves. Whenever in these verses you encounter the phrase "what your right hands possess" or a variation thereof it means slave-girls. Slave-girls are captives of war; the wives of an enemy defeated in battle or females given as settlement of a debt or other obligations such as compensation to resolve a blood-feud. There are no revealed truths, to my knowledge, that offer *specific* advice on the treatment and disposal of male slaves.

The second type of verse on slavery deals mainly with situations where a slave might be freed; as penance for example. These revelations, if you are so inclined, can be interpreted as Allah encouraging slave owners to grant their human chattel their freedom. This interpretation notwithstanding, the Koran unambiguously allows slavery, including the enslavement of young women and girls and, what the Koran allows no one can deny, not even God's Messenger; that would be like contradicting God. Yet, in many verses like those that follow, Allah appears to go out of his way to find excuses for freeing slaves. He even, in the following revelation, calls "righteous" those who would spend their money to buy a slave's freedom.

> 2:177 Righteousness is not to turn your faces towards the East and the West; the righteous is he who believes in Allah, the Last Day, the angels, the Book and the Prophets; who gives of his money, in spite of loving it, to the near of kin, the orphans, the needy, the wayfarers and the beggars, and <u>for the freeing of slaves</u>; who performs the prayers and pays the alms-tax. Such are also those who keep their pledges once they have made them, and endure patiently privation, affliction and in times of fighting (in the Way of Allah). Those are the truthful and the God-Fearing.

Allah's suggestion about what believers should do with their money would have meant little, if anything, for female slaves. Under normal circumstances, you only freed slaves that had the means to look after themselves. In traditional Islamic society, the forced seclusion of women and their property-like status meant that a female slave could never be expected to be able to look after herself. Therefore, her slave status was more or less a lifetime thing, unless she was a believer and her proprietor decided to make her one of his four permanent wives or give her in marriage to another believer in return for some benefit or to settle an obligation.

One of the ingenious contrivances which Allah uses to compel slave owners to free some of their slaves is requiring the freedom of a slave as penance for a transgression. In the following verse Allah makes the freeing of a believing slave part of the payment for the accidental killing of a believer by another believer.

> 4:92 It is not given to a believer to kill another believer except by mistake; and he who kills a believer by mistake should free a slave who is a believer and pay blood-money

to his relatives, unless they remit it as alms. If he happens to belong to a people who are your enemies, but he is a believer, then you should free a believing slave. If he belongs to a people bound with you by a compact, then blood-money should be paid to his relatives and a believing slave should be freed. As for him who has not the means, he should fast for two consecutive months, as a penance from Allah. Allah is All-Knowing, Wise!

A slave could also find freedom in death as retribution for the deliberate killing of another slave-owner's property.

2:178 O believers, retaliation for the slain is prescribed for you; a free [man] for a free [man], a slave for a slave and a female for a female. But if he is pardoned by his brother (the aggrieved), usage should be followed (capital punishment would be replaced by blood-money) and he should pay him (the aggrieved) liberally and kindly. This is remission and mercy from your Lord. He who transgresses after that will have a painful punishment.

The freeing of a slave is also the penance if you ignore your wife's sexual needs, claiming she reminds you of your mother, and then wish to get back together to indulge in more than social intercourse. These revelations, which do not stipulate whether the slave to be freed must be a believer, are found in the somewhat aptly named surah, *The Pleading Woman*.

58:2 Those of you who ignore their wives saying: "You are like our mother's back", should know that they are not really their mothers. Their mothers are only those women who gave them birth, and they are certainly making a reprehensible statement and a lie. But Allah is indeed All-Pardoning, All-Forgiving.

58:3 And those who say of their wives: "You are like our mother's back", then retract what they said, have to free a slave before touching each other. That is what you are admonished, and Allah is Fully Aware of what you do.

A slave could also be freed as penance for a broken oath.

5:89 Allah will not take you to task for what is unintentional in your oaths, but will take you to task for the oaths you intentionally take. Expiation for it, is feeding ten poor people with such average food as you would feed your own families, clothing them or freeing one slave. But he who cannot find [the means] should fast three days. That is the

> expiation for your oaths when you have sworn (those oaths which you have not kept). Keep your oaths; that is how Allah makes clear His Revelations to you, that you may be thankful.

If you have a choice between marrying a believing slave or an unbelieving free-woman, Allah recommends that you marry a believing slave. This could also be construed as Allah again, doing what he can to free the slaves, in this instance a female slave, by making her a respectable women. Considering the significant demands placed on "free" Muslim women in traditional Islamic society, for many, this change of status may not have been an improvement. For example, unlike the female slave who could be given as a token offering to an *unbeliever* thereby perhaps improving her lot in life, a *free* woman could not marry an unbeliever.

> 2:221 Do not marry unbelieving women (polytheists) until they believe. A believing slave-girl is certainly better than an unbelieving woman, even if the latter pleases you. And do not give your women (believing women) in marriage to polytheists[51] until they believe. A believing slave is certainly better than a polytheist, even if the latter pleases you. Those (the polytheists) call to the Fire and Allah calls to Paradise and Forgiveness by His Leave; and He makes clear His Revelations to mankind so that they may be mindful.

For a believing woman, revelation 2:221 is a divine imperative; for a believing man, not necessarily so. An unbelieving female in the midst of believers would face extreme pressure to convert – slavery and death not being excluded – and become eligible to be claimed by a believing man for matrimonial purposes.

You should be kind to your slave-girls.

> 4:36 Worship Allah and do not associate with Him anything. Show kindness to the parents, to kinsmen, to orphans, the destitute, the close and distant neighbour, the companion by your side, and those whom your right-hands possess. Allah does not love the arrogant and the boastful,

> 4:37 Those who are niggardly, and order other people to be niggardly, and conceal what Allah has given them of His

---

[51] Fakhry's translation of verse 2:221 is the only translation consulted that uses the term polytheists i.e. idol worshippers instead of unbelievers. In his translation "marrying your women" to Christians and Jews would appear to be permitted. Since this seldom happens in practice, I side with what appears to be a majority of translators that a believing women cannot be given in marriage to a non-Muslim.

Bounty, We have prepared for the unbelievers a demeaning punishment.

Kindness does not extend to sharing the extra that Allah may have given you with your slave-girls.

> 16:71 Allah has favoured some of you over the others in provision; but those favoured will not give their provision to those [slaves] whom their right hands possess so as to be equal therein. Will they then deny Allah's blessings?

And being kind did not necessarily prohibit having non-consensual sex.

> **Abu Sirma said to Abu Sa'id al Khadri** (Allah be pleased with him): 0 Abu Sa'id, did you hear Allah's Messenger (may peace be upon him) mentioning al-'azl?
>
> He said: Yes, and added: We went out with Allah's Messenger (may peace be upon him) on the expedition to the Bi'l- Mustaliq and took captive some excellent Arab women; and we desired them, for we were suffering from the absence of our wives, (but at the same time) we also desired ransom for them.
>
> So we decided to have sexual intercourse with them but by observing 'azl (withdrawing the male sexual organ before emission of semen to avoid conception).
>
> But we said: We are doing an act whereas Allah's Messenger is amongst us; why not ask him?
>
> So we asked Allah's Messenger (may peace be upon him), and he said: It does not matter if you do not do it, for every soul that is to be born up to the Day of Resurrection will be born.
>
> *Imam Muslim 8:3371*

Why Slavery Cannot Be Simply Abolished

The question remains: "Why did Allah, in revelations that were meant to guide mankind for thousands of years, not simply abolish slavery?" Believers would say it is because Allah sees nothing wrong in enslaving your fellow men, women and children as long as it is done in accordance with the standard slavery practices prescribed in the Koran; and they are probably right.

Also, in the brutal, inescapable logic of Islam, how could a believer make amends for a transgression where a slave is part of the penance if he was not allowed to own slaves in the first place?

And then, there is revelation 30:30, the single most significant and probably insurmountable obstacle to the Islamic World formally renouncing slavery in all its forms, for it would be altering the original nature of Allah's Creation, of which slavery always was and is an integral part.

> 30:29 Yet, the wrongdoers have followed their fancies without knowledge. Who, then, will guide those whom Allah has led astray and who have no supporters?
>
> 30:30 So, set you face towards religion uprightly. It is the original nature according to which Allah fashioned mankind. There is no altering Allah's Creation. That is the true religion; but most men do not know.
>
> 30:31 Returning unto Him. Fear Him, perform the prayer and do not be like the idolaters;
>
> 30:32 Those who have rent their religion asunder and split into factions, each party rejoicing in what they had.

The Koran is not so much a philosophy of life as a set of rules. Allah will judge the believers based on their strict adherence to these rules. A slaver who follows Allah's revelations, including those governing slavery, is being a good Muslim.

The Koran's explicit condoning of slavery and the increase in the number of slaves around the world, especially in countries where traditional Islam finds acceptance, has to be particularly worrisome for non-traditional believers and unbelievers alike.

Slavery and the Prophet

Judging from a sample of the sayings and examples of the Prophet, God's Messenger is unequivocal in his approval of slavery. Remember, in Islamic law, where the Koran is ambiguous, the Prophet's saying or example is the law.

The Prophet rebuked a woman for freeing (manumitting) a slave-girl instead of giving her to an uncle.

> **Narrated Kurib:**
>
> The freed slave of Ibn 'Abbas, that Maimuna bint Al-Harith told him that she manumitted (freed) a slave-girl without taking the permission of the Prophet. On the day when it was her turn to be with the Prophet, she said, "Do you

know, O Allah's Apostle, that I have manumitted my slave-girl?"

He said, "Have you really?"

She replied in the affirmative.

He said, "You would have got more reward if you had given her (i.e. the slave-girl) to one of your maternal uncles."

Bukhari 47.765

The Prophet helped a man in need of money by selling his slave for him.

Narrated Jabir bin Abdullah:

A man decided that a slave of his would be manumitted after his death and later on he was in need of money, so the Prophet took the slave and said, "Who will buy this slave from me?"

Nu'aim bin Abdullah bought him for such and such price and the Prophet gave him the slave.

Bukhari 34.351

The Prophet cancelled a dying man's wish that six of his slaves be freed, manumitting only two and keeping the other four for himself or for someone else.

Imran b. Husain reported that a person who had no other property emancipated six slaves of his at the time of his death. Allah's Messenger (may peace be upon him) called for them and divided them into three sections, cast lots amongst them, and set two free and kept four in slavery; and he (the Holy Prophet) spoke severely of him.

Muslim 4112

The Prophet cancelled the freeing of a slave and sold it on behalf of its owner who had no other chattel.

Narrated Jabir:

A man manumitted a slave and he had no other property than that, so the Prophet cancelled the manumission (and sold the slave for him). No'aim bin Al-Nahham bought the slave from him.

Bukhari 41.598

One last hadith about what the Prophet had to say about slavery; and it's somewhat of a confounding one.

Narrated Anas bin Malik:

The Prophet said: "The freed slave belongs to the people who have freed him."

Bukhari 80.753

The Babylonian Exile and the Roman Diaspora

17:2 We gave Moses the Book and made it a guidance to the Children of Israel [saying]: "Do not take besides Me any other guardian."

17:3 O progeny of those whom We caused to be carried along with Noah; He was truly a very thankful servant.

17:4 And We decreed for the Children of Israel in the Book: "You shall make mischief in the land twice, and you shall become very haughty."

In 586 B.C. Nebuchadnezzar [634 – 562 BC] destroyed the *First Temple* and took the Jews into captivity to Babylon. The "mischief" in the Bible for this unfortunate turn of events was rebelling against God and disobeying his commandments.

17:5 And when the punishment for the first [making of mischief] became due, We sent forth against you servants of Ours possessing great might who went after you in your country. Thus our threat was accomplished.

In 539 B.C. Cyrus the Great proclaimed what has been called *The Edict of Cyrus* allowing all people who had been taken into captivity by the Babylonians to return home. It was not a military success, as intimated by the following revelation that allowed the Jews to return to Jerusalem and Judea, but a simple act of goodwill; a kindness for which the Jews honoured Cyrus in the Bible with the name Messiah (Isaiah 45:1)

17:6 Then, We gave you back your turn against them and aided you with wealth and children and increased you in number.

In A.D. 70, during the reign of the Roman Emperor Titus, it was time for the punishment again. Allah's servants this time around would be Roman legions who would destroy the rebuilt *Second Temple* and send the Jews into exile to no specific place.

17:7 [And We said]: "If you do good, you do good for yourselves, and if you do evil, you do it for yourselves too.

> And when the punishment for the second [making of mischief] became due, [We send our men again] to afflict you, and to enter the Mosque (Temple) as they entered it the first time and to utterly destroy what they conquered.

There is hope, but don't push it, or the unbelievers will really get it!

> 17:8 It may be that your Lord will have mercy on you; but if you go back [to mischief], We shall come back and make Hell a prison for the unbelievers.

Just follow the guide and believe, and pray for good not evil, and don't be hasty for God-sake!

> 17:9 Surely, this Qur'an guides to that which is most upright and announces to the believers who do good works the good news that they shall have a great reward.

> 17:10 And those who do not believe in the Hereafter, We have prepared for them a very painful punishment.

> 17:11 Man prays for evil, just as he prays for good; and man is very hasty.

Trees to Impress a God

With so many different types of trees on earth and so few trees mentioned in the Koran, it is assumed that those who are worthy of Allah's notice are the most impressive.

Author

The palm tree, the olive tree, the lotus tree, the acacia, a "gourd tree" and perhaps the banana tree, are the only variety of trees found on earth which Allah mentions by name in the Koran; with palms being the most often mentioned by a wide margin. In five translations consulted, two, Mohsin Khan's and Shakir's, interpret "talh" to mean banana tree. In Fakhry's, talh (acacia in Yemeni Arabic) is taken to be the genus acacia which does not contain any banana growing trees or scrubs.

The banana tree was first cultivated in the Mediterranean region around the year 650. The Prophet died in 632. Unless it's another miracle of the Koran that Allah was aware of the eminent arrival of banana cultivation in the Middle East, His Messenger was unlikely to be familiar with the fruit. And even if he was, having heard about it during his travels, it is questionable that he would have favoured the propagation of a Dark Age equivalent of Donovan's Electrical Banana among believers by having it mentioned in the Koran, considering the Prophet's aversion to phallic symbols and his legendary prudishness. God's Messenger was even worried about flutes as phallic symbols. He warned believers about the seductive power of musical instruments which resembled a man's penis, such as a flute, into which you blew or used your fingers to coax out a tune. This is why he banned the playing of all wind instruments.

Acacias (or banana?) trees are one of the rewards of the people of heaven, along with the lotus tree.

56:27 As for the Companions of the Right (people in heaven); and behold the Companions of the Right?

56:28 They are in the midst of thornless (sic) Lotus trees,

56:29 And braided acacias,

There is one extraordinary lotus tree in heaven, whose blossoms may be even unknown to Allah. This lotus tree marks the farthest boundary of the seventh level of Paradise, and near which the Prophet is said to have seen the angel Gabriel.

> 53:13 He has indeed seen him (Gabriel) a second time;
>
> 53:14 By the Lotus Tree of the outermost limit.
>
> 53:15 Close by it is the Garden of Refuge.
>
> 53:16 As the Lotus Tree was covered by that which covers it;

It is not known if Allah kept the infamous tree of Adam and his wife's fame, the "Tree of Immortality". As in the Book of Genesis, the type of tree is not mentioned in the Koran. There was no apple tree in Genesis and there is no apple tree in the Koran. Not so for the olive tree. Allah does not initially name the tree that produces olive oil and olives but He will tell you where you can find it, revelation 23:20, on earth, if not in heaven.

> 23:18 And We send down water from heaven in measure, then lodge it in the ground, although we are Able to allow it to drain away.
>
> 23:19 Then through it We produce for you gardens of palm trees and vines, from which you get many fruits whereof you eat.
>
> 23:20 And a tree (the olive tree) growing out of Mount Sinai that produces oil and condiments for eaters.

A by-product of the fruit of the olive tree powers Allah's Light.

> 24:35 Allah is the Light of the heavens and the earth. His light is like a niche in which there is a lamp, the lamp is in a glass, the glass is like a glittering star. It is kindled from a blessed olive tree, neither of the East nor the West. Its oil will almost shine, even if no fire has touched it. Light upon light, Allah guides to His Light whomever He pleases and gives the examples to mankind. Allah has knowledge of everything.

All conifers, evergreen and such are lumped into a general category of "green trees" whose main use is as firewood.

> 36:80 It is He Who produces fire from green trees for you; and behold you are kindling flames from it.

Hell has one tree. The Tree of Zaqqum can be found in the depth of Allah's Hell. Its unnamed fruit, when eaten, cooks your stomach from the inside.

44:43 The Tree of Zaqqum (the Tree of Bitterness) will certainly be

44:44 The food of the sinner.

44:45 Like molten lead, which boils in the bellies;

44:46 Like boiling water.

Trees, with perhaps the assistance of a strong wind, like everything else in Allah's creation (except for some stubborn human beings), bow down to Him.

55:6 And the shrubs (or stars) and the trees prostrate themselves.

22:18 Have you not seen that to Allah bows down whoever is in the heavens and whoever is on earth, as well as the sun, the moon, the stars, the mountains, the trees, the beasts and many of the people? And for many the punishment has been decreed. And he whom Allah humiliates, will have no one to honour him. Allah does whatever He pleases.

If trees were pens:

31:27 Were all trees on earth so many pens and the sea, coupled by seven other seas, supplying them with ink, Allah's Words would not be exhausted. Allah is, indeed, All-Mighty and Wise.

You Are What You Eat

The Table Is Set

The longest surah about what a believer can and cannot eat, dining etiquette and what he should do before partaking of Allah's edible bounty is appropriately titled *The Table*. The first revealed truth about food consumption and preparation is a decree outlawing the eating of game while on pilgrimage. The reason for this being a sin is not clear; but it may have something to do with not being tempted to interrupt your pilgrimage to go hunting for dinner.

THE TABLE

5 *Al-Mâ'idah*

*In the Name of Allah,
the Compassionate, the Merciful*

5:1 O believers, fulfil your obligations. Lawful to you are the beast of the flock, except what is being recited to you now: "Game is unlawful to you while you are on pilgrimage." Allah decrees whatever He pleases.

5:2 O believers, do not violate the Rites of Allah, or the Sacred Month, or the sacrificial offerings, or the animals with garlands, or those who repair to the Sacred House seeking the bounty and pleasure of their Lord. When you are through with the rites of pilgrimage, you can go hunting. And let not the hatred of those who debar you from the Sacred Mosque prompt you to transgress. Help one another in righteousness and piety, but not in sin and aggression. Fear Allah; Allah is Severe in retribution.

The longest verse in the Koran on what foods are halal (allowed) and what foods are haram (prohibited):

5:3 You are forbidden the eating of carrion, blood, the flesh of swine as well as whatever is slaughtered in the name of anyone other than Allah. [You are forbidden] also the animals strangled or beaten to death, those that fall and die, those killed by goring with the horn or mangled by wild beasts, except those which you slaughter and those sacrificed on stones set up [for idols]. [You are forbidden] to use divining arrows[52]; it is an evil practice. Today, those who disbelieve have despaired of your religion; so do not fear them, but fear Me. Today, I have perfected your religion for you, completed my Grace on you and approved Islam as a religion for you. Yet, whoever is compelled by reason of hunger (to eat what is forbidden), but not intending to sin, then surely Allah is All-Forgiving, Merciful.

What your dog, or trained falcon for example, catches for you, you can eat.

> 5:4 They ask you (O Muhammad) what is lawful to them. Say: "The good things are lawful; and such hunting birds or hounds that you have taught, as Allah has taught you. You may eat whatever they catch for you, mentioning Allah's name over it. Fear Allah, for Allah is, indeed, Quick in reckoning!"

What scholars believe is the last verse revealed to God's Messenger is about food, and about the women a believer can marry – go figure.

> 5:5 This day the good things have been made lawful to you; the food of the People of the Book is lawful to you, and your food is lawful to them; and so are the believing women who are chaste, and the chaste women of those who were given the Book before you, provided you give them their dowries and take them in marriage, not in fornication or as mistresses. If any one denies the faith, his work shall be of no avail to him, and in the Hereafter he will rank with the losers.

Allah's food guide includes only good and pleasant things. You should not eat anything else or deny the foods Allah allows, if you know what is good for you!

> 5:87 O believers, do not forbid the good things that Allah has made lawful to you and do not transgress; for Allah does not like the transgressors.

Do not be fooled by the pleasing, undoubtedly delicious fare that Allah has provided into thinking that He is not a god to be feared.

---

[52] Arrows used by pre-Islamic Arabs to cast lots. Divining arrows were strips of wood without points usually marked with values, inscriptions or symbols. These arrows were usually thrown haphazardly to divide the spoils, to foretell the future, to know the opinion of gods and so on.

> 5:88 Eat of the pleasant things which Allah has given you; and fear Allah in whom you believe.

Wine is not one of the good things!

> 5:90 O believers, wine, gambling, idols and divining arrows are an abomination of the Devil's doing; so avoid them that perchance you may prosper!

> 5:91 The Devil only wishes to stir up enmity and hatred among you, through wine and gambling, and keep you away from remembering Allah and from prayer. Will you not desist, then?

Allah's revelations pertaining to the decreed diet for the believers was probably delivered, like much of what He had to reveal, during one of His Messenger's homilies, where it would have been advisable to stay until the end.

> 5:92 Obey Allah and obey the Messenger and beware; but if you turn back, then know that is the duty of Our Messenger to deliver the clear Message.

The following somewhat convoluted revealed truth seems to imply that straying from Allah's decreed diet may not be that big of a deal if you do all the other things that He expects of a believer. But, I would not take a chance. Allah is a fickle God, it could also be a test.

> 5:93 Those who believe and do the good deeds are not to blame for what they eat, if they are God-fearing, believe and do the good deeds, then fear God, and believe, then fear God and do good. Allah loves the charitable.

Allah will tempt those performing the pilgrimage with game to confirm if they do what they are told when they think He is not looking.

> 5:94 O believers, Allah will certainly test you with some game that your hands or lances may catch, so Allah may know who fears Him unseen. Whoever transgresses thereafter shall be painfully punished.

The range of punishments for breaking Allah's injunction against catching and killing game during the pilgrimage:

> 5:95 O believers, do not kill game while you are on pilgrimage. Whoever of you kills it willfully will have to give the like of what he killed of cattle, as determined by two just men from yourselves, to reach the Ka'ba as an offering; or will have to feed as expiation a number of poor men, or the equivalent of that in fasting so that he may taste

the evil consequences of his action. Allah will pardon what is past; but he who offends again, Allah will wreck vengeance upon him. Allah is Mighty, Capable of Retribution.

Catching fish is not the same as catching land game when you are on pilgrimage.

> 5:96 Lawful to you is the catch of the sea and its food as an enjoyment for you and for travellers; but unlawful to you is the game of the land so long as you are on pilgrimage. Fear Allah unto Whom you shall be gathered.

The aptly named surah *The Table* is, of course, not the only place you find revelations as to what a believer can or cannot eat or drink. It would not be the Koran otherwise. In the surah *The Bees*, Allah prohibits the consumption of wine while lauding its production.

> 16:67 And from the fruits of palms and vines, you get wine and fair provision. Surely, there is in that a sign to a people who understand.

To keep within Allah's injunction that "You are forbidden ... whatever is slaughtered in the name of anyone other than Allah", revelation 5:3, the person killing an animal whose meat is destined for a believer's table must not only be a believer but must also praise Allah using the Arabic invocation "Bismillah Allah-u-Akbar" (In the name of God, And God is the greatest).

To "eat from that over which the Name of Allah has not been mentioned" is running the risk of being labelled an idol worshipper and all the bad things that entails.

> 6:121 And do not eat from that over which the Name of Allah has not been mentioned; it is indeed sinful. The devils shall insinuate to their followers to dispute with you; but if you obey them, then you will surely be polytheists.

A believer was not at fault if he ate any of the proscribed foods if it was not his intention to do so, or if it was a matter of necessity e.g. if he was "constrained" and could not avoid running afoul of Allah's Decree.

> 2:172 O believers, eat of the good things which We have provided for you and give thanks to Allah, if He is the One Whom you worship.
>
> 2:173 He has only forbidden you [to eat] carrion, blood, pork and that over which (when slaughtered) any name other than that of Allah is invoked. But he who is constrained (constrained to eat those forbidden things)

without intending to disobey or transgress, will commit no sin. Allah is Forgiving, Merciful.

16:114 Eat then from the lawful and good things which Allah provided you, and give thanks for Allah's blessing, if you truly worship Him.

16:115 He has forbidden you carrion, blood, the flesh of swine and that over which any other name than that of Allah is invoked. But whoever is compelled while neither transgressing nor exceeding the bounds, Allah is All-forgiving, Merciful.

Can only men feed on live-born calf or is it just those others gods sowing confusion as to what is haram and what is halal?

6:138 And they (other gods) say: These cattle and tilth (crops) are taboo, and none shall eat them except those we wish," as they claim. And there are cattle whose backs are forbidden, and others over which they do not mention the Name of Allah. Such is their fabrication about Him. [But] He will punish them for their lies.

6:139 And they say: "What is in the bellies of these cattle is lawful to our males, but forbidden to our wives. If it is still-born both can share it." [Allah] will punish them for what they attribute [to Him]. He is surely Wise, All-Knowing.

By killing your children foolishly you deprive them of the good things Allah has provided for them.

6:140 Those who kill their children foolishly without knowledge are real losers; and they forbid what Allah has provided for them, thus fabricating lies against Allah. They go astray and they are not well-guided.

Answering a Question with a Question and Pork is for Other Gods

Some listeners obviously had questions for the Prophet after he announced Allah's dietary rules. As He often does when asked a difficult question, Allah advises His Messenger to do what politicians do all the time, answer the question with a question and impute ulterior motives to the questioner, such as wanting to make Allah out to be a liar, by asking the question in the first place.

6:143 [Take] eight in pairs: of sheep two and of goats two. Say: "Has He forbidden the two males, or the two females, or what the womb of two females contain? Tell me if you a truthful."

> 6:144 And [take] of camels two and of cows [and oxen] two. Say: "Has He forbidden the two males, the two females, or what the womb of females contain? Or have you been witnesses when Allah commanded you to do this?" Who then is more unjust than he who imputes falsehood to Allah, in order to lead people astray, without knowledge? Surely, Allah will not guide the wrongdoing people.

Pork is for other gods, as Allah has His Messenger make clear in revelation 6:145 which appears to be in response to a question about a specific food which the Prophet skirts by repeating the general prohibitions Allah decreed in revealed truths 2:173 and 16:115 (remember the order of a revelation is not normally an indication of when it was received). Again, the questioner may also have been concerned about eating a forbidden food under duress i.e. "constrained", for Allah to request His Messenger to yet again provide assurance that if a believer has a bite about what only other god's eat because he has no choice, He will be forgiven!

> 6:145 Say: "I do not find in what has been revealed to me anything forbidden to an eater to eat from, unless it is carrion, or running blood, or the flesh of swine – which are unclean. For it is profane and slaughtered to [gods] other than Allah. However, he who is constrained, intending neither to commit a sin nor to exceed the bounds, then surely your Lord is All-Forgiving, Merciful.

Also, there is always the possibility that Allah's general prohibition about eating "carrion, or running blood, or the flesh of swine" was only communicated once, but because of the way the Koran was put together (appendix - *The First Koran*) remembered slightly differently by three different witnesses to what the Prophet said..

Vegetarians are not Muslims

Believers who do not eat what Allah has allowed e.g. meat are not real Muslims; and not only that, they may lead others astray by following "their fancies", revelation 6:119.

> 6:118 Eat, then, of that upon which the name of Allah has been mentioned, if you really believe in His Revelations.

> 6:119 And why is it that you do not eat from that upon which Allah's name is mentioned, when He has explained to you what is unlawful to you, except for what you are

compelled to [eat]? Indeed many shall lead others astray by their fancies, without any knowledge. Surely, your Lord knows best the transgressors.

A hadith confirming that those who do not eat what Allah has allowed, with the Prophet singling out eating meat as one of the four things he eats as a Muslim, are not believers:

> Three women approached the Prophet one day. One of them said, "O Prophet! My husband has shunned the company of his wife." The second said, "My husband has stopped eating meat!" The third said, "My husband has stopped using perfume!"
>
> Hearing the women, the Prophet was upset. He saw that misguided ideas were beginning to take root amongst his followers.
>
> Although it was not the time for any mandatory prayer, he proceeded to the mosque. He went in such a great hurry that even his cloak was not properly placed on his shoulder and one end of it was touching the ground. He ordered the people to assemble in the mosque. People rushed there leaving aside their tasks.
>
> The Prophet ascended the pulpit and said," I have heard that my companions are getting wrong ideas." He added, "I am Allah's Messenger, I eat meat and delicious food! I wear good clothes! I wear perfumes and keep the company of my wives and have conjugal relations with them! Whosoever opposes my ways is not my follower!"
>
> The Prophet has repeated this sentence on several occasions: "One who does not adopt my ways is not a Muslim".
>
> *Wasa'il*

Figs were a favourite food of the Prophet, not only for their taste but for their medicinal properties.

> If I had to mention a fruit that descended from paradise I would say this is it because the paradisiacal fruits do not have pits ... eat from these fruits for they prevent hemorrhoids, prevent piles and help gout.
>
> *Bukhari*

Pits or no pits melon, again according to Bukhari, "was among one of the fruits most often eaten by the prophet" and the same could be said for citrus fruits. The Prophet compared eating a "citrus" to reading the Koran.

> The parable of a believer who reads the Koran regularly is like that of a citrus it has a good taste and a good fragrance.
>
> *Bukhari*

What Do the Jews Have To Do With It!

At one point in time, Yahweh and Allah were in almost complete agreement as to the foods that the believers in both flavours of god (Jews and Muslims) could eat.

> 3:93 All food was lawful to the Children of Israel, save what Israel forbade itself before the Torah was revealed. Say: "Bring then the Torah and recite it, if you are truthful."
>
> 3:94 Whoever, afterwards, fabricates falsehood against Allah, those are truly the evildoers.

Why Allah imposed additional restrictions as to what Jews can eat.

> 6:146 We have forbidden the Jews every [animal] with claws; and the fat of oxen and sheep except what their backs or entrails carry, or what is mixed with bones. This was the punishment We inflicted on them on account of their aggression. We are surely Truthful.

Jesus of Nazareth did away with much of the dietary rules of the Old Testament. In one interpretation of Mark 7:19, Jesus declares all food clean therefore permissible, and in Acts 10:15, God in a vision to the apostle Peter, is said to declare that all formerly unclean animals are now clean therefore may be consumed: "Do not call anything impure that God has made clean". Therefore, the reference to "the food of the People of the Book is lawful to you" probably means the food of the Jews.

Leviticus in the Hebrew Bible contains many of the same restrictions as the Koran as to what an observant Jew can eat, the most obvious being the prohibition against pork and pork by-products – the most glaring difference being Allah's interdiction of intoxicants (the cautionary tale of Noah getting drunk after disembarking from the Ark would indicate that the God of the Old Testament expects the *People of the Book* to exercise moderation when consuming such beverages).

> 2:219 They ask you about wine and gambling, say: "In both there is great sin and some benefit for people. But the sin is greater than the benefit." And they ask you about what they

should spend, say: "What you can spare." Thus Allah makes clear to you His Revelations so that you may reflect,

2:220 Upon this world and the Hereafter ...

Eating of the good stuff not allowed by Allah and saying it is, as the Jews did, will give you momentary pleasure but lead to an eternity of hurt, unless you were not aware you were committing evil and repented afterwards.

> 16:116 And when you speak do not lie by saying: "This is lawful and this is unlawful", in order to impute lies to Allah. Surely those who impute lies to Allah will not prosper.
>
> 16:117 A little enjoyment and then a great punishment is store for them.
>
> 16:118 We forbade the Jews what We have related to you earlier. And We did not wrong them, but they wronged themselves.
>
> 16:119 Surely, with respect to those who commit evil in ignorance, and later repent and make amends, your Lord thereafter is All-Forgiving, Merciful.

Allah's dietary rules would have met with Abraham's approval.

> 16:120 Indeed, Abraham was a model [of virtue], obedient to Allah and upright; and he was not one of the polytheists.
>
> 16:121 [He was] thankful for His Blessings, and Allah elected him and guided him to a Straight Path.
>
> 16:122 We made him praiseworthy in this world, and in the Hereafter he will be one of the righteous.
>
> 16:123 Then We revealed to you (Muhammad): "Follow the religion of Abraham, the upright; for he was not one of the polytheists,"

Moududi:

> Prophet Muhammad (Allah's peace be upon him) was commanded to follow the way of Abraham and not the way of the Jews, and they themselves knew than these things were not unlawful in the law of Abraham. For instance, the Jews did not eat the flesh of camel but this was lawful according to Abraham. Likewise, ostrich, hare, duck, etc., were unlawful in the Jewish law, but they were lawful according to Abraham.

Where You May Dine

> 24:61 The blind are not at fault, the lame are not at fault, the sick are not at fault, nor are you if you eat in your houses, the houses of your fathers, the houses of your mothers, the houses of your brothers, the houses of your sisters, the houses of your paternal uncles, the houses of your paternal aunts, the houses of your maternal uncles, the houses of your maternal aunts, those of which you are in possession of the keys or those of your friend. You are not at fault if you eat altogether or separately, but if you enter any houses, greet each other with a blessed and good greeting from Allah. That is how Allah makes clear to you the Signs, that perchance you may understand.

Why Some Gods Go Hungry

Allah being the top god means that if you make Him an offering, along with an offering to lesser gods whose existence He both grudgingly acknowledges and vehemently denies throughout the Koran, the offering never reaches Him but it reaches these lesser gods (associate-gods in the following revelation) in whatever heaven they call home..

> 6:136 They assigned to Allah a share of the tilth (crop) and cattle He created, saying: "This is for Allah," - as they declare - "and this is for our associate-gods." And while that which is assigned to their associate-gods does not reach Allah, that which is set aside for Allah would reach their associate-gods. How evil is what they judge!

Two Once Extraordinary Verses About Tolerance

Of all the incongruities that devotees of a religion steeped in incongruities have to accept, the concept of abrogation has to be the most outlandish. Abrogation, i.e. retraction, annulment, cancellation ... is common in the real world as better information replaces old information. In the world of revealed truths, immutable facts revealed to a mortal by a god, abrogation should not even be the exception, it defies logic. Nevertheless, in the study of the Koran, a consensus of scholar agrees: superseding unassailable Divine communications have to be taken into account. Two verses of the more than two hundred abrogated verses which cannot be ignored, are revealed truths 2:62 and 109:6 which appear to sanction tolerance of practitioners of other religions.

> 2:62 The believers (Muslims), the Jews, the Christians and the Sabians – whoever believes in Allah and the Last Day and does what is good, shall receive their reward from their Lord. They shall have nothing to fear and they shall not grieve.

> 109:6 "You have your religion and I have mine."

Revelation 2:62 is said to be abrogated by 3:85:

> 3:85 Whoever seeks a religion other than Islam, it will never be accepted from him, and in the Hereafter he will be one of the losers.

Revelation 109:6 is said to be abrogated by the Verse of the Sword:

> 9:5 Then, when the Sacred Months (these are the four months during which war was prohibited in pre-Islamic times) are over, kill the idolaters wherever you find them, take them [as captives], besiege them, and lie in wait for them at every point of observation. If they repent afterwards, perform the prayer and pay the alms, then release them. Allah is truly All-Forgiving, Merciful.

According to the imminent Egyptian theologian Abu al-Fadl Abd ar-Rahman Jalal ad-Din as-Suyuti (d. 1505), "Everything in the Qur'an about forgiveness and peace is abrogated by verse 9:5."

No study of the Koran is complete without an introduction to the concept of abrogation, which is why I recommend you read *Let Me Rephrase That! Your Guide to Abrogations*, Boreal Books, 2015.

Even without taking the impact of abrogation into consideration, these two revelation about tolerance are not all they seem to be.

Revelation 2:62

When you come across a verse like reveal truth 2:62 you are taken aback because the message it appears to convey is so different from what you have been reading. Like all of Allah's seemingly universal declarations, there is a catch. Those who do not believe in an omnipotent monotheistic deity whose name is Allah e.g. Indians (Hindus), animists, atheists, agnostics… can do all the good they can, and live an exemplary life, it won't matter a whit. Allah may not even write their good deeds down. What would be the point!

> 20:112 And he who does the righteous deeds, <u>while a believer</u>, will fear neither injustice nor inequity.
>
> 21:94 Whoever does what is good, <u>while a believer</u>, his endeavour will not be denied, and We are indeed writing it down for him.
>
> ----
>
> 22:50 <u>Those who believe</u> and do the righteous deeds will receive forgiveness and a bountiful provision,
>
> 22:51 But who strive against our Revelations defying Us – those are the people of Hell.

Then, there are the ambiguous verses about the actual status of the people of the Book: believers, unbelievers or evildoers (people who associate other gods with Allah such as Christians obviously qualify).

> 29:46 Do not dispute with the people of the Book save in the fairest way; except for those of them who are evildoers. And say: "We believe in what has been sent down to us and what has been sent down to you. Our God and your God are one and to Him we are submissive."
>
> 29:47 And thus We have sent down to you the Book. Those to whom We gave the Book (the people of the Book, Jews and Christians) believe in it, and of these (the Prophet's

Meccans contemporaries) some believe in it. Our Signs are only denied by the unbelievers.

Then there is verse 45:14:

> 45:14 Tell the believers to forgive those who do not hope for Allah's Days (evil days from Allah, *Moududi*, calamities mostly, *Fakhry*), that He may reward a people for what they used to earn.

Is Allah really expecting the believers to forgive the unbelievers, and who is the reward for, and what is the reward? Is Allah being facetious? Moududi:

> The commentators have given two meanings of this verse and the words of the verse admit of both: (1) "That the believers should pardon the excesses of this wicked group so that Allah may reward them for their patience and forbearance and nobility from Himself and recompense them for the persecutions they have suffered for His sake." (2) "That the believers should pardon these people so that Allah may Himself punish them for their persecutions of them."
>
> Some other commentators have regarded this verse as repealed. They say that this command was applicable only till the Muslims had not been permitted to fight. Then, when they were permitted to fight, this command became abrogated.

Authors like Fouad Laroui ask us to forget all that other stuff, the nasty and pedantic stuff found in the Koran, what he calls, "window dressing", and concentrate on the good things the Koran has to say about getting along and doing God's work, such as:

> 2:215 They ask you (the question was put to the Messenger by a wealthy old man) what they should spend. Say: "Whatever bounty you give is for the parents, the near of kin, the orphans, the needy and the wayfarer. And whatever good you do, Allah is fully cognizant of it."

> 2:256 There is no compulsion in religion; true guidance has become distinct from error. Thus he who disbelieves in the Devil and believes in Allah grasps the firmest handle that will never break. Allah is All-Hearing, All-Knowing.

If only that were possible! Consider a revelation which contains a plea, a prayer; a somewhat amenable near-universal prayer if you ignore the last line. Pity!

2:286 Allah does not charge any soul beyond its capacity. It gets [rewarded for] what [good] it has earned, and is called to account for what [evil] it has committed. Lord, forgive us if we have forgotten or erred. Lord, do not lay on us a burden like that You laid on those before us, and do not burden us with what we cannot bear. Pardon us, forgive us and have mercy on us. You are our Protector. Give us victory over the unbelieving people.

Revelation 109:6

THE UNBELIEVERS
109 Al-Kâfirûn

*In the Name of Allah,
the Compassionate, the Merciful*

109:1 Say: "O unbelievers,

109:2 "I do not worship what you worship,

109:3 "Nor do you worship what I worship;

109:4 "Nor do I worship what you have worshipped,

109:5 "Nor do you worship what I worship[53],

109:6 "You have your religion and I have mine."

Unfortunately, revelation 109:6 is from a Meccan surah, a surah revealed during the Prophet's time in Mecca when he had few friends and only his say-so to convince his tribesmen that he was God's Messenger charged with delivering His final instructions for mankind, the Koran.

As he became more powerful, after fleeing Mecca for Medina, the Prophet discovered the persuasive power of the sword and Allah became a lot less tolerant, as is evident in the Medinan surah, *The Clear Proof*.

THE CLEAR PROOF
98 Al-Bayyinah

*In the Name of Allah,
the Compassionate, the Merciful*

98:1 The unbelievers, among the People of the Book and the idolaters, would not desist till the clear proof comes to them;

---

[53] Yes, except for the punctuation, verses 109:3 and 109:5 are exactly the same.

> 98:2 A Messenger (*the Prophet Muhammad*) from Allah reciting purified scrolls,
>
> 98:3 Wherein are valuable books.

Both Jews and Christians were not willing to accept Allah's contention, communicated via His latest self-proclaimed spokesperson, the Prophet Muhammad, and contained within the Book itself, that He sent the Koran to correct errors that had allegedly crept into an earlier scriptural manuscript of His: the Bible.

> 98:4 Those who were given the Book (*the Bible*) did not diverge except after the clear proof (*the Qur'an*) came to them.

For their refusal to accept the Koran as the overriding Message i.e. "the clear proof", and Islam as the superior religion i.e. "the religion of truth" they will be joining the idolaters in Hell, revelation 98:6.

> 98:5 And they were only commanded to worship Allah, professing the religion sincerely to Him as upright believers, to perform the prayers and give the alms. That is the religion of truth.
>
> 98:6 The unbelievers, among the People of the Book and the idolaters, shall be in the Fire of Hell, dwelling therein forever. Those are the worst of creatures.
>
> 98:7 Those who have believed and did the righteous deeds – those are the best of creatures.
>
> 98:8 Their reward with their Lord will be Gardens of Eden, beneath which rivers flow, dwelling therein forever. Allah is well-pleased with them and they are well-pleased with Him. That is the lot of whoever fears His Lord.

One more revelation about those who "quarrelled after the clear proofs came to them" being severely punished, revelation 3:105, a revealed truth in which the "clear proof" has morphed into "the clear proofs".

> 3:100 O believers, if you obey a group of those who have received the Book, they will turn you, after you have believed, into unbelievers.
>
> 3:101 How could you disbelieve, while God's revelations are recited to you, and His Messenger is in your midst? He who holds fast to Allah has been guided to a straight path.
>
> 3:102 O believers, fear Allah as He should be feared, and do not die except as Muslims.

3:103 And hold fast to Allah's Bond (his religion), all of you, and do not fall apart. And remember Allah's grace upon you; how you were enemies, then He united your hearts (by becoming Muslims) so that you have become, by His Grace, brethren. You were on the brink of the pit of Fire, but He saved you from it. Thus Allah manifests to you His Revelations so that perchance you might be rightly guided!

3:104 And let there be among you a nation calling to goodness, bidding the right and forbidding the wrong. Those are the prosperous.

3:105 And do not be like those who fell apart and quarrelled, after the clear proofs came to them. For those a terrible punishment is in store.

Tidbits Meccan Surahs

Tidbit: "A small and particularly interesting item of information"

While the Koran offers little in terms of a timeline, Scholars have grouped Allah's revealed truths into two time periods; what he revealed to the Prophet during His Messenger's time in Mecca, and what He later communicated to him after His latest and greatest spokesperson took up residence in Medina.

Allah taketh away and Allah giveth back.

> 6:46 Say: "Tell me! If Allah were to take away your hearing and sight and seal your hearts, what god other than Allah would give them back to you?" Behold, how We make plain Our Revelations, but they turn away.

How Allah puts the arrogant and the wealthy to the test.

> 6:53 Likewise, We test some of them through others[54] so that they may say: "Are these the ones whom Allah has favoured among us?" Does not Allah know best the thankful?

If Allah is Merciful to the evildoers who repent and mend their ways it is because, according to Moududi, He has to be; it is "incumbent" i.e. obligatory.

> 6:54 And when those who believe in Our Revelations come to you, say: "Peace be upon you. Your Lord has prescribed Mercy upon Himself (made mercy incumbent upon Himself, *Moududi*), that he who perpetrates evil in ignorance, repents afterwards and mends his ways [will find Him] All-Forgiving, Merciful.

Now you know how to spot the criminals in your midst, the vast majority will be those who do not believe in Allah's revelations.

---

[54]By enabling the poor and the indigent, the people who have a low station in society to precede others in believing, God has put those who wax proud of wealth and honour to a severe test. *Moududi*

6:55 And thus We expound the revelations so that the way of the criminals becomes clear.

Allah the Best-Decision-maker knows who to punish and when, as a good decision maker should.

6:57 Say: "I have clear proof from my Lord, and you deny Him. I do not possess that which you seek to hasten [punishment]. Judgement is Allah's alone; He determines the right, and He is the Best-Decision-maker."

6:58 Say: "If I possessed that which you seek to hasten, the matter between you and me would have been settled; and Allah knows best the wrongdoers."

Allah delivers people from the depths of both land and sea; a comfort for both sailors and miners, I am sure.

6:63 Say: "Who will deliver you from the dark depths of the land and the sea? You call upon Him humbly and secretly saying: 'If He delivers us from this we will certainly be thankful.'"

6:64 Say: "Allah delivers you from this and from every distress; yet you associate [other gods with Him]."

That Allah is responsible for armed conflicts and the ensuing death and destruction is self-evident, and is another of Allah's many signs that He is not a figment of someone's imagination, that He really does exist.

6:65 Say: "It is He Who has the power to inflict upon you punishment from above you or from under your feet; or to mix you up dividing you into factions, and make you taste the might of one another." See, how We make plain our revelations, that, perchance they might understand.

Fear the Author of the "true guidance", for He is more than just a guide, and you have His Messenger's word on that.

6:71 Say: "Shall we call, besides Allah, on what neither profits nor harms us, and turn on our heels after Allah has guided us?" [We shall then be] like one who, being tempted by the devils in the land, is bewildered though he has friends who call him to guidance [saying]: "Come to us." Say: "Guidance from Allah is the true guidance. And we are commanded to submit to the Lord of the Words;

6:72 "And perform the prayers and fear Him; for He is the One unto Whom you shall be gathered."

> 6:73 It is He who created the heavens and the earth in truth, and the Day He says: "Be", it will come to be. His Word is the Truth, and His is the sovereignty on the Day the trumpet is blown (Judgement Day). The Knower of the Unseen and the Seen, He is the Wise, the Well-Aware [of all things].

Allah and that vision thing (remember Bush junior):

> 6:103 Vision does not attain Him, but He attains the vision, and He is the Kind, the All-Knowing.

Allah love His Messengers, one has to assume, even if He does not care to reign in the enemy He assigns to each.

> 6:112 Likewise, We have assigned to every Prophet an enemy, the devils of men and jinn, revealing one to the other tawdry speech in order to deceive; but had your Lord willed, they would not have done it. So leave them to what they invent;
>
> 6:113 So that the hearts of those who do not believe in the Hereafter may incline to it and accept it; as well as to perpetrate that which they themselves are perpetrating.

Allah is the only judge you want; He wrote the Book on justice!

> 6:114 Shall I seek a judge other than Allah, when He is the one Who sent down the Book fully expounded? Those to whom We have given the Book (the Torah) know that it is revealed from your Lord in truth. Do not then be one of the doubters.
>
> 6:115 The Word of your Lord has been completed in truth and justice; no one can change His Words. He is the All-Hearing, the All-Knowing.
>
> 6:116 And were you to obey most people on earth, they will lead you away from the Path of Allah. They follow nothing but conjecture, and they only lie.
>
> 6:117 Your Lord knows best who strays from His Path, and He knows best who are the rightly guided.

Allah establishes leading sinners in every city, which He will, more often than not, then destroy, pitilessly slaughtering every men, women and child because of the presence of wrongdoers He placed among them.

> 6:123 And thus We have set up in every city its leading wicked sinners so as to plot therein. However, they only

plot against themselves, although they do not realize it.

Allah refused to favour with a spectacle to awe his audience, as He did for Moses and lesser prophets, His greatest and last Messenger, the Prophet Muhammad, leaving some to wonder why.

> 6:124 And if a sign comes to them, they say: "We will not believe, until we are given the like of what Allah's Messengers have been given." Allah knows best where to place His Message. Those who commit sins will suffer humiliation and severe punishment from Allah on account of their plotting.

If your heart feels constricted as if rising in the air, that is Allah's doing.

> 6:125 Whomever Allah wants to guide, He opens his heart up to Islam, and whomever He wants to lead astray, He makes his heart extremely constricted, as though he were ascending to heaven. Thus Allah inflicts His punishment upon those who do not believe.

> 6:126 This is the Path of your Lord, perfectly Straight. We have expounded the revelations to people who take heed.

> 6:127 Theirs is the abode of peace with their Lord and He is their Protector, for what they used to do.

If you take devils for patrons you might think you are being righty guided. But, you would be wrong, and you have Allah's Word on it!

> 7:30 "A group of you He has guided and another group was doomed to error; for they have taken the devils for patrons, apart from Allah, and they still think that they are rightly guided."

Allah controls His Universe from a seated position.

> 7:54 Your Lord is truly Allah, Who has created the heavens and the earth in six days, then He sat upon the Throne. He covers the day with the night, which pursues it relentlessly. The sun, the moon and the stars are made subservient by His Command. To Him belongs the Creation and the Command. Blessed is Allah the Lord of the Worlds.
>
> ----
>
> 10:3 Truly, your Lord is Allah Who created the heavens and the earth in six days, then He sat on the Throne controlling all things. There is no intercessor without His Leave. That is Allah, your Lord; so worship Him. Do you not pay heed?

Call on Allah humbly in secrecy, in fear and hope etc.

> 7:55 Call on your Lord humbly and secretly. He certainly does not like the aggressors.

> 7:56 And do not sow corruption in the land after it has been put in order. Call on Him with fear and hope. Allah's Mercy is indeed close at hand for the beneficent.

People are so ungrateful!

> 10:12 And if hardship afflicts man, he calls Us lying down, sitting or standing; but when We lift his hardship, he passes on, as if he never called Us to [lift] a hardship that afflicted him. Thus what the transgressors do seems fair to them.

Aggressive ungrateful people whom He saves from drowning and provides with a safe landing only to have them resort to unjustified violence.

> 10:22 It is He who makes your journey on land and on sea; so that when you are in the ships and they sail with them driven by a fair wind, and they rejoice in it, a stormy wind comes upon them and waves surge over them from every side, and they think that they are being overwhelmed. Then they call upon Allah, professing submission to Him sincerely: "If you save us from this, we shall be truly thankful."

> 10:23 But when He saves them, they resort to aggression in the land wrongfully. O people, your aggression shall recoil upon yourselves. It is what you enjoy in the present life; then unto Us shall be your return; whereupon We will inform you about what you were doing.

Allah has an illiterate's fascination with books and writing, even what animals do and when is recorded in the Book.

> 11:6 There is no beast on earth but its sustenance is [provided] by Allah; and He knows its resting place and its repository. All is in a Manifest Book.

Allah's Throne floats, or hovers.

> 11:7 And it is He Who created the heavens and the earth in six days, and His Throne was upon the water, that He might try you [and see] which one of you does the best work. And if you (the Prophet) say: "You will surely be raised up after death", the unbelievers will say: "This is nothing but manifest sorcery."

Allah is a whimsical God who "does whatever He pleases".

> 14:27 Allah confirms those who believe with the firm word in the present life, and in the life to come; but He leads the wrongdoers astray. Allah does whatever He pleases.
>
> 14:28 Have you not seen those who turn Allah's Grace into disbelief and lead their people to the abode of ruin (Hell)?
>
> 14:29 In Hell they will burn, and what a wretched abode!
>
> 14:30 And they set up equals to Allah in order to lead people away from His Path. Say: "Take your pleasure; for your fate is the Fire."

Allah is a god who just keeps on giving; but, are you grateful. Nooo ...

> 14:34 He gives you all you ask Him for. And were you to count Allah's favours you will never be able to exhaust them. Man is truly unjust and ungrateful.

How Allah creates things out of nothing.

> 16:38 And they solemnly swear by Allah that Allah will not raise from the dead anyone who dies. Surely, His is the true promise, but most people do not know.
>
> 16:39 [They shall be raised up] so as to make clear to them that whereof they differ, and that the unbelievers may know that they were lying.
>
> 16:40 Indeed, when We want a thing to be, We just say to it: "Be", and it comes to be.

Angels are not too proud to prostrate themselves before Allah.

> 16:49 And before Allah all creatures in the heavens and on the earth, together with the angels, prostrate themselves, and they are not proud.
>
> 16:50 They fear their Lord, high above them, and they do what they are commanded.

Allah has instructions for bees and knows about the healing properties of honey as did His Messenger[55].

---

[55] **Narrated Ibn Abbas:**

(The Prophet said), "Healing is in three things: A gulp of honey, cupping, and branding with fire (cauterizing). But I forbid my followers to use (cauterization) branding with fire."

Bukhari 71.584

> 16:68 And your Lord revealed to the bees: "Build homes in the mountains, the trees and in what men construct for you.
>
> 16:69 "Then eat from all the fruits and follow your Lord's smoothed paths." From their bellies comes out a syrup of different hues, wherein is healing for mankind. Surely, in that there is a sign for a people who reflect.

You will one day forget Who is responsible for you forgetting.

> 16:70 Allah created you, then He will cause you to die. For some of you will be brought back to the worst age, so that they will no longer know anything, after having acquired knowledge. Surely, Allah is All-Knowing, All-Powerful.

Allah provides the brides who will provide you what you and He prefer: sons and grandsons.

> 16:72 Allah has given you wives from among yourselves, and from your wives, sons and grandsons, and has provided you with all the good things. Will they believe in falsehood, then, and deny Allah's Blessings?
>
> 16:73 And they worship, besides Allah, what cannot provide anything for them from the heavens or the earth and can do nothing.

Allah's heart may be in the right place; but, what about all the poor unbelievers who do good?

> 16:97 Whoever does a good deed, whether male or female, while a believer, We shall make him live a good life; and We will give them a better reward than what they have done.

Those over whom the "accursed Devil" has no authority:

> 16:98 When you recite the Qur'an, seek refuge with Allah from the accursed Devil.
>
> 16:99 He has no authority over those who believe and have put their trust in their Lord.
>
> 16:100 His authority is only over those who befriend him and who associate others with Him (Allah).

Allah will amply reward those who have a death wish, even if their striving for the Hereafter leaves them stranded in the here-and-now, they will be rewarded with an increase in rank. Death, however, holds promises of a higher ranking.

> 17:19 But as for those who desire the Hereafter and strive

for it, as they should, while they are believers, their effort will be appreciated.

17:20 For them all – these and those – We shall provide from Allah's Bounty; and the Bounty of your Lord will not be denied to anyone.

17:21 Behold how We have made some of them surpass the others, although the Hereafter is far higher in rank and more preferable.

If Allah saves you from this or that peril, remember to give thanks, or you may find yourself in a worse mess.

17:66 Your Lord who drives for you the ships at sea, that you may seek His Bounty. He is indeed Merciful to you.

17:67 And if you are touched by adversity at sea, those you call upon other than He will wander away; but when He delivers you to land safely, you turn away. Man is ever thankless.

17:68 Are you, then, assured that He will not cause the land to cave in under you, or release a sandstorm upon you, and then you will find no one to protect you?

17:69 Or are you assured that He will not return you to it a second time, releasing upon you a roaring wind and drowning you, on account of your disbelief. Then you will find no one to defend you against us.

Allah speaks plainly and clearly:

THE CAVE

18 Al-Kahf

*In the Name of Allah,
the Compassionate, the Merciful*

18:1 Praise be to Allah, Who revealed the Book to His servant and did not leave in it any crookedness.

18:2 He has made it straight to warn of severe punishment from Himself and announce the good news to the believers, who do righteous deeds, that they shall have a good reward (Paradise).

18:3 Abiding therein forever.

What is better than wealth and children?

18:46 Wealth and children are the adornment of the present

life, but the everlasting good works are better in your Lord's Sight in reward and better in expectations.

A lesson for mankind explained:

> 21:92 This, your community is indeed a single community and I am your Lord; so worship Me.
>
> 21:93 They fell apart into factions; but they will all return unto Us.

Moududi:

> [these verses address] the whole of mankind. It means: "O mankind, in reality all of you belonged to one community and had one and the same religion and all the Prophets brought one and the same Creed which was this: `Allah alone is the Lord of all mankind: therefore they should worship Him alone."' But afterwards the people corrupted this Creed and invented and adopted the things they liked and mixed their own theories, whims and practices in it. This brought into being countless communities and religions.

The sound of light! Allah is the only god who could have brought you daylight. Do you not hear? Do you not see? So give thanks!

> 28:71 Say: "Have you considered, what if Allah had made the night to last for you continuously until the Day of Resurrection? What other god than Allah will bring you light? Do you not hear?"
>
> 28:72 Say: "Have you considered, what if Allah had made the day to last for you continuously until the Day of Resurrection? What other god than Allah will bring the night to rest in? Do you not see?"
>
> 28:73 It was out of His Mercy that He created the day and the night, so that you may rest in it and seek some of His Bounty, that perchance you may give thanks.

Allah will test those who say "We believe" in private.

THE SPIDER

29 Al `Ankabut

*In the Name of Allah,
the Compassionate, the Merciful*

29:1 Alif – Lam – Mim.

29:2 Have the people supposed that they will be left alone to say: "We believe", and then they will not be tested?

29:3 We have indeed tested those who preceded them; and Allah shall certainly know those who speak the truth and shall know those who lie.

29:4 Or have those who do the evil deeds supposed that they will outstrip Us? Wretched is what they judge!

Those who say they will bear your sins are liars!

29:11 And Allah certainly knows the believers and He knows the hypocrites.

29:12 The unbelievers said to the believers: "Follow our path and let us bear your sins"; but they will not bear any of their sins. Indeed they are liars.

29:13 They shall bear their own burdens, plus burdens upon burdens, and they will be questioned on the Day of Resurrection concerning what they used to fabricate.

It is a righteous deed to honour your parents; that is, unless they believe in Allah's obsession: the damned associates.

29:8 We have commanded man to be kind to his parents; but if they strive with you to associate with Me that of which you have no knowledge, then do not obey them. Unto Me is your return and I will tell you what you used to do.

29:9 Those who believe and do the righteous deeds, We shall admit them into the company of the righteous.

Allah knows what is in the "breasts of all of mankind".

29:10 There are some people who say: "We believe in Allah", but if one of them is injured on account of Allah, he reckons the persecution of men similar to Allah's punishment. If, however, victory comes from your Lord, they will say: "We were with you." Does not Allah know better what is in the breasts of the whole of mankind?

Allah's earth may be vast, but it is still not vast enough for more than one god.

29:56 O my servants who believe and do the righteous deeds, My earth is vast, so worship Me alone.

Allah provides for both beasts and humans.

> 29:60 How many a beast does not bear its provision, yet Allah provides for it and for you. He is All-Hearing, All-Knowing.

A taste of mercy!

> 30:33 When people are visited by some adversity, they call upon their Lord, turning to Him; but when He lets them taste a mercy from Him, behold, a group of them associate [other gods] with their Lord;

> 30:34 So as to be ungrateful for what We have given them. Indulge yourselves, then. For you shall certainly know!

> 30:35 Or have We sent down to them an authority, and he speaks about that which they were associating with Him?

> 30:36 If We let people taste a certain mercy, they rejoice at it; but if misfortune befalls them, on account of what their hands have perpetrated, behold, they are in despair.

> 30:37 Have they not seen that Allah expands and restricts the provision for whomever he wishes? Surely, there are in that signs for a people who believe.

> 30:38 So, give the kinsman his due, as well as the destitute and the wayfarer. That is better for those who desire the Face of Allah. Those are the prosperous.

Why Allah will allow some to keep ill-gotten-gains:

> 30:41 Corruption has appeared in the land and the sea, on account of what men's hands have earned; so that He may let them taste the reward of some of their deeds, that perchance they may return.

Sandstorms are supposed to make you believe in God. Where snow falls, a wind turning white should serve the same purpose.

> 30:51 And were We to send forth a wind and they saw it turning yellow, they would continue thereafter to disbelieve.

Some people never go gray. Must be the devil's doing or Grecian formula.

> 30:54 It is Allah who created you from a weak substance, then gave you strength after weakness, then after strength weakness and grey hair. He creates what He pleases and He is the All-Knowing, All-Powerful.

How Allah creates night and day:

> 31:29 Have you not seen how Allah causes the night to phase into the day, and the day to phase into the night; and He has subjected the sun and the moon, each of them running to an appointed term, and that Allah is Well-Aware of what you do?
>
> 31:30 That is because Allah is the Truth and what they call upon, apart from Him, is the falsehood and that Allah is the All-High, the Great.

> 35:13 He causes the night to phase into the day and the day to phase into the night and He has subjected the sun and the moon, each running for an appointed term. That is Allah, your Lord to whom belongs the dominion, whereas those you call upon, from Him, do not possess a date's crust.

Allah may send down the rain, know when He will bring about Judgement Day, know if you are pregnant, know what will become of the fetus; but claiming that no "living soul know in what land it shall die" can't be right – two example of people knowing their time and place of death are those who take their own lives instead of keeping to some mythical god's timetable and the condemned man.

> 31:34 Allah surely has the knowledge of the Hour and He sends down the rain. He knows what is in the wombs, whereas no soul knows what it shall earn tomorrow; nor does any living soul know in what land it shall die. Allah is All-Knowing, Well-Informed.

Allah is a real Know-it-all:

THE CITY OF SHEBA

34 Saba'

In the Name of Allah,
the Compassionate, the Merciful

> 34:1 Praise be to Allah, to whom belong whatever is in the heavens and whatever is on earth, and praise be to him in the Hereafter. He is the All-Wise, the All-Informed.
>
> 34:2 He knows what penetrates into the earth and what goes out of it, what descends from heaven and what ascends to it. He is the All-Merciful, the All-Forgiving.

For the Knower of the Unseen, not even a particular of dust will escape His attention.

> 34:3 The unbelievers say: "The Hour will not come for us." Say: "Yes, indeed, it will come, by my Lord, Knower of the Unseen, from Whom not the weight of a speck of dust will escape in the heavens or on earth; nor is anything smaller or bigger than that but is in a Manifest Book."

And by the way, if you have to barter you provision in the performance of some righteous deed, we have to assume, Allah will replace it, no questions asked because of the good provider He is.

> 34:39 Say: "It is my Lord Who expands the provision to whomever of His servants He wishes and restricts it. Anything you spend, He will replace it. He is the Best of Providers."

Present, past, future tense, it's all the same to Allah. The Hereafter should come after:

> 34:51 If you could see how they were terrified. There was no escape, and they were seized from a near place[56].

> 34:52 And they say: "We believe in it", but whence can they attain it (the belief) from afar?[57]

The different hues of fruits, animals and people is Allah's doing.

> 35:27 Have you not seen how Allah sends water down from the sky, and then We bring forth thereby fruits of diverse hues. And of the mountains there are lanes, white and red, of diverse hues, and some pitch dark.

> 35:28 And of people, beast and cattle, some are of diverse hues also. Indeed, of His servants, only the learned fear Allah. Allah is All-Mighty, All-Forgiving.

As every businessman and merchant knows, you have to spend money to make money. Praying may also be beneficial to the bottom line.

> 35:29 Surely, those who recite the Book of Allah, perform the prayer and spend of what we provided for them, secretly and publically, may hope for a trade which does not slacken.

---

[56] "On the Day of Resurrection, every culprit will be seized in a way as though he lay in hiding close by." *Moududi*

[57] "They should have believed when they lived in the world; they have come a long way away from it. After having arrived in the Next World how can they get a chance to repent and believe?" *Moududi*

> 35:30 That He might pay them their wages and increase them from His Bounty; He is indeed All-Forgiving, All-Thankful.

Allah's Way is the only way, and that will never change, and there is nothing you can do about it. To even try to make Allah adapt to changing circumstances and a more enlightened constituency is to invite retaliation on a genocidal scale!

> 35:42 They (the Arabs, *Moududi*) swore their most earnest oaths that if a warner came to them they would surely be more guided than a certain nation (the Jewish or Christian nation). But when a warner came to them, that only increased their aversion.
>
> 35:43 Out of arrogance in the land and evil cunning. Yet the evil cunning will only recoil upon its perpetrators. Do they then look to anything other than the way of the ancients? For you will never find any alteration of Allah's Way, and you will never find any deflecting of Allah's Way.
>
> 35:44 Have they not travelled in the land to see what was the fate of those who came before them and were even mightier than they? Nothing in the heavens or the earth can thwart Allah; He is indeed All-Knowing, All-Powerful.

If in old age you have lost a few centimeters in height, that is also Allah's doing, don't you know.

> 36:68 Whoever We grant old age, We would cause to shrink in form. Do they not understand, then?

Angel groups you may have never heard of ("The majority of the commentators are agreed that all these three groups (revelations 37:1-3) imply the groups of the angels" *Moududi):*

THE RANGERS

37 As-Sâffât

*In the Name of Allah,
the Compassionate, the Merciful*

> 37:1 By the rangers ranged in rows;
>
> 37:2 By the reprovers (sic) reproving;
>
> 37:3 By the reciters of a Reminder;
>
> 37:4 Your God is surely One,
>
> 37:5 The Lord of the heavens and the earth and what lies between them, Lord of the Orients.

37:164 There is not one of us but has a well-known station.

37:165 And we are indeed the rangers.

37:166 And We are those who glorify.

The bounteous who will have a bounty in both worlds.

39:10 Say: "O My servants who have believed, fear your Lord. Those who have been bounteous in this world will have a bounty, and Allah's earth is vast. The steadfast will be paid their wages in full, without reckoning."

The good and bad about the Word!

39:17 Those who shunned the worship of idols and turned in repentance unto Allah, theirs is the good news. "Announce, then, the good news to My servants."

39:18 Those who hear the Word and follow the fairest of it; those are the ones whom Allah has guided and those are the people of understanding!

39:19 He upon whom the Word of punishment has been uttered, are you able to deliver from the Fire?

Allah's discourse leaves a palpable harsh imprint followed by a mellowing effect on both the skins and hearts of those who hear it.

39:22 Now, what of one whose breast Allah has dilated unto Islam, so that he basks in light from his Lord? Woe betide then the hard-hearted, upon Allah's mention. Those are in manifest error.

39:23 Allah has sent down the fairest discourse as a Book, both insistent and corroboratory, from which the skins of those who fear their Lord shiver. Then their skins and hearts mellow at the mention of Allah. That is the guidance of Allah whereby He guides whomever He wishes; and he whom Allah leads astray will have no guide.

With Allah, bad deeds don't have to be a deal breaker. Paradise can still be yours if you have enough offsetting good deeds.

39:32 Who, then, is more unjust than one who imputes lies to Allah and denounces the Truth as a lie when he hears it? Is not in Hell an abode for the unbelievers?

39:33 But he who brings the Truth and believes in it – those are the true God-fearing people.

> 39:34 They shall have what they wish from their Lord. That is the reward of the beneficent.
>
> 39:35 That Allah might remit their worst deeds and reward them their due according to the fairest deeds they used to do.

Allah's punishment is not only lasting, it is downright degrading.

> 39:40 "Whoever is visited by punishment will be degraded by it and a lasting punishment will befall him."

Allah can't be bribed, and don't even try.

> 39:47 Had the wrongdoers possessed all that is on earth and the like of it too, they would have redeemed therewith themselves from the terrible punishment of the Day of Resurrection, and there would have appeared to them from Allah that which they did not count on.
>
> 39:48 And there would have appeared to them the evils of what they have earned, and what they scoffed at would have afflicted them.

If Allah mends an injury, don't think it is because you are special, that you have "some knowledge" that others don't have. If you do, you may be smitten by something much worse.

> 39:49 When an injury touches a man, he calls upon Us. Then if We accord him a bounty from Us, he says: "I have been granted it on account of some knowledge." However, it is a mere trial, but most of them do not know.
>
> 39:50 Thus those who preceded them have said it, but what they have earned did not avail them.
>
> 39:51 And so the evils of what they had earned smote them, and the evil-doers among these will be smitten by the evils of what they earned; and they will not frustrate Us.

Don't expect Allah's Mercy in the Hereafter if you have not repented in the here-and-now.

> 39:53 Say: "O My servants, who have been excessive against themselves: Do not despair of Allah's Mercy; Allah remits all sins. He is indeed the All-Forgiving, the All-Clement.
>
> 39:54 "Return to your Lord and submit to Him before punishment visits you then you will have no support.

> 39:55 "And follow the fairest of what has been sent down to you from your Lord, before punishment visits you suddenly while you are unaware."

Allah's considers His creation of the heavens (seven of them to be exact) and the earth a greater accomplishment than creating life from dirt.

> 40:57 Surely, the creation of the heavens and the earth is greater than the creation of mankind, but most people do not know.

Allah does not have to be the only one with the fairest of speeches.

> 41:33 Who is fairer in speech than one who calls unto Allah and performs the righteous deeds and says: "I am one of those who submit."

The furthest astray are those who argue about the provenance of Allah's Koran.

> 41:52 Say: "What do you think? If it (the Qur'an) is from Allah and then you disbelieve in it, who is more astray than one who is given to profound contention?"

Forget everything you have learned about the role of X and Y chromosomes at conception; Allah decides on the sex of the child you conceive, if He even deigns to allow you to bear children.

> 42:49 To Allah belongs the dominion of the heavens and the earth. He creates whatever He pleases, and grants whomever He wishes females, and whomever He wishes males.

> 42:50 Or He marries them, males and females, and makes whomever He wishes sterile. Indeed, He is All-Knowing, All-Powerful.

Remember Allah often if you don't want unwanted company in the here-and-now and in Hell.

> 43:36 And he who is blind to the remembrance of the All-Compassionate, We shall assign to him a demon, who will be his constant companion.

> 43:37 They (the demons) will certainly bar them from the Path, while they think they are well-guided.

> 43:38 But when he comes to Us, he will say: "Would that between me and you is the distance between East and West." What a wretched companion!

43:39 Today, it will not avail you, being wrongdoers, that you are partners in punishment.

Allah's superior conniving may have something to do with stealth snitches who can write.

43:78 We brought you (Meccans, *Moududi*) the Truth, but most of you were adverse to the Truth.

43:79 Or had they contrived some scheme. We are certainly contriving too.

43:80 Or do they think that We do not hear their secret and their private counsels. Yes, indeed, and Our Messengers (angels) are in their midst writing down.

You are doubly evil if you think Allah will consider your evilness on a par with those who do good and believe in Him.

45:21 What, do those who have perpetrated the evil deeds believe that We shall regard them as equal to those who have believed and done the righteous deeds, whether in their life or death (making their lives and deaths alike, *Moududi*)? Evil is their judgement.

Be the best you can be and Allah may overlook your evil deeds; but don't believe you will be raised up from the dead and you are literally toast.

46:16 Those from whom We accept the best of what they do and overlook their evil deeds shall be reckoned among the companions of Paradise, this being the promise of the truth which they were promised.

46:17 But as for him who says to his parents: "Fie upon you. Do you promised me to be raised up (from the dead), while generations have already gone before me?" They both call upon Allah to help them: "Woe unto you, have faith. Allah's promise is true." But he will say: "These are merely legend of the ancients."

The Creation did not weary Allah one bit, and He will do it again.

50:15 Were We wearied by the first creation? No, they are in doubt regarding a new creation (the new world order after the Day of Resurrection, *Moududi*).

50:38 Indeed, We have created the heavens and the earth and what is between them in six days, and We were not touch by weariness.

Had Allah wished you would be a totally different person, or not a person at all.

> 56:60 We have decreed death upon you and We would not be outstripped;
>
> 56:61 Had We wanted to change the like of you and form you afresh in a fashion you do not know.
>
> 56:62 You have already known the first fashioning; if only you would remember.

You reap what Allah sows!

> 56:63 Have you seen what your till?
>
> 56:64 Do you sow it yourselves, or are We the Sowers?
>
> 56:65 Had We wished, We would have reduced it to rubble, and so you would have remained wondering:
>
> 56:66 "We are penalized, indeed;
>
> 56:67 "No, we are being deprived."

The wood which you use to make a fire, that too is from Allah (desert-dwellers should be particularly grateful).

> 56:71 Or did you see the fire which you kindle?
>
> 56:72 Did you make its timber to grow or were We the Growers?
>
> 56:73 We have made it a reminder and a boon to the desert-dwellers.
>
> 56:74 Glorify, then, the name of your Great Lord.

Allah knows what He has created, thank goodness!

> 67:13 Conceal your words or proclaim them, He knows very well the secrets of the breasts.
>
> 67:14 Does He not know what He has created, though He is the All-Subtle, the All-Informed?

But, then again, with Allah, you never know.

> 67:16 Are you sure that He Who is in heaven will not cause the earth to cave in upon you? Behold how it quakes!
>
> 67:17 Or are you sure that He Who is in heaven will not let loose upon you a squall of pebbles? Then you shall know how My Warning sounds.

Allah admitting that much of what He does is an abomination.

> 67:18 Those who preceded you have disbelieved. How then was My Abomination?

You, and what army?

> 67:20 Or who is this who is a sentinel (your army, *Moududi*) for you to protect you against the Compassionate. The unbelievers are simply in error.
>
> 67:21 Or who is this who will provide for you, if He withholds His provision? Rather they have persisted in arrogance and aversion.

If you earn a living working the night shift, this may not be what Allah wished.

> 78:9 And made your sleep a period of rest?
>
> 78:10 And made the night as a garment?
>
> 78:11 And made the day a source of livelihood?

> 25:47 It is He who made the night a raiment for you, and sleep a period of rest, and made the day a rising up.

Allah swears to the stages of life and death and beyond.

> 84:16 No, I swear by the twilight,
>
> 84:17 And by the night and what it brings forth,
>
> 84:18 And by the moon when it is full,
>
> 84:19 That you will mount stage by stage.

Moududi:

> You will not remain in one and the same state, but will have to pass through countless stages gradually, from youth to old age, from old age to death, from death to barzakh (the intermediary state between death and Resurrection), from barzakh to Resurrections from Resurrection to the Plain of Assembly, then to the Reckoning, and then to the meting out of rewards and punishments.

Did Allah witness the burning of believers and did nothing?

THE CONSTELLATIONS
85 Al-Burûj

*In the Name of Allah,
the Compassionate, the Merciful*

85:1 By the heaven of the many constellations;

85:2 And by the Promised Day;

85:3 And by every witness and what is witnessed.

85:4 Perish the companions of the Pit,

85:5 The fire well-stoked;

85:6 While they sat around it,

85:7 And were witnessing what they did to the believers.

85:8 They did not begrudge them except that they believed in Allah, the All-Mighty, the All-Praiseworthy;

85:9 To Whom belongs the dominion of the heavens and the earth. Allah is witness of everything.

Allah is a Mighty Schemer, and what He is scheming about is no joking matter!

86:8 Surely, He has the power to bring him back,

86:9 When the consciences of men shall be tested.

86:10 Then, he will have no power and no supporter.

86:11 And by the heavens which alternates (recurring cycle of rain, *Moududi*);

86:12 And the earth which is split up (ever bursting with verdure, *Moududi*).

86:13 It is indeed a decisive discourse;

86:14 And it is no joking matter.

86:15 They are indeed scheming mightily,

86:16 And I am scheming mightily.

86:17 So, give the unbelievers some respite. Respite them slowly.

Why Allah "straightens" out the provision:

89:15 As for man, whenever His Lord tests him, honouring him and favouring him with bounties, he says: "My Lord has honoured me."

89:16 But when He tests him, straitening his provision, he says: "My Lord has despised me."

89:17 Not at all: you do not actually honour the orphans;

89:18 And do not advocate the feeding of the destitute;

89:19 And you devour the inheritance greedily;

89:20 And you love wealth ardently.

It!

THE SUN
91 Ash-Shams

*In the Name of Allah,
the Compassionate, the Merciful*

91:1 By the sun and its forenoon brightness,

91:2 And the moon when it follows it,

91:3 And the day when it exhibits its light,

91:4 And the night when it obscures it;

91:5 And by the heaven and Him who erected it;

91:6 And the earth and Him who spread it out,

91:7 And the soul and Him who fashioned it well,

91:8 Inspiring it to profligacy and piety.

91:9 Prosperous shall be He who purifies it,

91:10 An ruined he who corrupts it.

Who is Allah talking too?

COVETOUSNESS
102 At-Takâthur

*In the Name of Allah,
the Compassionate, the Merciful*

102:1 Covetousness has distracted you,

102:2 Till you visited the graveyards.

102:3 No; you shall surely know.

102:4 Again, no; you shall surely know.

102:5 No; if only you knew with certainty,

102:6 You would surely have perceived Hell (and ended up in Hell, *Moududi*).

102:7 Then, you will have perceived it with visual certainty.

102:8 Then, on that Day (*Judgement Day*) you will surely be questioned about the Bliss (My Bounties you enjoyed, *Moududi*).

Believe, do good by Allah and be steadfast and you will avoid falling prey to perdition.

THE AEON

103 Al`Asr

*In the Name of Allah,
the Compassionate, the Merciful*

103:1 By the aeon (time),

103:2 Man is, indeed, a prey to perdition,

103:3 Except for those who believe, do the righteous deeds, urge each other to seek the truth and urge each other to be steadfast.

If the following surah was Medinan, then the following revelations could be considered instructions from Allah to His Messenger not to attack the Meccans caravans during certain months; but it's a Meccan surah. Pity!

QURAYSH

106 Quraysh

*In the Name of Allah,
the Compassionate, the Merciful*

106:1 For Quraysh's customary journey,

106:2 The journey of the winter and summer,

106:3 Let them worship the Lord of this House,

106:4 Who has fed them when they were hungry and secured them against fear.

Tidbits Medinan Surahs

Allah's Face is everywhere even if He never laid claim in the Koran to being the owner of the North and the South.

> 2:115 To Allah belongs the East and the West. So whichever way you turn (while praying), there is Allah's Face. Indeed, Allah is Omnipresent and Omniscient.

Allah's Quid Pro Quos:

> 2:152 Remember Me (by glorifying Me) then I will remember you (by rewarding you). Give thanks to Me (by obeying Me) and do not be ungrateful (by disobeying Me).

> 2:186 And when my servants ask you about Me, say: I am near; I answer the prayer of the supplicant when he calls; so they should answer My Call (by obeying me) and believe in Me, that they might be rightly guided.

Your fathers and forefathers were ignoramuses!

> 2:170 When it is said to them: "Follow what Allah has revealed", they say: "We would rather follow that which we found our fathers doing." What, even though their fathers understood nothing and were not rightly guided!

> 5:104 And if they are told: "Come now to what Allah has revealed and to the Messenger", they reply: "Sufficient unto us what we found our forefathers doing", even if their forefathers knew nothing and were not rightly guided!

Don't bribe the judge!

> 2:188 Do not devour each other's money unjustly or offer it to the judges in order to devour a part of other people's money sinfully and knowingly.

Satan = Poverty, Allah = Bounty

> 2:268 Satan induces you to expect poverty and orders you to be niggardly, and Allah promises you His Forgiveness and His Bounty. Allah is Munificent, All-Knowing.

Why some people are smart and others less so.

> 2:269 He gives wisdom to whom He wills. And he who receives wisdom has received an abundant good. But none take heed except people of understanding.

If anyone other than the Prophet Muhammad, one has to assume, seeks to lord it over them – including angels who would be Lord of an earthly realm – they are twisting Allah's Words or making it up.

> 3:78 And there is a group of them who twist their tongues while reading the Book, so that you may suppose it is part of the Book; whereas it is not part of the Book. They also say: "It is from Allah", whereas it is not from Allah; they only speak falsehoods against Allah knowingly.

> 3:79 It is not given to any mortal that Allah should give him the Book, the judgement and the Prophethood and then he should say to the people: "Be servants to me, rather than to Allah"; but rather: "Be learned men, by virtue of what you used to teach of the Book and what you used to study."

> 3:80 Nor would he enjoin you to take angels and the Prophets as lords. Would he enjoin you to be unbelievers after you have become Muslims?

If you are not willing to part with something you cherish, no matter how religious or reverent you are, Allah will not consider you among the pious.

> 3:92 You will not achieve piety until you spend part of what you cherish; and whatever you spend, Allah knows it very well.

Could "the upright people" of revelation 3:113, be the Sabians, who, along with the Jews and Christians, Allah considers people of the Book; not the Koran, but the Bible, or perhaps another book of revealed truths revealed by the one and only god to a mortal .e.g. the Avesta?

> 3:113 They are not all alike. For of the People of the Book, there is an upright nation who recite Allah's Revelations, throughout the night, while prostrating themselves.

> 3:114 They believe in Allah and the Last Day, bid the right and forbid the wrong and hasten to do the good deeds. Those are among the righteous people!

> 3:115 And whatever good they do, they will not be denied. Allah knows well the God-fearing!

A somewhat uncharacteristic admonition from Allah, that women, whom the Koran considers in most circumstances nothing more than chattel, like men, have "a share of what they earned".

> 4:32 Do not covet that with which Allah has favoured some of you over the others. Men have a share of what they earned, and women a share of what they earned. And ask Allah to give you of His Bounty. Allah indeed has knowledge of everything!

Allah does not like show-offs, or perhaps unbelievers who are show-offs.

> 4:38 And for those who spent their wealth in order to show off, and do not believe in Allah and the Last Day. He who has the Devil as a companion, an evil companion has he!

On at least nine occasions, Allah will remind His readers, but not in the following revealed truth, that He is indeed a well-informed god. His knowledge about a wide range of subjects is evident in His use of the word atom from the Greek átomos to describe something infinitely small in the following revelation.

> 4:40 Surely Allah will not wrong anyone an atom's weight; and if it is a good deed, He will multiply it and give from Himself in addition a great reward.

Allah exhorts you to judge justly.

> 4:58 God commands you to deliver trusts to their owners and, if you judge between people, to judge justly. Splendid is Allah's exhortation to you. Allah is indeed All-Hearing, All-Seeing.

Allah has no objection to lawyers, for example, sharing in the proceeds of a successful litigation or mediation.

> 4:85 He who offers a good intercession (he who intercedes for people in accordance with Muslim law) shall have a share of it; and he offers a bad intercession shall suffer from its consequences. Allah has power over everything.

Allah on the use of foul language:

> 4:148 Allah does not like the public uttering of foul words (*evil*), except by one who has been wronged. Allah is All-Hearing, All-Knowing.

> 4:149 Whether you do good openly, or secretly, or pardon an evil deed, Allah is indeed All Pardoning, All-Powerful.

Moududi:

> ... if a wronged person speaks out against a wrong-doer, he is quite justified in doing so. Even though this is a person's right, it is more meritorious to continue to do good both in public and in private, and to ignore the misdeeds of others.

On Judgement Day, Allah will tell you what you should already know.

> 5:105 O believers, take care of yourselves; you will not be harmed by him who has gone astray, if you are well-guided. To Allah you will all return; then He will tell you what you were doing.

Those who are cursed by Allah are in for a really, really bad time, including running the risk of being transformed into monkeys and pigs.:

> 5:60 Say: "Shall I tell you about those who will get a worse punishment from Allah? Those whom Allah cursed and on whom He poured forth His Wrath, transformed them into monkeys and swine, and worshippers of the Devil. They are worse off and farther astray."

Is Allah the flip side of God?

> 5:98 Know that God is Severe in punishment and that Allah is All-Forgiving, Merciful.

It is not *the* evil per se that is the problem, it is its abundance; and no, the use of the determinate article "the" does not imply that Allah is "the evil" which you must fear. If that was the case, the first letter of evil would be capitalized.

> 5:100 Say: "The evil and the good are not equal, even if the abundance of the evil should appeal to you." Fear then Allah, O people of understanding, that perchance you may prosper.

Allah does not believe in reincarnation. Enough said!

> 13:5 Should you (Muhammad) wonder, the wonder is their saying: "What, if we turn into dust, will we be created anew?" Those are the ones who disbelieve in their Lord, and those are the ones around whose necks are chains, and those are the people of the Fire, abiding therein forever.

Allah knows what you say and what you don't say.

> 13:10 It is the same whether any of you conceals his words or utters them, and whether he hides by night or goes forth by day.

Allah assigns guardian angels to protect your front and your back at all times.

> 13:11 There are guardian [angels] before him and behind him, guarding him by Allah's Command. Allah does not change the condition of a people until they change what is in their hearts. And if Allah wills to afflict a people with a misfortune, it cannot be turned away, and they have, apart from Allah, no protector.

Allah imitating Jupiter:

> 13:12 It is He who shows you the lightning, inspiring fear and hope, and originates the laden clouds.

> 13:13 And the thunder sounds His praise and the angels, too, in awe of Him. And He sends forth the thunderbolts smiting with them whomever he pleases. Nevertheless, they dispute about Allah, but he is Mighty in prowess.

It is only logical that shadows would prostrate themselves before Allah.

> 13:15 Those in the heavens and on the earth prostrate themselves to Allah willingly or unwillingly, and so do their shadows morning and evenings.

> ----

> 16:48 Have they not considered all the things Allah has created, casting their shades right and left, and prostrating themselves before Allah in humility?

> ----

> 25:45 Have you not considered your Lord, how He has stretched out the shadow? Had He willed, He would have made it still, then made the sun a signal thereof.

> 25:46 Then, We would have drawn it towards Us slowly.

Allah can't be bribed, and don't even try; more or less what He revealed in the Meccan verses 39:47-48.

> 13:18 To those who obey their Lord belongs the best [reward (Paradise)], but those who disobey Him, were they to have all that is on earth plus its equal, would offer it as

ransom. To those a bad reckoning is reserved, and their abode will be Hell, and what a miserable resting-place!

Those who dispute with Allah have the devil for a friend.

> 22:3 And there are some people who dispute regarding Allah without any knowledge, and follow every rebellious devil.

> 22:4 It has been written against him (the Devil) that whoever takes him for a friend, he will lead astray and guide him to the punishment of Hell.

What you risk losing if your worship of Allah is half-hearted i.e. tepid.

> 22:11 And of the people, there are some who worship Allah tepidly. When good fortune comes his way, he is pleased with it, but if an ordeal befalls him, he turns around (goes back to disbelief) losing both this world and the world to come. That is the manifest lost.

Allah chooses His Messengers from among angels and men and knows what is behind and in front of them.

> 22:75 Allah chooses from angels and men Messengers; Allah is All-Hearing, All-Seeing.

> 22:76 He knows what is before them and what is behind them, and to Allah are all things returned.

Everyone and everything prays to Allah in its own way. That chirping you hear …

> 24:41 Have you not seen how Allah is glorified by whatever is in the heavens or the earth, and by the birds in flight. He knows the prayer of each and its glorification. Allah knows well what they do.

Allah is responsible for the alternation of night and day.

> 24:44 He alternates the night and day. In that there is a lesson for those who have eyes to see.

> 39:5 He created the heavens and the earth in truth. He wraps up the night around the day and He wraps the day around the night . He has subjected the sun and the moon, each running for an appointed term. He is indeed the All-Mighty, the All-Forgiving.

An order of closeness:

> 33:6 The Prophet is closer to the believers than their own selves and his wives are like their mothers. The kinsmen are closer to each other, in Allah's Book, than the believers or the Emigrants; unless you are doing your friends an honourable deed, that has already been inscribed in the Book.

Allah's angels extend His blessings on the believers. There may also be those, who, when they encounter their Lord express a wish for "Peace", and for good reason.

> 33:43 It is He Who blesses you, with His angels (His angels invoke blessings on you, *Moududi*), that He may bring you out of the shadows of darkness into light; and He is Ever Merciful towards the believers.

> 33:44 Their greeting, when they encounter Him is: "Peace", and He has prepared for them a generous reward.

Allah expects you to break up fights among believers, unless...

> 49:9 If two parties of the believers should fight one another, bring them peacefully together; but if one of them seeks to oppress the other, then fight the oppressor until it reverts to Allah's Command. If it reverts, then bring them together in justice and be equitable; for Allah loves the equitable.

> 49:10 Surely, the believers are brothers; so bring your two brothers together and fear Allah, so that you may receive Mercy.

Calling each other names, including sobriquets, is considered ungodliness.

> 49:11 O believers, let not one people scoff at another people, lest they be better than they; nor women at other women, lest they be better than they. Do not slander yourselves and do not revile each other with false names. Wretched is the name of ungodliness, after belief! He who does not repent, such are the wrongdoers, indeed.

Allah says He created nations and tribes in an effort to get people to get to know each other. The logic of creating divisions to foster understanding escapes me; but, I sure Allah knows what He is doing, even if earlier, revelation 6:65, He said, in effect, that it was to foster conflicts.

49:13 O mankind, We have created you male and female and made you nations and tribes, so that you might come to know one another. Surely the noblest of you in Allah's Sight is the most pious. Allah indeed is All-Knowing, All-Informed.

Before Allah creates a disaster, He writes it down in a book.

57:22 Not a disaster befalls in the earth or in yourselves but is in a Book, before We create it. That for Allah is an easy matter.

57:23 So that you may not grieve for what you missed, and rejoice in what came your way. Allah does not like the conceited and the boastful;

57:24 Those who are niggardly and bid people to be niggardly. He who turns away, Allah is All-Sufficient, Praiseworthy.

Why Allah sent iron down from heaven.

57:25 We have sent forth our Messengers with clear proofs and sent down with them the Book and the Balance, so that people might act equitably. We have also sent down iron, which has mighty power and benefits for mankind, and that Allah might know who supports Him and His Messengers invisibly. Allah is indeed Strong and Mighty.

Forget Allah, and you will forget who you are.

59:18 O believers, fear Allah and let each soul consider what it has forwarded for the morrow. Fear Allah; He is Aware of what your do.

59:19 Do not be like those who forgot Allah, and so He made them forget themselves. Those are indeed the sinners.

Allah is not a modest god; but you already knew that.

35:10 Whoever wishes Glory, it is to Allah that the glory utterly belongs. Unto Him good words ascend and the righteous deeds uplifts it. Those who contrive evil deeds will incur terrible punishment and the contriving of these will come to grief.

If it's a choice between Allah and your children!

63:9 O believers, let not your possessions or your children distract you from the remembrance of Allah. Whoever does that – those are the real losers.

The money you paid to the Catholic Church in the bad old days, for so-called indulgences, which came with a sin-forgiving guarantee went mostly to pay for monuments. The money Allah requests in revelation 64:17 served mainly to fund Islam's defence and later its wars of expansion. The Catholic Church's request for sin-forgiving monetary contribution was a man-made law, therefore the aberrant practice was largely abandoned earlier on thanks in part to the Protestant Reformation and Martin Luther. Allah's variation of the Catholic Church's indulgences are permanent, for revealed truths are immutable and eternal.

> 64:17 If you lend Allah a fair loan, He will multiply it for you and forgive you. Allah is All-Grateful, All-Clement;

If you have aching joints, it is not because Allah did not fasten them well.

> 76:28 We have created them and fastened their joints well; and if We wish We change their likes completely.

> 76:29 This indeed is a reminder; so he who wishes will follow, unto His Lord, a path.

You wish in tandem with Allah.

> 76:30 Yet, you do not wish unless Allah wishes. Allah is truly All-Knowing and Wise.

> 76:31 He admits into His Mercy whomever He wishes; and for the wrongdoers He has prepared a painful punishment.

AFTERWORD

It Wasn't Always Like That

It wasn't always like that – the hate, the intolerance, the brutality found in the Koran that many now associate with Arabs in particular and Muslims in general.

Arabs, Before and After

> 45:20 This (Qur'an) is an illumination for mankind, a guidance and mercy unto a people who believe with certainty.

Virgil Gheorghiu in his admiring biography of the Prophet, *La vie de Mahomet,* writes about a pre-Islamic Arabia that was home to a multitude of cultures and religions. For this author, pre-Islamic Arabs were dynamic, creative, fun-loving and tolerant. Ernest Renan (1823–92), French historian and critic, writing about pre-Islamic Arab society, described it this way (my translation).

> I am not aware in the entire history of civilisation of a more gracious, more loving, more vibrant society than that of the Arabs before Islam ... [it was a time] ... of unbound freedom, lofty sentiments, a nomadic and chivalrous way of life, [a land] of fantasy, joy, mischievousness, bawdy impious poetry, refined love-making ...
>
> Ernest Renan, cf. Robert Montagne, *La Civilisation du désert*

Barnaby Rogerson paints a similar picture of the inhabitants of the peninsula and the Middle East before the Islamic conquest in his flattering biography *The Prophet Muhammad*. His vivid travel-log-like writing has you imagining that you are with the Prophet on his voyages throughout the Middle East, meeting the people he meets, hearing the stories he hears – stories that will find their way into the Koran. It's a magical, fantastical place, a good time to be alive. So what happened? Islam happened. Islam became the religion of the inhabitants of the peninsula and the Arabs, in T.E. Lawrence's words, became a people of "primary colours."

> They were a people of primary colours, or rather of black and white ... They were a dogmatic people, despising

doubt, our modern crown of thorns. They did not understand our metaphysical difficulties, our introspective questioning. They only knew truth and untruth, belief and unbelief, without our hesitating retinue of finer shades.

This people was black and white not merely in clarity, but in apposition. Their thoughts were at ease only in extremes ... they never compromised; they pursued the logic of several incompatible opinions to absurd ends, without perceiving the incongruity.

They were a limited, narrow-minded people, whose inert intellect lay fallow in curious resignation. Their imaginations were vivid, but not creative.

T.E. Lawrence, *Seven Pillars of Wisdom*

Even in the Koran you get a glimpse of the Arabs before Islam, not as unthinking pagans as Allah would have us believe, but as rational to the core, spiritual human beings in the best sense of the word. This is evident in their coherent, logical, reasoned response – which Allah denounces as following their fancies – when asked to accept, without question, the world view of the self-proclaimed, writing-enamoured, illiterate mouthpiece of a do-it-all, know-it-all, owner-of-everything god.

A group of Meccan men's fancy, of which Einstein would have approved and which remains my favourite, was their explanation of aging and life and death, revelation 45:24.

> 45:22 Allah created the heavens and the earth in truth, so that every soul may be rewarded for what it has earned; and they shall not be wronged.

> 45:23 Have you seen him who has taken his fancy as his god and Allah has led him astray knowingly, and set a seal upon his hearing and his heart, and placed a veil upon his sight. Who, then, will guide him besides Allah? Do you not remember?

> 45:24 They say: "There is nothing but this our present life. We die and we live and we are only destroyed by time." However, they have no certain knowledge of this; they are only conjecturing.

Conjecturing about the Seen and the Unseen, to use Allah's terminology, about what we know and what we don't know, has been associated with the beginning of wisdom by Western philosophers and Eastern sages since man started to look beyond the superstitions which purported to describe his surroundings and a possible world beyond. Many Meccans, despite being told not to think too much or they would be held to account, revelation 17:36, were comfortable with conjecture and said so, revelation 45:32.

17:36 Do not pursue what you have no knowledge of. Hearing, sight and the heart – all these [you] shall be questioned about.

45:25 And when Our Signs are clearly recited to them, their only argument is to say: "Bring our fathers back, if you are truthful."

45:26 Say: "Allah gives you life, then causes you to die, then musters you unto the Day of Resurrection, which is undoubted. Yet most people do not know."

45:27 To Allah belongs the dominion of the heavens and the earth, and when the Hour shall come, on that Day the negators (sic) shall lose.

45:28 And you will see every nation kneeling; each nation being called unto its Book: "Today, you shall be rewarded for what you used to do.

45:29 "This is Our Book which speaks against you truly. In fact, We used to record what you were doing."

45:30 As to those who believed and did the righteous deeds, their Lord will admit them into His Mercy. That is the manifest triumph.

45:31 But as for those who disbelieved [they will be asked]: "Were not My Signs recited to you, but you waxed proud and were a criminal people?"

45:32 And when it was said: "Allah's Promise is true and the Hour is undoubted", you said: " We do not know what the Hour is. We only conjecture and are by no means certain."

45:33 Then the evil of their deeds shall appear to them and they will be smitten by that which they used to mock.

45:34 And it will be said: "Today We forget you, as you forgot the Encounter of this your day, and your abode is the Fire and you will have no supporters.

45:35 "That is because you took Allah's Signs in jest and the earthly life lured you." So today they will not be brought out of it and they will not be allowed to repent.

> 45:36 Praise, then, be to Allah, the Lord of the heavens and the Lord of the earth, the Lord of the Worlds.
>
> 45:37 Unto Him is the grandeur in the heavens and on the earth, and He is the All-Mighty, the All-Wise.

Allah would not tell them when the Hour would strike and bring about the "Encounter" i.e. Judgement Day and therefore it is only logical – the pre-Islamic Arabs being a reasonable confident people – that they would admit to not knowing. Such a rational people could be expected to speculate about the time, the place and how Allah would pull off such a thing, if such a thing was even possible.

In Allah's Universe, you may not even conjecture about what He tells you you do not know; and what He tells you is the truth which you must believe "with certainty", no matter the incongruity.

The disincentive that is Allah's blanket embargo against seeking knowledge of what He tells you you do not know, and not to question what He reveals as to how His Creation functions, may be partly responsible for the Muslims world, which constitutes 21 percent of the world's population (2011), having produced only 10 Nobel Prize laureates, with only two in the physical sciences (1979 physics, 1999 chemistry). Another is the inordinate amount of worship and glorification time Allah demands (if prayer is the answer, than the world may eventually owe Islam an enormous debt).

Not to be overlooked is the requirements of an Islamic education where priority is given to learning Arabic and attempting to memorise the Koran in its entirety; the negative impact on critical thinking just as damaging, if not more, than the time not available to non-religious subjects which Islamists consider very much a pre-occupation of the ignorant.

The period before Islam, on the Arabian Peninsula, is generally referred to by Muslims as Jahiliya, the time of ignorance when world views as numerous and as varied as the colours of the rainbow flourished. Then Allah sent His last messenger and that multi-coloured view of the universe changed to black and white and humankind's relationship with its Creator was demoted to that of mere supplicants of a vain and vengeful God.

The Prophet's flight from Mecca to Medina in 622 with his followers marks this alleged transition from ignorance to enlightenment. The year of this exodus is known as the Hijra or Hegira. The Hegira begins the Muslim calendar and is represented as 1 AH or 1 al-Hijra. As you read the revelations surrounding the Meccan unbelievers' statement about the ravages of time, and about expressing doubts, you may be left to wonder as to the meaning of ignorance.

Muslim tradition holds that the Koran and the instructions it contains are unchanging and carved for eternity on a golden tablet in Paradise. The bases of this tradition are the verses that end surah 85, *The Constellations*, a short panegyric to Allah.

> 85:21 Yet, it is a glorious Qur'an,
>
> 85:22 In a Well-Preserved Tablet.[58]

The master copy of the Koran in heaven is also referred to as the *Mother of the Book*; and then, there is the *Master Register* ("Umm al-Kitab or al-Lawh al Mahfuz. Whether they are one of the same is a matter of conjecture.

> 36:12 It is We Who bring the dead back to life and write down what they have advanced and their vestiges too. Everything We have enumerated in a clear Master Register.

The Koran received by the Prophet Muhammad is believed to be a clone of the *Mother of the Book* and therefore error-free.

> 39:28 We made it an Arabic Qur'an without any defect that perchance they might be God-fearing[59].

Competing World Views

Muslim tradition holds that the Koran and the instructions it contains are unchanging and carved for eternity on a golden tablet in Paradise. The bases of this tradition are the verses that end surah 85, *The Constellations*, a short panegyric to Allah.

> 85:21 Yet, it is a glorious Qur'an,
>
> 85:22 In a Well-Preserved Tablet.[60]

---

[58] A saying of the Prophet would place the Tablet on Allah's Lap or close to His Eminence and the Tablet appears to contain a last minute entry which may be a dedication of sorts.

Narrated Abu Huraira:

Allah's Apostle said, "When Allah completed the creation, He wrote in His Book which is with Him on His Throne, 'My Mercy overpowers My Anger.'"

Bukhari 54.416

[59] Allah may have been wary about delivering His Koran to the Arabs of Montagne.

> 43:5 Shall We then divert the Reminder from you mercifully, because you are an extra-vagant (*wanton, extravagant in other translations*) people.

[60] A saying of the Prophet would place the Tablet on Allah's Lap or close to His Eminence and the Tablet appears to contain a last minute entry which may be a dedication of sorts.

The master copy of the Koran in heaven is also referred to as the *Mother of the Book;* and then, there is the *Master Register* ("Umm al-Kitab or al-Lawh al Mahfuz. Whether they are one of the same is a matter of conjecture.

> 36:12 It is We Who bring the dead back to life and write down what they have advanced and their vestiges too. Everything We have enumerated in a clear Master Register.

The Koran received by the Prophet Muhammad is believed to be a clone of the *Mother of the Book* and therefore error-free.

> 39:28 We made it an Arabic Qur'an without any defect that perchance they might be God-fearing[61].

Depending on how you see the world, this new unchanging, perfect, divinely ordained world-order decreed in a book allegedly "without any defect" and our place in it was a good or a bad thing. For the believers, western civilization's questioning, multi-coloured world-view is a product of the time of ignorance. The Koran's dogmatic black and white world-view was to usher in a new age of enlightenment. Both world-views cannot peacefully co-exist and never have.

When the 17th century welcomed the *Age of Reason* it was thought that one world-view had triumph over the other. Islam has proven this assumption to be wrong and the outcome of the battle between reason and dogma is still very much in doubt.

The Renaissance, which marked the end of the Catholic Church's dominance in Europe allowing for a flowering of the arts and sciences, and the Enlightenment which ushered in the Age of Reason may turn out to have been a short detour, taken by a relatively small segment of humanity in the march of history; a fragile exception writes Mark Lilla, professor of the humanities at Columbia University in *The Stillborn God: Religion, Politics and the Modern West* (2007):

> After centuries of strife, the West has learned to separate religion and politics – to establish the legitimacy of its leaders without referring to divine command. There is little

---

Narrated Abu Huraira:
Allah's Apostle said, "When Allah completed the creation, He wrote in His Book which is with Him on His Throne, 'My Mercy overpowers My Anger.'"
Bukhari 54.416

[61] Allah may have been wary about delivering His Koran to the Arabs of Montagne.
43:5 Shall We then divert the Reminder from you mercifully, because you are an extra-vagant (*wanton, extravagant in other translations*) people.

reason to expect the rest of the world – the Islamic world in particular – will follow.

We in the West find it incomprehensible that theological ideas still inflame the minds of men, stirring up messianic passions that can leave societies in ruin. We had assumed that this was no longer possible, that human beings had learned to separate religious questions from political ones, that political theology died in 16th-century Europe. We were wrong. It's we who are the fragile exception.

If you believe that the Koran's world-view is the correct one, you only have to do nothing for this point of view to triumph. Islam's blanket rejection of abortion and birth control; its approval of polygamy, early marriages and large families; its promise of death to those who would even contemplate leaving the perfect religion for one less perfect or for no religion at all mean the community of believers will always be expanding. In fact, except for a temporary halt at the gates of Vienna in 1683, a small setback in Spain during the reign of Isabella and Ferdinand and a temporary reversal during the Mongol invasions, Islam has never looked back.

With all it has going for it, not to mention the paralyzing fear of random death as the more fanatical followers of the Prophet Muhammad threaten violence if Islam is not allowed to recruit in the "land of war", the land of the unbelievers, in Islam you have the making of a winner.

This is a forgone conclusion for authors like Mark Stein. In his book *America Alone*, he writes that the future belong to Islam because "the Muslim world has youth, numbers and global ambition. The West is growing old and enfeebled, and more and more lacks the will to rebuff those who would supplant it."

If you don't believe that the Koranic world-view should prevail, what should you do? Informing yourself of what is at stake is a start. Another would be acknowledging that Muslims are not your enemy. Religion, to paraphrase Nobel Laureate Steven Weinberg, can make good people do bad things. Your enemy is a religion that was not allowed to grow beyond its desert roots; to become more than what Irshad Manji, in her plea for reform, *The Trouble With Islam. A Wake-up Call for Honesty and Change*, calls "desert Islam."

The Cartoon Protest

I mentioned earlier that the Koran was a set of rules to be rigidly adhered to, but of course, it is more than that, it is also one man's idea of what your relationship with God should be. Like any profound idea, good or bad, it will easily take root if it offers some benefit to a large enough collective and is left unopposed.

Until the last century, Islam was mainly spread by the sword, the Ottoman Empire spearheading the most recent assault into Europe. Today, desert Islam is subjugating the West not through the force of arms although intimidation, mainly through terrorist acts, still plays a role, but through complicity of the Western democracies. The West has implicitly, if not explicitly, accepted desert Islam's argument that limits should be placed on criticism of religious beliefs, thereby allowing desert Islam to advance almost unchallenged. This gradual surrender of basic freedoms in the face of religious intolerance is slowly neutering the most effective weapons against the spread of this type of tyranny: freedom of expression and freedom of speech.

Winston Churchill, after the end of the Second World War, when the war still had no official name, was asked what they should call the war that had just ended and cost more than 30 million lives. He said "the unnecessary war." Like Churchill, I believe that if the democracies had stood steadfast in the face of Hitler's demands instead of rewarding aggressive behaviour there would have been no Second World War.

I was reminded of Churchill's response when viewing a demonstration by Muslims in London during the so-called "cartoon protest." Some of the demonstrators carried signs demanding that the now infamous Danish cartoonists be slaughtered, others that they be butchered for mocking Islam – for drawing mostly inoffensive cartoons of the Prophet Muhammad. I am sure that Churchill, if he were still alive, would have labelled the democracies' timid response, which involved mainly apologizing for their citizens exercising their right to freedom of expression, as rewarding aggressive behaviour.

Will the outcome be the same, a bloody, global war to dwarf all wars to try to regain cherished freedoms carelessly thrown away? Not if you fight the real enemy now, using the bloodless weapons that you still have at your disposal: your right to freedom of speech, your right to freedom of expression, your right to express an opinion with which others might disagree. And who is your enemy? Those of any faith, of any religion or of no faith, who would deny you your right to criticize an idea, a person or a book, in your own words or through your art, simply because the idea, the person or the book is deemed by the defenders of the status-quo to be sacred and off-limits.

APPENDICES

Pillars

Pillars of Faith

To be a Muslim is also to admit to the following beliefs which are often referred to as the Pillars of Faith (not to be confused with the Five Pillars of Islam which are not beliefs but mandatory activities to be performed at pre-determined intervals):

1) Belief in God;

2) Belief in the Angels;

3) Belief in the revealed Books of the Prophet;

4) Belief in God's many prophets[62];

5) Belief in a Last Day;

6) Belief in the divine measurement of human affairs;

7) Belief in a life after death.

Pillars of Islam

1. Shahadah, declaring allegiance to God.

2. Salat, daily prayers.

3. Zakat, annual charity.

4. Saum, month-long fasting.

5. Hajj, the pilgrimage to Mecca.

---

[62] Some communities of believers combine the 3rd and 4th beliefs into one: "Belief in God's books and God's Messengers."

The First Koran

Abridged excerpt from *1,001 Sayings and Deeds of the Prophet Muhammad*, Boreal Books, 2104

The Koran was put together in a hurry from what could be considered mainly second-rate sources after those who remembered Allah's' revelations best were killed putting down a rebellion against Muslim rule known as the *War of the Apostates*. In the last phase of that war, 7,000 apostates were surrounded and shown no mercy.

The believers' opponents were not into extermination, therefore Muslim casualties tended to be less, but still, at the battle of Yamama 70 or so fanatics of the Koran, the professional reciters of Islam's Holy Book, were killed. The loss of the best "Koranic memories" meant that the young man tasked with putting together the first and only approved version of the Koran had to depend on less reliable sources to create a written record of what Allah first told the angel Gabriel, and which he, in turn, revealed to the Prophet Muhammad.

Narrated Zaid bin Thabit Al-Ansari who was one of those who used to write the Divine Revelation:

Abu Bakr sent for me after the (heavy) casualties among the warriors (of the battle) of Yamama (where a great number of Qurra (reciters of the Koran) were killed). Umar was present with Abu Bakr who said, "Umar has come to me and said, 'The people have suffered heavy casualties on the day of (the battle of) Yamama, and I am afraid that there will be more casualties among the Qurra (those who know the Qur'an by heart) at other battle-fields, whereby a large part of the Qur'an may be lost, unless you collect it. And I am of the opinion that you should collect the Qur'an."

Abu Bakr added, "I said to Umar, 'How can I do something which Allah's Apostle has not done?'"

Umar said (to me), "By Allah, it is (really) a good thing. " So Umar kept on pressing, trying to persuade me to accept his proposal, till Allah opened my bosom for it and I had the same opinion as 'Umar.

(Zaid bin Thabit added:) Umar was sitting with him, Abu Bakr, and was not speaking to me).

"You are a wise young man and we do not suspect you (of telling lies or of forgetfulness): and you used to write the Divine Inspiration for Allah's Apostle. Therefore, look for the Qur'an and collect it (in one manuscript)."

By Allah, if he (Abu Bakr) had ordered me to shift one of the mountains (from its place) it would not have been harder for me than what he had ordered me concerning the collection of the Qur'an. I said to both of them, "How dare you do a thing which the Prophet has not done?"

Abu Bakr said, "By Allah, it is (really) a good thing." So I kept on arguing with him about it till Allah opened my bosom for that which He had opened the bosoms of Abu Bakr and Umar. So I started locating Quranic material and collecting it from parchments, scapula, leaf-stalks of date palms and from the memories of men (who knew it by heart).

I found with Khuzaima two Verses of Surat-at-Tauba which I had not found with anybody else, (and they were): "Verily there has come to you an Apostle (Muhammad) from amongst yourselves. It grieves him that you should receive any injury or difficulty He (Muhammad) is ardently anxious over you (to be rightly guided)" (9:128)

The manuscript on which the Quran was collected, remained with Abu Bakr till Allah took him unto Him, and then with Umar till Allah took him unto Him, and finally it remained with Hafsa, Umar's daughter.

Bukhari 60.201

The finished product appears to have been put together in a haphazard manner. There is no timeline. The only allowance given to any kind of order is the sequencing of most of the 114 chapters from longest to shortest. Because no attention seems to have been given to arranging the chapters and verses in some kind of chronological order, you often get answers to questions that have yet to be asked. And duplicates, triplicates, quadruplicates and even quintuplets abound. There is little scholarship evident in its production, although, some editing may have been done in producing copies for distribution from Thabit's original which the daughter of Caliph Umar kept under her bed. It was retrieved on order of Uthman who succeeded Umar as caliph.

Narrated Anas bin Malik:

Hudhaifa bin Al-Yaman came to Uthman at the time when the people of Sham and the people of Iraq were Waging war to conquer Arminya and Adharbijan. Hudhaifa was afraid of their (the people of Sham and Iraq) differences in the recitation of the Qur'an, so he said to 'Uthman, "O chief of the Believers! Save this nation before they differ about the Book (Quran) as Jews and the Christians did before."

So Uthman sent a message to Hafsa saying, "Send us the manuscripts of the Qur'an so that we may compile the Qur'anic materials in perfect copies and return the manuscripts to you."

Hafsa sent it to Uthman. Uthman then ordered Zaid bin Thabit, Abdullah bin AzZubair, Said bin Al-As and 'Abdur Rahman bin Harith bin Hisham to rewrite the manuscripts in perfect copies.

Uthman said to the three Quraishi men, "In case you disagree with Zaid bin Thabit on any point in the Qur'an, then write it in the dialect of Quraish, the Qur'an was revealed in their tongue."

They did so, and when they had written many copies, Uthman returned the original manuscripts to Hafsa.

Uthman sent to every Muslim province one copy of what they had copied, and ordered that all the other Qur'anic materials, whether written in fragmentary manuscripts or whole copies, be burnt.

Said bin Thabit added, "A Verse from Surat Ahzab was missed by me when we copied the Qur'an and I used to hear Allah's Apostle reciting it. So we searched for it and found it with Khuzaima bin Thabit Al-Ansari. (That Verse was): 'Among the Believers are men who have been true in their covenant with Allah.'" (33:23)

Bukhari 61.510

The opinion of two eminent historians on the end product:

A confused, jumble, crude, incondite, endless iteration...

Thomas Carlyle [1795 - 1881]

As toilsome a reading a I ever undertook; a wearisome confused jumble.

Edward Gibbon [1737 - 1794]

...

www.ingramcontent.com/pod-product-compliance
Lightning Source LLC
LaVergne TN
LVHW011344080426
835511LV00005B/123